357

Vegetables and fruits

1. Apple
2. Tomato
3. Kantola
4. Carrot
5. Bottlegourd, white pumpkin
6. Bittergourd
7. Drumstick
8. Capsicum
9. Brinjal, eggplant
10. Red pumpkin
11. Yam - elephant
12. Yam - ordinary
13. Padwal
14. Ginger
15. Dill
16. Fenugreek leaves
17. Curry leaves
18. Mint
19. Spinach
20. Coriander leaves
21. Lemon
22. Valol
23. Chickoo
24. Pear
25. French bean
26. Onion (Small baby onion)
27. String bean
28. Green chillies
29. Lady fingers
30. Ridge gourd
31. Guava
32. Custard apple
33. Papaya
34. Pomegranate
35. Cucumber (brownish red skin)
36. Cucumber (small green)
37. Cucumber (big monsoon variety)
38. White radish
39. Raw mango
40. Sweet lime
41. Sweet potato
42. Colocassia leaf
43. Garlic
44. Lettuce
45. Spring onion
46. Turnip

WONDERWORLD OF VEGETARIAN COOKING

Preparation and Enjoyment of Indian
&
International Cooking
with
THE ART OF VEGETABLE & FRUIT CARVING

JYOTI NIKUNJ PAREKH

WONDERWORLD OF
VEGETARIAN COOKING

Published by The Western India Mfr'rs Agency (Pvt.) Ltd.
Peerbhoy Mansion, 456, Sardar V. P. Road,
Bombay-400 004, India

First published 1989 2nd Printing 1992

Photographs   : Swapan Mukherji
                Nikunj S. Parekh, Sonali N. Parekh
Art Direction : Alka Shah, Babuji Shilpi,
                Dina Ambani, Sonali N. Parekh
Line Drawings : Mona Patel, Sripal Munshi

Printed and bound in India by M/s Conway Printers Pvt. Ltd., New Bombay.

SOLE DISTRIBUTORS FOR INDIA:
THE WESTERN INDIA MFR'RS AGENCY (PVT) LTD.
Peerbhoy Mansion, 456, Sardar V.P. Road,
Bombay-400 004, INDIA.

EXCLUSIVE OVERSEAS DISTRIBUTORS OUTSIDE INDIA :
EASTERN OVERSEAS CORPORATION
16, Onlooker Bldg., 2nd Floor,
Sir P.M. Road, Bombay-400 001. INDIA.

ISBN 81-81-85304-46-7

CONTENTS

ACKNOWLEDGEMENTS

This book is a result of persistent demands and requests from my innumerable students to author a vegetarian cookery book, containing simple, quick and inexpensive but timetested recipes which also presents the art and techniques of fruit and vegetable carving. I wish to express my thanks to one and all who offered help in preparation of this book, but most important asset for any endeavour is the GRACE OF GOD ALMIGHTY, who gives us the strength to carry our onward march towards perfection.

I would like to thank my husband NIKUNJ, who constantly inspired me and helped me in every way, without whose help the production of this book would have been impossible.

My sincere thanks also to my sisters-in-law, NEELA KHAMBHLA and SEEMA SHIRODKAR, for their suggestions and initially sharing their culinary knowledge. SONALI, my daughter, gave her valuable suggestions and ideas on preparing the layout of the book and some line drawings. My mother-in-law SHAKUNTALA PAREKH, has always been a pillar of strength. KIRAN SHAH, my brother, helped me with his expertise in printing. JAYSHREE SHAH helped in preparing the recipes under my instructions during the long photography sessions.

My special thanks to BABUJI SHILPI, an eminent interior designer and ALKA SHAH, my friend for the most valuable assistance to get proper props and arrangements for photography, to Mr. SHANBAUG of Strand Book Stall for his sound advice in preparing the book. MILIND VAZE of National Typesetters for typing the manuscript and to SMITA AMBANI, MINAL BAJAJ, MAITHILI DESAI, SHAILA JHAVERI, MUMTAZ KACHWALA, UMKA KHANNA, LEELA PATEL, PURNIMA PATEL, ALKA PODDAR, MEENA SHAH, PADMA SHAH, SURBHI SHARMA, HEMU SHIPLI, NILOUFER SHROFF, VILOO SHROFF and SAVITRI ZAVERI for the help in procuring crockery, cutlery and items of table decoration, during the photography sessions. MR. AND MRS. KARTIKEYA MAHADEVIA for their help on health foods.

Despite busy schedules many well wishers, friends came forward to assist me in fulfilling the task of preparing this book.

— *JYOTI NIKUNJ PAREKH*

INTRODUCTION

The word *vegetarian* comes from the Latin word *Vegetus*, meaning "whole, sound, fresh or lively". The original meaning of the word implies a balanced philosophical and moral sense of life, a lot more than just a diet of vegetables and fruits.

These feelings have an ancient tradition, manifest in the Hindu and Sikh religions. As the front dust jacket of this book depicts, the way we Indians, serve our meals on flat circular plates with shallow rims known as 'Thalis'. The liquid foods such as curries, dals are poured into bowls known as 'katoris', which can either be arranged on or near the *thali*. On festive occasions, the *thali* and *katoris* are arranged on a raised stand made of wood known as *patla*. Another *patla* is arranged at the rear side for the person eating the meal to sit on. The festive border design on the floor is either *rungoli* or *alpana* - an ancient art of India - which is hand drawn with powdered marble, sand or rice paste. Generally, all items of food including the *puris, dals,* curries, sweets, savouries and kachumbar (salad) etc., accompaniments are served together, except the rice and papudums, which are offered separately.

Food is eaten with fingers of the right hand only and left hand is kept clean for taking additional helpings of the prepared dishes and picking up a glass of drinking water.

It is the usual practice amongst the devout in India, to offer the prepared dishes first at the altar of the Lord to seek blessings and thank the Almighty for the food. Only then this *prasadam* - the mercy of God, is distributed to family members and friends for partaking.

The rear dust jacket of this book depicts, a typical western meal. As communication in the jet age has made rapid progress, more and more people get exposed to the culinary secrets of far off places. Vegetarian food has gained popularity and a synthesis of many Indian dishes alongside with western dishes has become possible.

In urban India, we observe that housewives and chefs adapt and create exciting new dishes out of the most common vegetables, grains, legumes, pulses, herbs, fruits and spices. A dinner can start with a soup and its accompaniments, at the same time the dinner table will have puris, curries side by side with western style salad, savouries like croquettes or even a baked dish all perfectly co-existing. Such a co-existence, with perfectly laid out, well decorated food creates an atmosphere of gaiety and happiness for the guests to enjoy.

Many philosophers, writers and thinkers like Leonardo da Vinci, Pythagoras, Leo Tolstoy, George Bernard Shaw, Benjamin Franklin, Henry David Thoreau, Mahatma Gandhi, Albert Schweitzer and Albert Einstein, thought that vegetarianism is an essential step towards a better society.

Lord Buddha, Emperor Ashoka preached non-violence, even the Shojin cookery of the Zen sect developed from the prohibition against killing any living being. Today the Buddhist temples and shrines of China, Korea, Japan and Thailand still use vegetables and seaplants to create wholesome vegetarian dishes for the priests as well as common people.

Readers, this vegetarian food, sustains us without hurting any living creature and at the same time gives pleasure in life to one and all. There are certain combinations of vegetables, legumes, pulses and grains that are necessary for a sound diet, which can be a harmless alternative to a diet full of meat, fish and eggs.

'WONDERWORLD OF VEGETARIAN COOKING' is an effort towards getting tasty dishes for both the diet conscious and to the most fastidious entertainers. The book includes 335 recipes of vegetarian dishes alongwith nearly 75 illustrated drawings and more than 20 colour pictures, which also takes you to the enchanting world of carving of fruits and vegetables. Before trying out the recipes, I request each newcomer to read the recipes carefully and then try your hand at it. I am confident the dishes thus prepared will give you, your family members and friends the satisfaction and happiness of having memorable meals.

- JYOTI NIKUNJ PAREKH

EXPLANATION OF COOKERY TERMS

AJI-NO-MOTO (Monosodium glutamate)
A white crystalline seasoning that enhances the natural flavours of many foods. It is very popular in Chinese dishes and salads.

APPETIZER
The first course of a meal of titbits served before a meal. Drinks, cocktails are also called appetizers.

ASPIC
A transparent savoury jelly.

AU GRATIN
A dish prepared and transferred into a baking dish. It is then covered with a sauce, breadcrumbs or cheese, before baking or grilling.

BAKING POWDER
It is a mixture of soda-bicarbonate with some suitable acid, like cream of tartar. It is then diluted with corn flour to a suitable strength before packing and marketing. Baking powder is used as a raising agent in baked dishes like cakes, biscuits etc. Generally, 1 or 2 teaspoons of baking powder is used per half kilo of flour.

BATTER
A mixture of flour and liquid of such consistency that it can be beaten or stirred or poured. It may be sweet or savoury.

BIRYANI
A rich rice dish cooked usually on festive occasions. Originally, it is a combination of rice, meat of chicken pieces with lots of spices. But biryani c an be prepared with mixed vegetables also.

BREADCRUMBS
Dry roast bread in 150 degree C oven until crisp but not brown. Make course powder either with electric grinder or with 'khal dasta' (similar to mortar and pestle). To store, refrigerate in an air tight bottle.

CANAPES
Small dainty pieces of toast, fried bread, crackers or pastry on which little savouries are served.

CARAMEL
It is prepared by heating sugar until it turns dark brown. It is used for flavouring sweet dishes.

CASSEROLE
An ovenproof baking dish with a tight fitting lid. Used for cooking stews etc. in the oven. The food is usually served directly from casserole.

CEREALS
An ovenproof baking dish with a tight fitting lid. Used for cooking stews etc. in the oven. The food is usually served directly from casserole.

CHARLOTTE RUSSE
It is type of pudding where a mould is lined with sponge cake or sponge fingers and filled with a mixture of cream, fruits and jelly.

CHOWDER
An American style stew or soup made with potatoes and other vegetables. Milk and various seasoning are added to it. Crackers or crisp croutons are generally added just before serving.

COCHINEAL
Red colour.

CONDIMENTS
Spices and seasonings.

CONSOMME
A light coloured clear soup.

CREPES
A fancy name given to pancakes. Similar to 'puda' or 'dosa'.

CROQUETTES
A soft mixture of vegetables and seasoning, rolled into small oval shapes. They are coated with breadcrumbs or vermicelli or semolina and golden brown.

CROUTONS
Bread cut into small pieces or fancy shapes and fried or toasted. They are used as a garnish for soups.

FALOODA
It is a transparent vermicelli made out of corn flour. It is used as a garnish with Indian icecream like kulfi and cold drinks made out of milk.

FATS AND OILS

(A)   FATS

Margarine, butter, ghee, vanaspati ghee (hydrogenated oils).

Butter, ghee and vanaspati ghee has been explained in the heading 'Milk'.
Margarine — Margarine is made entirely from vegetable oils, processed to give desirable spreading and cooking properties. In many recipes margarine and butter can replace each other, although in certain recipes like cakes, butter gives better flavour and consistency. But margarine only from a store that keeps it refrigerated. Store covered, in a refrigerator.

(B)   OILS

Refined groundnut oil, coconut oil, refined sesame (til) oil, mustard oil, salad oil.

Many different kinds of oils are used as a cooking medium in India. Each oil has its own characteristic flavour which influences the taste of the dish. When it is mentioned in the recipe just 'oil' it means either refined seasame oil or refined groundnut oil. Salad oil is used in some of the western style recipes. Coconut oil is used in some of the south Indian recipes, while mustard oil is used for north western Indian recipes.

FLAN
It is a pastry case prepared in a flat tin and later filled with a sweet or savoury mixture.

FOOL
A sweet made with sieved fruit, whipped into frothy light mixture with cream or custard.

FRITTERS
Vegetables or fruits coated with batter and deep fried.

FROSTING
A sugar icing either cooked or uncooked used to cover and decorate cakes etc.

GELATINE
Unflavoured gelatine is sold in four to five envelopes to a packet. Generally, one envelope (about 1 tablespoon) gelatine is used for every two cups of liquid. It is also advisable to follow the instructions on the packet.

Fruit flavoured gelatine packets, generally known as jelly crystals, are readily available in many delectable flavours.

For the successful use of gelatine, following points are worth remembering :

(1)   Before melting gelatine, always soak it in the liquid for a few minutes, then put over hot water. It will melt with heat. Stir till all the grains are dissolved. Never get tempted to melt directly on the gas. Burnt gelatine will give out very bad smell.

(2)   While preparing puddings, both - melted gelatine and milk, should be at room temperature, otherwise the milk might curdle.

(3)   Use hot melted gelatine while mixing in the very chilled mixture, otherwise, it will form strands and will not mix with the liquid.

(4)   Always set the jelly in a wet mould. To unmould gelatine desserts, immerse mould, almost to rim, in a bowl of warm water for a few minutes (if mould is glass, use hot water). Remove gently loosen gelatine with a thin knife on all sides. If it does not loosen after dipping, repeat the process. Then place serving dish, upside down on top of the mould. Invert carefully lift off mould, leaving jelly on dish. It is a good idea to keep surface of the serving plate wet, before unmoulding the gelatine, you can move it to centre of dish more easily if it has fallen off centre.

GLACE
Best example is glace cherries. A thin sugar syrup is cooked to the cracked stage and then used as coating.

GREEN CHILLI-GINGER PASTE
Many Indian recipes require freshly chopped or ground chillies as well as ginger. To save time on chopping and grinding everytime, it is convenient to prepare paste as follows and store in an air-tight jar for a few days in the fridge.
-       100 grams green chillies
-       1-1/2 inch ginger
-       1/2 teaspoon salt
-       1 teaspoon lemon juice
Grind to a paste all the above ingredients.

HORS D'OEUVRE
These are small savoury titbits, usually cold, served as appetizers.

ICING
Sugar coating used to decorate a cake.

KEBAB
Spiced pieces of food grilled in a tandoor or over open iron grill.

KOFTA
Vegetable balls.

MARZIPAN
A sweet or an icing made out of ground almonds and sugar bound into a paste.
MASALA
Mixed spices.

MILK
Milk has been called 'Nature's perfect food". No other food consumed alone, can support human life than milk. That is why it is one of the major ingredients in preparing number of recipes; sweet as well as savoury. Milk is not only used directly in food preparation but it is also changed into different products like butter, curds, ghee, paneer etc. before using. The following explanations will serve as general guide and will help you in many recipes.

BUTTER
Butter has always been a favourite because of its unique flavour and its ability to enhance the texture and flavour of so many everyday dishes.

Salted or unsalted butter is available in ready packets. It can be easily prepared at home. Collect fresh cream from the milk in a vessel. When sufficient amount is collected, mix one tablespoon of sour curds in two cups of cream. Leave aside for four to five hours. Then beat the entire mixture with a wooden spoon. Water will separate leaving lump of butter. Strain and store in a covered bowl. Homemade butter contains a good deal of moisture. It should have a sweet, fresh taste. If kept too long or in an unsuitable storage place, it will turn rancid. Always store butter in a cool place.

Cream
A layer of thick cream removed from top of the chilled milk.

Curd
Plain yoghurt is a good substitute for curds. Curds is used extensively in Indian cooking. It improves digestion and has a cooling effect against the hot spicy food. Beat and break lumps of curds before mixing with the ingredients. Sometimes, it may curdle if cooked for too long or at high temperature. Though this will not look good, it will not harm the taste and flavour of the dish.

Heat 1/2 litre of milk to lukewarm. Take about one tablespoon of curds (for culture) and smear it along the base and sides of a bowl. Pour warm milk and stir gently. Cover the bowl and leave in a warm place overnight. Next morning when ready, store in fridge.

Note: Curds can be made by mixing a small pinch of powdered alum in little curd that is used as culture.

Condensed Milk
Evaporated milk to which sugar has been added before canning is called condensed milk. It is convenient to use condensed milk in preparing many delicious desserts. It is readily available in cans. Use according to the directions on the can as well as follow the recipe carefully. Condensed milk will keep for a week or so after the can has been opened as the sugar acts as a preservative.

Ghee-Clarified butter
Ghee is available at any Indian grocery shop, but homemade ghee has a special flavour.

Heat unsalted homemade butter over low heat (see 'butter' above) in a thick based vessel. Ghee will separate leaving creamish residue at the bottom. Remove from heat and strain. Cool Store in an airtight bottle and use as required. It keeps well for a long period.

Hydrogenated oils (Vanaspati ghee) can be used instead of homemade pure ghee.

Khoya
It is also called 'mawa'. It is readily available in India. Boiling milk in a think, broad vessel, stirring often, until a thick residue left is called mawa. Use of a non-stick pan is ideal , although occasional stirring is

necessary. One can put a few drops of lemon juice in the boiling milk to hasten the process.

Paneer or chena (homemade cottage cheese)
Many sweets are made out of chhena. When the chhena is flattened, pressed and set, it is called paneer. Paneer is used in many curried and savoury dishes.

Paneer is readily available in India. If not, one can easily make it at home. Take half a litre of milk and bring it to a boil. Reduce heat and stir in half tablespoon of lemon juice mixed with quarter cup of curds. (One can use quarter teaspoon of citric acid instead of lemon juice). Stir till milk curdles and very light greenish water separates. Remove from heat strain through a cheese cloth. The small lump that remains in the cloth is 'chhena' and the liquid called whey will drain out. It will make approximately (depending on the cream content of the milk) three-fourth cup of chhena. Whey has lot of nourishment. It can be used instead of water in preparation of dals (pulses), rice, curries, soups etc. Chhena is wrapped in the cheese cloth and flattened to form a square shape. A heavy weight is placed over it and left aside for three hours, to drain out the water content completely. Unwrap carefully and cut into small cubes as required.

Cheese
Cheese is one of the most popular ingredients in cooking, as it easily blends with many other food flavours. It is (1) sprinkled over vegetable soups (2) added to sauces with vegetables (3) in savoury dishes with macaroni, spaghetti, rice, cheese pies, cheesecakes etc. (4) sometimes mixed with breadcrumbs or directly sprinkled as a topping in cooked vegetable dishes, which are then browned under dry heat (5) with salads (6) in sandwiches (7) or just plain cubes with drinks. Hence it is very important to know more about this versatile ingredient.

Cheese is made from milk which has been naturally or artificially soured. Colouring and salt are added during the process. Natural souring is brought about by keeping milk in a warm place overnight. Harmless bacteria turns milksugar into lactic acid which causes curdling. Artificial souring is brought about by adding an enzyme. Rennet is the enzyme most generally used. On souring, whey is drained off. The curd which remains is cut and pressed into moulds and then ripened or cured. There is an immense variety of cheese made world over by varying fat contents, adding flavours and pressures during the manufacturing processes as cheese is normally bought readymade. Following tips will help in preparing many dishes with cheese.

Processed cheese is the most commonly used. It is hard, which has been finely divided and heated with water and emulsified until a homogeneous liquid is formed. This is poured into moulds lined with silver foil or directly in cans. This cheese stores well, because heating has pasterised it and the bacteria have been destroyed.

Processed cheese is normally served after meals. It is good for cooking too. It melts smoothly and quickly without separation or stringiness. It is uniform in flavour and texture.

All cheese require special care in handling. Once the packet or can is opened it should be stored properly. Cheese, if left open, will soon go dry and mouldy. Though one can slice off the harmless mouldy part and use the remaining cheese. The best policy is to rewrap in original paper and place in refrigerator. Cheese should not be served cold. It tastes good at room temperature.

For cooking purposes it is useful to have grated cheese stored in an airtight box, ready in the fridge. Cheese must be dry and hard for grating. The harder the cheese the finer it will grate and stores for a longer time.

MOUSSE
A light spongy dish made with sweetened and flavoured cream. It is whipped and frozen.

PAPAD OR PAPUDUMS
Very paper thin crisp rounds of about 8" diameters are prepared out of flour of pulses and legumes. Spices like black pepper, green chillies, garlic, asafoetida etc. are added while making dough. They are dried in sun and stored. For serving they are either roasted or deep fried.

PARFAIT
Icecream served in a tall glass and decorated with a variety of nuts and fruits.

PUREE
A smooth mixture obtained by sieving cooked fruits or vegetables.

PULSES
Vegetables that grow in pods like peas, beans, lentils etc.

PURIS
It is a very common bread made throughout India. A dough is made out of wheat flour with or without spices. Small rounds of about 3" diameter and 1/2" thick are rolled out on a wooden board and deep fried. They will puff out on frying. Many times reference is made in some recipes to make 'dough like puris' or 'roll like puris'.

RAITA
Beaten curds mixed with grated vegetables like carrots, cucumber, boiled potatoes etc. or fruits like bananas. It is mildly flavoured with mustard paste and salt.

SHORBET
It is a frozen mixture of fruit juice, sugar, milk or water.

SHORTENING
Fat suitable for baking is sometimes called shortening.

SLIVERS
Long thin slices normally obtained from nuts like almonds, pistachios etc.

SOUFFLE
It is a very light fluffy dish prepared by incorporating lots of air. It can be a hot baked dish or a cold dish.

STOCK
A liquid in which vegetables are cooked. This stock is used as a foundation for soups, sauces and stews etc.

YEAST
Yeast consists of microscopic, unicellular plants. When yeast is kept in favourable conditions, it is capable of rapid multiplication. That is why it is used to ferment the dough, specially of breads. It puffs up the dough, so that it spreads and rises and becomes full of holes, thus making it light and not close and heavy. The holes are retained during cooking.

There are two types of yeast available: (1) Dried yeast (2) Fresh yeast or compressed yeast.

Dried yeast
It is in granular form. It can be stored in a dry cool place for several weeks. When mixed with lukewarm water and sugar it becomes active. This mixture is allowed to ferment for sometime before using in dough preparation.

Fresh yeast
It is a beige coloured compressed yeast. It has a fresh yeasty smell. It should be used in fresh condition. When it is stale, it changes to darker colour and gives out bad smell. To keep fresh yeast in good condition, wrap in a clean plastic bag and place in the ice compartment of your refrigerator. It stays fresh for at least 2 months. In deep freezer, it stays for more than 6 months.

Fresh yeast remains active and will grow and multiply rapidly when added to dough. It can be directly rubbed into flour or blended in liquid and then mixed with flour.

While preparing bread dough, all the ingredients used have their effect on the action of the yeast. The effect is as follows.

<u>Water</u> - Always use lukewarm water. Too hot water will kill the action of yeast and in cold water yeast will not become active.

<u>Flour</u> - Flour (maida) gives satisfactory results in most of the breads. Wheat flour does not make light textured breads if used alone. So mix equal amount of flour with it to get good bread..

<u>Sugar</u> - Sugar is added to hasten the activity of the yeast, to improve flavour and taste. Too much sugar retards the action of the yeast.

<u>Salt</u> - It is used to improve the flavour and taste of the bread. Too much salt retards the action of the yeast

<u>Fat</u> - Margarine, butter, ghee or refined oil can be used according to the recipe. The volume of a bread is much improved by small amount of fat. Fat in large quantity slows down yeast action, reduces the rise and gives a softer dough and smaller bread. But the right amount enriches the dough, gives bread a silky texture and delays staling.

EXPLANATION OF COOKING METHODS

TO BAKE

Food cooked in the hot dry air of an oven. The temperature is controlled to get the right type of cooking. Foods like breads, cakes, pastries, puddings, biscuits, etc. are cooked in an oven. A good cook should learn to know his own oven and to know how the heat varies in different parts. Usually, the top shelf and sides are hottest as hot air rises. Temperature is little low in the centre and front side near the door. Food placed in the right position or shifted as required will give satisfactory results.

Ovens are operated by either gas or electricity. The chart on Pg. 34 will help to convert temperatures according to the recipes. In this book temperatures are given in centigrades.

TO BARBECUE

Food pieces basted with a highly seasoned sauce and grilled over open charcoal flame.

TO BASTE

To apply melted fat over food during cooking to keep it moist.

TO BEAT

A thin liquid mixed with an eggbeater or a fork to incorporate air and to thicken it gradually, e.g. egg or fresh cream. This method is also used to make a mixture smooth and free from lumps. A wooden spoon is best for beating thick mixtures.

TO BLANCH

A method to remove difficult skin, e.g. almonds. The ingredient is soaked into a bowl of boiling water for about five minutes. Water is drained before removing the skin.

TO BLEND

Two or more ingredients are thoroughly mixed together.

TO BOIL

The best method of boiling is to plunge the vegetables into boiling liquid. Cover the vessel and allow to reboil. Then reduce heat and simmer till cooked. The liquid left at the end of cooking contains some nutrient and flavour. As far as possible, this should not be wasted. It can be used as a stock for soup or for preparing curries and dishes containing gravy.

For boiling vegetables for salads and vegetables for garnishing, it is very important to retain colour of the vegetables. The best method is to boil vegetables with little salt and a pinch of soda bicarb. Boil uncovered on fast flame. Remove in a colander as soon as they are cooked. Pour cold water over them.

TO BRUSH

A thin, even coating of milk or ghee is applied to pies, buns, etc., just before they are placed in the oven. This is done to make them glossy in appearance and help them to brown more quickly and deeply. Special pastry brushes are available in the market.

TO CHILL UNTIL SET

A liquid mixed with gelatine, jelly or custard, becomes solid especially by keeping in the fridge.

TO CHOP

Food cut into very small pieces with no regards to shape or size. Sometimes a fine chopping is mentioned for herbs like coriander leaves, parsley etc.

TO COAT

Cover food with thin layer.

TO CREAM

Margarine, butter or ghee softened and beaten with a wooden spoon. Then sugar is mixed into it. This method is used for preparing cake mixtures.

TO CUT
Vegetables or fruits are cut into different smaller sizes with a knife or scissors.

TO CUT IN
Cold fat like margarine or butter is cut with a knife and added to the flour. This method is used for preparing pastry mixtures.

TO GRATE
Making food into very small pieces with the help of a grater.

TO KNEAD
This method is used to mix ingredients thoroughly into a dough. The dough is pressed with knuckles and also pressed, pulled and stretched to make the mixture smooth and light.

TO MARINATE
A mixture of vinegar, oil, herbs, spices, curds, etc. is prepared. Food pieces are soaked in it before cooking for a few hours. This makes them tender, and improves flavour and texture.

TO MASH
Reducing soft cooked food into a pulp like boiled potatoes, carrots, peas etc.

TO MINCE
Food cut into extremely small pieces with the help of an electric or an ordinary mincer.

TO PARBOIL
To boil food until only partly cooked.

TO RUB IN
This method is used in preparing pastry like shortcrust pastry. Here the margarine or butter is mixed in the flour very lightly with the help of finger tips and thumbs, as a result the mixture looks like breadcrumbs.

TO SAUTE
Food is tossed and lightly browned in shallow fat.

TO SEMISET
Food is cooled to partly solid state, e.g. jellied pudding or salad is kept in the fridge till semiset before mixing other ingredients, so that there is equal distribution of solids in the jellied food.

TO SCOOP
A process of removing the inner portion and make a hollow with a round spoon or a special scooper.

TO SIFT
To pass through a fine sieve to break or remove lumps.

TO SHRED
Cut food in this long strips with a knife or a shredder.

TO SIMMER
To cook just below the boiling point.

TO SLICE
Cut food into thin long slices but not as fine as shredding.

TO STEAM
Food cooked by the steam rising from boiling water. Food is steamed in a pressure cooker. Special vessels

are available to put food in and lowered into a pressure cooker with little water. It is steamed with or without pressure, as done for idlis.

Sometimes a big deep vessel is filled with a little water. A ring is placed in the centre to put the plate or colander of uncooked food. Then the vessel is tightly covered before steaming. This method is used for making dhoklas and muthias. Special steam boxes are also available for convenient cooking.

TO STONE
To remove seed from the fruit.

TO TOSS
Two or more ingredients are mixed together without mashing. It is done either with a fork or by shaking the vessel, e.g. for salads.

TO WHIP OR WHISK
To beat cream or any other liquid until it is frothy.

TO STIFF BUT FLOWING
Cream is beaten with an eggbeater until it is stiff, i.e. it falls in peaks on picking, but peaks flow down. This type of cream is good for mixing in puddings.

CONDIMENTS AND NUTS

Spices play a very important role in cooking. It brings out the original flavour and makes the food aromatic, attractive, appetizing and most important-digestive. Indians have mastered the art of using right combination of spices without masking the natural taste of the basic ingredients or their nutritive values. Most of the spices have some medicinal value. An expert housewife knows how to use them in cooking to balance the food value and taste. For example, vegetables like 'papdi' and cereals like 'val' cause gastric problems. But adding a teaspoon of carom seeds (ajwain) and a pinch of asafoetida while cooking reduces the effect.

Spices should be stored in airtight containers and should be kept in a dry, dark and cool place. Freshly ground spices give out good aroma. They lose their flavour on keeping for a long time. So it is advisable to buy 'whole' spices and grind them as required. If you have to buy spices in powder form, then buy in small quantities, making sure that they are fresh at the time of purchasing.

Nuts like almonds, cashews, pistachios are used in many sweet as well as savoury dishes. They make the dishes tasty but rich in calories.

Given below are the essential and common condiments and nuts used in western and Indian cooking. Hindi names are given in brackets.

ALMONDS (*Badam*)
Among all types of nuts, almonds are very widely used in cooking. They taste good in sweets, like icecreams, confectioneries, Indian sweets etc. Almonds combine successfully with savoury dishes, vegetable preparations, soups as well as salads. Almonds are used whole, blanched, flaked, slivered or toasted.

ALFALFA
It is a light-brown coloured legume with delicious nutty flavour. It is sprouted and used in making salads and sandwich fillings.

ANISE (*Suwa*)
It is a golden-brown, tear shaped, aromatic seed. It is believed to have the property to help in digestion and stimulate the appetite. In India, a spoonful mixture of roasted anise seeds mixed with roasted dry coconut and poppy seeds are eaten after meals as mouth freshener. It is also recommended for nursing mothers, as it has the property to increase milk supply.

ANISEED (*Saunf*)
It is a small sweet smelling, light green coloured and oval shaped seed. In western countries, they are used to flavour wines and confectioneries. In India, it is roasted and eaten after meals as a mouth freshener and to stimulate digestion.

ASAFOETIDA (*Hing*)
It is a strong smelling, yellowish to brownish coloured resin. It is available in lump form as well as in grainy powdered form. It is a common practice to put one or two lumps in each bottle containing powdered spices like chillies, cummin seeds and coriander seeds and turmeric powder to preserve them for the whole year. Powdered asafoetida is used in very small quantity (just a pinch) for flavouring many vegetarian dishes.

BASIL (*Tulsi*)
It is a sacred plant for Hindus, with lots of medicinal properties. The leaves have sweet smell. Its tender fresh leaves are used as garnishing. It also makes very tasty cold drinks.

BAY LEAVES (*Tej Patta*)
The dry light green coloured long aromatic leaves are preserved in an airtight bottle. Mostly used in flavouring pullaos and some curries. The leaves are used whole and are not eaten. They are removed at the time of eating.

BLACK PEPPERCORNS (*Kala mirch*)

Fresh green peppercorns in bunches are used in pickles. But sun dried, hard, black, brittle seeds are commonly used in many western and Indian recipes. They are used whole or freshly ground in powdered form.

BLACK SALT (*Kala namak or Sanchal*)

It is a purplish brown coloured rock salt, with a distinctive flavour. Used in small quantities in snacks or pickles.

CARAWAY SEEDS (*Shahjeeru*)

They are dark brown very small seeds, smaller than common cummin seeds. They are used to flavour certain breads, biscuits and some vegetarian dishes.

CARDAMOMS (*Elaichi*)

It is an aromatic spice, generally sold in its pods. There are two types -one is dark brown and big (Badi Elaichi) with seeds inside and a strong flavour. It is used whole for flavouring pullao. The other one is small with light green pod with black seeds and pleasant smell. Creamish coloured and plumper variety is also available, but with little less aroma. Indians use cardamoms extensively in flavouring sweet dishes and also in many vegetables and rice dishes. Sometimes, they are used whole or black seeds are powdered before using in the recipe.

CAROB POWDER

It is made from the pulp of the dried carob beans. It is used in soft drinks and in confectioneries as substitute for chocolate powder.

CAROM SEEDS (*Ajwain*)

Very tiny brown seeds with strong smell. Very good in preparing many Indian vegetables and pulses.

CASHEWNUTS (*Kaju*)

One of the favourite nuts for preparing many western and Indian dishes. Its subtle flavour and taste blends very well in preparing many sweet as well as savoury dishes. It is a half round white nut with brown thin shell which comes out readily on roasting. One can buy shelled cashewnuts also. Roasted, salted cashewnuts are excellent to eat with cocktail drinks.

CHILLIES (*Hari mirch and lal mirch*)

Generally, two types of chillies are used in cooking. Fresh green ones (hari mirch) and dry red ones (lal mirch). Both varieties are quite pungent. If you want just the flavour without its pungentness then make a slit on the sides of the chilli and shake off the white seeds from the inside. Green chillies are used whole or cut into pieces or ground to a paste before using. Red chillies are either used whole or ground to a paste. Normally, Indian housewives buy chilli powder in quantity in the hot summer season and store for the whole year in an airtight bottle. In western countries, though chilli powder is available with the Indian grocer, cayenne pepper powder can be used in the recipe in place of chilli powder. Of course, one should use it with discretion.

CINNAMON (*Dalchini*)

It is a dried aromatic brown bark of cinnamon tree. It is used in stick or powder form in sweets, cakes and curries. Sticks used for flavouring pullao are not eaten, but removed at the time of eating.

CLOVES (*Laung or Lavang*)

It is a dried aromatic flower bud of a clove tree. It is used whole or in powder form in many sweets, savouries and spice powders. Clove oil can be extracted from cloves which has a lot of medicinal value.

COCONUT (*Narial*)

Coconut is very extensively used in many Indian sweets and savouries. Buy a coconut which has a lot of water inside. Break open in two. Grate coconut with special grater or separate kernels from shell by heating and then grate with grater or in food processor. Coconut is used in grated form or as coconut milk extract.

Method for extracting coconut milk is as follows :

Put one cup of grated coconut in a mixer with two cups of warm water. Blend till smooth. Sieve the milk thoroughly with hand. Dry residue is discarded. Some recipes ask for thin and thick coconut milk. In that case take one cup of grated coconut and one cup of warm water in the mixer. Blend and sieve out the thick milk. Take the same coconut back in the mixer with another cup of warm water. Blend and then sieve. Squeeze out thin coconut milk.

In Europe and America, one can buy tinned coconut milk and also creamed frozen coconut in small slabs. It can be preserved in the freezer for 2 - 3 months.

DESSICATED COCONUT (*Khaman*)
It is a dry white tiny flakes of coconut. It is easily available at the grocers. It is used mainly in preparing sweets like cakes, biscuits, puddings etc. Always preserve in an airtight box and keep in the refrigerator.

CORIANDER (*Dhania*)
Coriander leaves (hara dhania) are aromatic herb similar to parsley. Its leaves and tender stems are used in cooking and also used as a garnish. Coriander seeds (sabut dhania) whole and in powdered form are commonly used in many spice mixtures, savouries, vegetable dishes and pickles.

CUMMIN SEEDS (*Jeera or Zeera*)
Aromatic small seeds which give out more aroma when roasted or added to hot oil. Cummin seeds whole or in powdered form are very commonly used in Indian cooking.

CURRY LEAVES (*Meetha neem or Karipatta*)
Aromatic leaves used fresh in many Indian dishes, especially in the south. They are very fond of its flavour and use extensively in their cooking. Like bay leaves, they are added for their flavour and are kept aside while eating.

COCUM (*Garcinia indica*)
It is a dark purple coloured very acidic dried fruit. It is used to give sour taste to curries and pulses. Sometimes, they are added whole and are kept aside while eating or its extract is added to the recipe.

DILL (*Suwa bhaji*)
Dill is a feathery succulent of parsley family. The leaves can be fresh or dried and have a mild caraway like flavour. Used in many vegetable dishes, salads and soups.

FENNEL SEEDS (*Badi saunf*)
It is a bigger but milder variety of aniseed family. In India the fennel seeds are used in flavouring many vegetable dishes and pickles. It is roasted and eaten after meals as mouth freshener.

FENUGREEK SEEDS (*Methi*)
Yellowish brown, flat, squarish seeds, important for Indian cooking. They are used whole or broken in pickles and for flavouring vegetable and curries. But they are used sparingly as they have a bitter taste. Fenugreek leaves are used as vegetables and also in preparing Indian style breads. Fenugreek can be sprouted. Soak seeds for four to five hours. Drain water and put in a box and refrigerate. They will sprout very nicely within three days. It can make a tasty addition to salads. Fenugreek seeds have lot of medicinal value.

GINGER (*Ginger*)
It is a rhizome with a likeable pungent flavour. It is used in many Indian savoury dishes. Scrape the skin before grating or chopping very finely. It can also be crushed in an electric wet grinder. One can store ginger in the fridge placed in a paper bag for a long time.

Ginger is dried and powdered (Sounth). This powder is used in preparing confectioneries and biscuits like ginger biscuits etc.

GARLIC (*Lahsun*)

It is a strong smelling bulb with segments known as cloves. It has a lot of medicinal value. It is supposed to purify blood and reduce cholestrol. It enhances the flavour of curries, chutneys and pickles. It is also available in powdered form. This powder mixed with salt, tastes very good when sprinkled on dishes like pizza.

GROUNDNUTS OR PEANUTS (*Mungphali*)

They are roasted and rubbed over coarse cloth to remove skin, then stored in an airtight bottle. They are used in coarse powdered form in many savoury dishes. Sweets are also prepared out of them. Groundnut oil is also used very commonly in Indian cooking.

LEMON (*Nimbu*)

Lemon is very extensively used in all the Indian cuisines. It makes a refreshing drink during the summer months. The skin is used in making pickles. The fresh skin is sometimes grated (lemon rind) and used in certain recipes as flavouring.

LOTUS PUFFS (*Makhana*)

These are lotus seeds. They puff up while roasting. They are used in many sweets and savoury dishes.

MACE (*Javintri*)

It is the outer orange coloured membrane of nutmeg. It is powdered and used sparingly in sweets as well as savoury dishes, as it has a very strong flavour.

MANGO POWDER (*Amchoor*)

Raw, sour mangoes are peeled and cut into pieces and dried in scorching sun and then powdered.

MINT (*Pudina*)

It is a very aromatic herb, used in pickles, raitas, chutneys and also in certain vegetable dishes. Its crisp tender green leaves are used as a garnish.

MOLASSES (*Congealed jaggery or gur*)

Made out of sugarcane juice. Comes in light yellow to brownish colour in lump form. Store in an airtight bottle. It is used for sweetening many sweets and savoury dishes. It has better food value than sugar.

MUSTARD SEEDS (*Rye or Sarson*)

These are tiny round reddish brown to black coloured seeds. The one commonly used in Indian cooking and also in many western dishes. They are used as whole or broken to pieces or made into a paste or in powdered form. Its paste has a very pungent taste. In India, mustard is popular with vegetables, pulses and pickles. In north India, mustard plant leaves are used as vegetables.

NIGELLA SEEDS (*Kalongi or onion seeds*)

These are very tiny black seeds with peculiar flavour. They are used in flavouring some vegetarian snacks and pickles.

NUTMEG (*Jaiphal*)

Outer hard kernel is broken to take out nut like brown, pungent smelling seed from inside. It is powdered and used sparingly in sweets and savoury dishes - Indian as well as western.

OREGANO SEEDS (*Ajwain*)

These small tear shaped, light brown seeds are a pleasantly aromatic spice. They are popularly used in some vegetables and flavouring breads and popular dishes like pizza.

PAPRIKA

A bright red powder made from the special variety of capsicum peppers. Mild to very hot varieties are available. It's more popular with western dishes like cheese preparations, cocktail dips, dressings, sauces, soups etc.

PARSLEY

It is one of the most commonly used herb in western countries. There are many different varieties. The leaves and stems of the plant are used; of which stems have strongest flavour. The stem is chopped and used to flavour soups, sauces, salads etc. Fresh crisp leaves are used as a garnish. Dried parsley flakes are also available, but they do not have as strong flavour as the fresh ones.

PISTACHIOS (*Pista*)

Pistas are available either whole with hard shells or shelled. They are green from inside with reddish brown thin skin on top. Roasted and salted, they can be used as snacks. Pistachios taste good in icecreams and many other sweet dishes.

POMEGRANATE SEEDS (*Anardana*)

Pomegranate seeds are dried and stored for use as a spice. Powdered seeds give tangy flavour and dark colour to the recipe.

POPPY SEEDS (*Khus Khus*)

They are extremely tiny cream coloured seeds. They are used in recipes whole or made into paste. They are popular in sweet as well as savoury dishes like curries and snacks.

RAISINS (*Kismis*)

Dried seedless grapes are called raisins. Dried black grapes are called **black currants** and another variety is called **Sultanas** or **golden raisins**. All these are used in many Indian sweets and icecreams. They are popular in western dishes like salads, desserts and pies, etc.

SABJA SEEDS (*Tukmaria*)

Tiny black seeds, supposed to have a cooling effect in the stomach. They swell up on soaking and are very commonly used in 'Falooda'.

SAFFRON (*Kesar*)

Saffron is the most expensive spice. It imparts very pleasing flavour as well as golden yellow colour. Saffron is the dried stigma and part of style of the complete saffron flower. It is available in powdered form also. It is used for colouring and flavouring pullaos, sweets and puddings. It makes very pleasant cold drinks too.

ROSE WATER (*Gulab jal*)

It is a clear liquid available ready in bottles. It is distilled from fresh rose petals and is used in small amount for flavouring sweets and cold drinks. Pink fragrant fresh rose petals are also used to garnish certain Indian sweets.

SESAME SEEDS (*Til*)

The beige unpolished seeds are better for using in recipes than the white polished ones. They are very commonly used in Indian cooking. They give out very pleasant nutty flavour on roasting. A black variety is also available.

TAMARIND (*Imli*)

It is the fruit of tamarind tree. Its fresh tender green pods with sharp sour taste is very popular with children. It is used in chutneys also. The ripe brown pods are cleaned off its brittle brown skin and hard seeds. The inner portion obtained is applied with salt and made into balls. They are dried in Sun and then stored in bottles for future use. Required amount of tamarind for the recipe is taken and soaked in water for sometime and given a boil. The pulp is extracted for using in the recipe. Modern housewives, to save time, can extract very thick tamarind pulp in quantity and store in deep freezer. A spoonful can be taken out at the time of use. Tamarind is used in many vegetables, pulses, snacks, sauces and chutneys.

TURMERIC (*Haldi*)

Turmeric is a root having bright yellow colour. Chopped fresh root, mixed with lemon juice and salt is used as pickle. Turmeric root is dried and powdered to be used as spice. It is most commonly used in many vegetarian dishes.

VANILLA
It is an essence sold sometimes as dried pods in western countries or easily available in bottles. It is mainly used to flavour puddings, cakes, custards, milkshakes etc.

VINEGAR (*Sirka*)
Generally made from malt, acetic acid, cider or from wine or grape juice. It is common in western countries to flavour it with herbs, flowers, chillies, garlic sauces and to add sour taste to many other vegetable dishes.

WALNUTS (*Akhrot*)
One of the popular nuts. It is sold whole in its hard shell or shelled. They are excellent in salads, cakes, icecreams and other sweet dishes.

SELECTIVE NAMES OF FOODSTUFFS AND THEIR HINDI EQUIVALENTS

FRUITS

Apple	*Seb*
Apricot	*Khubani*
Banana	*Kela*
Custard apple	*Sitaphal*
Fig	*Anjeer*
Grapes	*Angour*
Guava	*Amrud*
Jackfruit	*Katahal, Fanas*
Lemon	*Meetha nimbu*
Lime	*Nimbu*
Mango	*Aam*
Olives	*Saitun*
Orange	*Narangi, Santra*
Peach	*Aaru*
Pear	*Naspati*
Pineapple	*Ananas*
Pomegranate	*Anar*
Sugarmelon	*Shakharteti*
Watermelon	*Kharbuja*

VEGETABLES

Beans	*Sem*
Beetroot	*Chuquander*
Bittergourd	*Karela*
Bottlegourd, white pumpkin	*Lauki*
Brinjal, eggplant or aubergine	*Baingan*
Cabbage	*Bandh gobi*
Capsicum	*Badi mirch or Simla mirch*
Carrot	*Gajjar*
Cauliflower	*Phool gobi*
Cluster beans	*Gawar ki phali*
Colocassia leaves	*Arvi ka patta*
Cucumber	*Kakri*
Drumstick	*Sahijan*
Fenugreek leaves	*Methi*
French beans	*Fanasi*
Kantola	*Kantola*
Mint	*Pudina*
Green peas	*Mattar*
Lettuce	*Salad leaves*
Lady finger	*Bhindi*
Mushroom	*Guchi, Dhingri*
Onions	*Pyaz*
Padwal	*Padwal*
Potatoes	*Aloo*
Radish	*Mooli*
Red pumpkin	*Kaddu*
Ridge gourd	*Tori, Turai*

Spinach	Palak
Spring onion	Hara pyaz
String beans	Chouli
Sweet potato	Shakharkand
Turnip	Shalgam
Valol	Valol
Water chestnut	Shingora
Yam : elephant	Zaminkand
Yam : ordinary	Ratalu or kand

CEREALS, PULSES AND LEGUMES

Barley	Jav
Bengal gram, whole	Chana
Bengal gram, whole green	Hara chana
Bengal gram, split	Chana dal
Bengal gram, flour or gram flour	Besan
Black eyed beans	Lobia or chola
Black gram	Udad
Black gram, split	Udad dal
Corn or Maize	Makkai
Field beans	Val
Green gram, whole	Moong
Green gram, split with skin	Moong dal chilke wali
Green gram, split, without green skin	Moong dal
Kidney beans	Rajma
Large white gram, chickpeas	Kabuli chana
Bengal gram roasted, puffed and split	Bhune hui channe ki dal, dalia
Lentil	Masoor dal
Millet	Bajara
Muth beans	Muth
Peas	Mattar
Red gram split	Arhar dal, tur dal
Rice puffed	Kurmura
Rice pressed	Poha
Sago	Saudana, sagodana
Semolina	Sooji, rava
Soya beans	Soya beans
Vermicelli	Sevai
Wheat flour	Gehu ka atta
Wheat flour refined	Maida

WEIGHTS, MEASURES AND TEMPERATURE GUIDE

In India, most experienced cooks do not exactly measure all their ingredients whilst preparing their dishes. Even if they measure they have their own way of doing so by using bowls, or any vessel they are used to in daily cooking. But as the new generation of educated cooks are venturing in the kitchen, they are particular in weighing and measuring the ingredients to get the satisfactory results. Some years back people used to make fun of a housewife if she followed a cookbook in the kitchen. Now thanks to the introduction and appreciation of many new national and international recipes, that a housewife can boldly follow a cookbook. A set of scales, measuring jugs and standard measuring cups and spoons are a must in every modern kitchen. In this book weights are given in grams or kilograms (kg) and standard cup measurements. Weighing is more accurate than measuring but for convenience, standard cups and spoons can be used. While measuring, it is better to use level measurement, as it is less subject to errors. For the convenience of the cook in some of the recipes, the weight in grams is rounded off to the nearest multiple of 25 gms or 5 gms depending on the ingredients.

A standard measuring cup indicating 8 ozs. is used or four separate cups of 1/4 cup (2 ozs.), 1/2 cup (4 ozs.), 3/4 cup (6 ozs.) and 1 cup (8 ozs.) are used depending on the individual's choice. Measurements are also given in millilitres (ml.) or litres in brackets.

Standard teaspoons and tablespoons are a great boon in every kitchen as the size of ordinary spoons vary with different manufacturers. In measuring, always use level measures unless it is indicated to use heaped spoon in the recipe.

Following chart will help you to follow recipes.

1 cup	=	8 ozs. (ounces)
2 - 1/2 cups	=	1 pint
1 pint	=	20 ozs.
1/2 litre	=	17 ozs. (approximately)
3 teaspoons	=	1 tablespoon
16 tablespoons	=	1 cup
1 litre	=	1000 millilitres
1 pound	=	16 ozs.
1 oz.	=	30 gms. (approximately)
1 kg.	=	35 ozs. (approximately)
1 kg.	=	2 - 1/2 pounds

Oven Temperatures	Temperature Grades		Gas Numbers
	°C.	°F	
Slow	50°-100°	225° - 230°	1/4
Slow moderate	150°	330°	2
Moderate	200°	375°	5
Moderately hot	250°	425°	7
Hot	330°	475° - 500°	9

The above chart indicates the oven temperatures in Fahrenheit and Centigrade degrees and gas mark. To understand the oven, best guide is the booklet given by the manufacturer. Secondly learn through experience. To know how the heat varies in different parts of it. Usually the top shelf is the hottest as hot air rises.

COCKTAILS AND COLD DRINKS

PUNGENT TOMATO JUICE (6 SERVINGS)

Pungent tomato juice with a raw taste of tomatoes.

INGREDIENTS

1 pint tomato juice from 1 kg. tomatoes

1/2 cup powdered sugar

4 tablespoons lemon juice

1/2 teaspoon Tabasco or Capsico sauce

1 teaspoon Worcestershire sauce

1/2 teaspoon salt

METHOD

(1) Cut tomatoes in big pieces and put them in a mixer and blend. Strain the juice.
(2) Mix all the remaining ingredients and chill in fridge.
(3) Serve in frosted glasses.

To frost:
Dip rim of each serving glass into water or lemon juice. Then dip into icing sugar. Allow to dry before pouring juice.

TROPICAL FRUIT PUNCH (8 SERVINGS)

Sweet and sour punch - a hit for a big party.

INGREDIENTS

1 cup sugar syrup

1/4 cup lemon juice

1 cup boiling water

1 teaspoon tea leaves

1-1/2 tablespoons ginger juice

1 cup orange juice

1 cup pineapple juice

2 bottles soda

TO DECORATE :

Sweet lime or lemon, sliced

A sprig mint leaves

METHOD

(1) Combine one cup water with sugar to make sugar syrup. Heat till sugar dissolves. Add a few drops of lemon to remove the scum. Strain and cool.
(2) Boil the remaining one cup of water. Remove from gas. Sprinkle tea leaves over. Leave aside for five to ten minutes, strain and cool.
(3) Combine all the juices with sugar syrup and tea. Chill. At the time of serving, mix cold soda and serve with lots of crushed ice.
(4) Decorate with slices of sweet lime or lemon and mint leaves.

FRUIT CUP (6 SERVINGS)

A treat for fruit lovers.

INGREDIENTS

1/2 cup orange pieces

1/2 cup sweet lime pieces

1/2 cup grapefruit

1/2 cup pineapple pieces

1 bottle lemonade

1 bottle gingerale or raspberry (red in colour)

METHOD

(1) Mix together all the fruit pieces and chill them.
(2) Add chilled lemonade and gingerale or raspberry to the chilled fruits at the time of serving.
(3) Serve in transparent individual cocktail glasses with fruit fork in each glass.

PINEAPPLE PUNCH (6 SERVINGS)

A refreshing punch with pineapple pieces to be eaten daintily with a tiny fruit fork.

INGREDIENTS

1 cup sugar

1 small can (450 grams) pineapple tidbits or slices

1/2 cup orange juice

3 tablespoons lemon juice

1 bottle soda

1 bottle lemonade

Few mint leaves

TO DECORATE :

A specially prepared cocktail-pick in an umbrella shape

METHOD

(1) Mix sugar into pineapple syrup (from can). Heat till sugar dissolves. Cool.
(2) Cut pineapple into small pieces.
(3) Mix orange and lemon juices.
(4) Mix these juices, with the pineapple syrup, fruit pieces and chill the mixture.
(5) Mix chilled soda and lemonade before serving.
(6) Serve in wide mouth glasses and don't forget to put a small fruit fork in each glass.
(7) For special occasions, you may decorate each glass with a long cocktail-pick made with an umbrella made out of sweetlime peel, carrot and a pea.

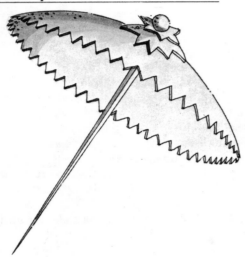
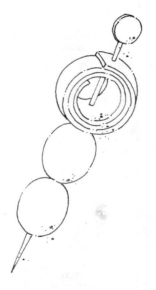

COOL COCONUT DRINK (6 SERVINGS)

A healthy drink for all seasons.

INGREDIENTS

4 fresh coconuts with thin cream

4 tablespoons sugar

TO DECORATE :

A specially prepared cocktail-pick with coconut cream and cherries.

METHOD

(1) Pour out water from the coconuts into a vessel and scrape out cream from inside.
(2) Take cream and sugar in a mixer jar and blend to a puree. To it add the coconut water and mix evenly.
(3) Chill before serving.
(4) Serve with a long cocktail-pick fitted with a curl of coconut cream and glazed cherries.

ICED ORANGE TEA (4 SERVINGS)

A refreshing drink for a hot summer day.

INGREDIENTS	METHOD
1 pint hot tea	(1) Make tea, adding sugar to it. Cool. (Sugar can be adjusted to taste).
6 teaspoons sugar	(2) Pour over crushed ice in a bowl.
Crushed ice	(3) Add orange juice and pour into tall serving glasses.
1/3 cup orange juice	(4) Serve with a slice of lemon and crushed mint leaves floating in each glass.
TO DECORATE :	**Note:**
Mint leaves and lemon slices	This tea can also be made with half a cup of lemon juice instead of orange juice.

GANGA-JAMUNA COCKTAIL WITH A DECORATIVE ICE BLOCK (6-8 SERVINGS)

A surprise for your guests and an opportunity to show them your culinary art.

INGREDIENTS

FOR THE COCKTAIL

1 cup orange squash

1 cup pineapple squash

3 bottles soda, chilled

FOR THE ICE BLOCK

Water

Pieces of orange or pineapple

Glaze cherries

A mould of suitable size

METHOD

FOR THE COCKTAIL

(1) Mix the two squashes together and keep them chilled.

(2) Pour soda at the time of serving and float the decorated ice block in the cocktail bowl.

FOR THE ICE BLOCK

Choose a square or round cake tin of a suitable size to fit in the cocktail bowl. Pour one inch of water into the mould and freeze it. Over it arrange the cherries, orange or pineapple pieces, decoratively. Cover with another thin layer of water and freeze again. When the decoration sets, pour another layer of cold water. Freeze and keep the mould, ready in the ice compartment. To unmould, hold the mould under running water. Float this ice block in the cocktail bowl at the time of serving.

One can make small ice cubes with little fruit pieces inside for individual serving.

GRAPES AND APPLE COCKTAIL (6 SERVINGS)

A delicious cold drink made when grapes are in plentiful.

INGREDIENTS

1/2 kg. green grapes (make 2 cups juice)

1/2 kg. black grapes (make 2 cups juice)

2 apples-extract juice with 1 cup water

1 cup crushed ice

6 tablespoons powdered sugar

Few drops cochineal red colour

Salt and pepper to sprinkle on top

TO DECORATE :

Few black and green grapes

METHOD

(1) Extract juice from both the grapes and strain.
(2) Extract apple juice by adding one cup water. Strain.
(3) Mix together all the juices, powdered sugar and red cochineal colour. Cool in fridge.
(4) Serve on crushed ice and sprinkle salt and pepper according to taste.
(5) Pierce alternately green and black grapes on a long cocktail-pick and put in each glass while serving.

KESARI RAW MANGO SHERBET (4 SERVINGS)

A sweet and sour raw mango sherbet - a refreshing summer drink.

INGREDIENTS

1 cup raw mango puree (obtained from 2 mangoes)

1/3 to 1/2 cup sugar - adjust according to the taste of mango

3 tablespoons cardamom and saffron syrup (see Pg. 280)

4 cups cold water

METHOD

(1) Peel and stone mangoes. Pressure cook them with one cup water. Blend to a fine puree in a mixer.
(2) Mix in all other ingredients and cool before serving.

TULSI-SUDHA (10 SERVINGS)

The good qualities of tulsi leaves are enhanced due to jaggery and lemon combination. The drink is not only tasty but is an excellent cure for colds, coughs, headaches and acidity. It also helps to improve one's blood-count and immunity against other diseases and improves digestion.

INGREDIENTS

10 cups water

3/4 cup jaggery

1/2 cup lemon juice

100 Tulsi leaves (basil), ground to a fine paste

1/2 teaspoon cardamom powder

METHOD

(1) Take 10 cups of hot water. To it add jaggery and let it melt.
(2) Mix in lemon juice, tulsi paste and cardamom powder.
(3) Chill tulsi-sudha for two hours and then strain it.
(4) Serve chilled or at room temperature.

HIBISCUS (JASWANTI) SHERBET (10 SERVINGS)

This colourful and tasty drink is very cooling and soothing, specially in summer. Heat strokes can be avoided by regular intake of this drink. It is also an effective cure for women's menstrual disorders.

INGREDIENTS

20 - five petal red hibiscus flowers

10 cups water

10-15 tablespoons sugar

10-15 teaspoons lemon juice

METHOD

(1) Take half the quantity of water and boil it. Remove from gas. Add hibiscus flower petals. (Remove green stems and centre portion). Cover and keep for 10 minutes. Remove flower. Water will have dull purplish red colour.

(2) To it add remaining water, sugar and lemon juice. Dissolve sugar and cool the sherbet. It will now have a nice red colour.

(3) Serve chilled.

(4) Hibiscus sherbet can be preserved in fridge for 15 days.

GOLDEN CREAMY DRINK TOPPED WITH ORANGE SHORBET (6 SERVINGS)

A very tasty, creamy drink, topped with orange shorbet cubes.

INGREDIENTS

FOR THE DRINK

4 bottles Goldspot (aerated orange)

1/2 cup vanilla icecream

A few pieces crushed ice

FOR THE SHORBET

2 teaspoons gelatine

90 grams (3 ozs.) sugar

150 ml. (5 fl. ozs.) water

3 tablespoons lemon juice (reduce lemon juice if oranges are sour)

1-1/4 cups orange juice

A pinch salt

Few drops orange colour and essence

METHOD

FOR THE DRINK

Combine Goldspot, vanilla icecream and crushed ice pieces in a liquidizer and blend well. Transfer into individual glasses. Top each glass with a cube of orange shorbet.

FOR THE SHORBET

(1) Mix gelatine, sugar and water in a vessel. Soak for a few minutes. Put on gas and stir till gelatine and sugar dissolves. Cool.

(2) Mix lemon juice, orange juice, salt, orange essence and colour. Pour in the ice tray and freeze till set.

COCKTAIL SNACKS AND APPETIZERS

MASALA PALAK ROLLS (MAKES 50 ROLLS)

Light to eat and yet full of proteins and other nutrients.

INGREDIENTS

2 cups moong dal with skin (split green gram with skin)

2 tablespoons green chilli-ginger paste

Salt to taste

1/2 cup sour curds, beaten

1 big onion, grated

2 tablespoons coriander leaves, chopped

2 bunches spinach leaves

Oil for shallow frying

Chaat masala as required (see Pg. 286)

METHOD

(1) Soak moong dal for about five hours. Wash out the skin and then grind to a paste with minimum water.

(2) Add chilli-ginger paste, salt, beaten curds, grated onion and coriander leaves to the paste and mix very well.

(3) Steam spinach leaves in a colander over boiling water. Steam a few leaves at a time.

(4) Take little oil and spread moong dal mixture like pancake (puda). Put spinach leaves all over and sprinkle with chaat masala. Remove the pancake on a board and make a tight roll when still hot. Cut into smaller pieces. Insert a toothpick in each roll. Similarly make other pancake rolls.

VEGETABLE MOCK PIZZA (MAKES 35 PIECES)

Small and spicy pizzas sure to be hit amongst your guests.

INGREDIENTS

FOR THE PIZZA

2 cups self raising flour

1/4 teaspoon salt

2 tablespoons mustard powder

5 tablespoons cheese, grated

5 tablespoons butter

About 3/4 cup milk

FOR THE TOPPING

2 tablespoons oil

1 cup cabbage, finely shredded

1/2 cup capsicum, long thin slices

1/2 cup onion, long thin slices

Salt to taste

1/4 teaspoon aji-no-moto

1 teaspoon chilli sauce

1 tablespoon soya sauce

Ketchup and grated cheese for the topping

METHOD

FOR THE PIZZA

(1) Mix flour with salt, mustard powder and cheese. Rub in butter till it resembles breadcrumbs.

(2) Gradually mix in milk and make a soft dough. Roll dough on a floured board, 8 mm. in thickness and cut small rounds with a cutter. Arrange pizza rounds on a greased baking tray and bake at 200°C till light brown in colour.

(3) Remove from the oven and put topping on each one and bake again on upper shelf till cheese melts. Serve hot.

FOR THE TOPPING

(1) Heat oil and add vegetables and saute over high flame. Mix in salt, aji-no-moto, chilli sauce and soya sauce. Remove after two minutes. Put one spoonful on each pizza piece. Top with ketchup and cheese.

(2) Bake at 200°C on the upper shelf till cheese melts. Serve hot.

CREAM CHEESE BALLS (MAKES 20 PIECES)

Simply sumptuous - the more you make them, the faster they'll vanish.

INGREDIENTS

1/2 cup flour

2 tablespoons cheese, grated

2 tablespoons tomato ketchup

1 teaspoon chilli sauce

Salt to taste

Milk to make a batter

20 very small potatoes, boiled

Little semolina for coating

Ghee for deep frying

METHOD

(1)   Combine flour, grated cheese, tomato ketchup, chilli sauce and salt in a vessel. Add milk little by little and make a creamy thick batter.

(2)   Dip each potato in the batter, then roll in semolina and deep fry in ghee. Serve with a toothpick in each ball.

SEMOLINA SAVOURY DOTS (MAKES 30 TO 35 PIECES)

Very attractive and delightful savoury dots - sure to win the heart of your guests !

INGREDIENTS

1-1/4 cup mixture of water and milk

2 pinches powdered nutmeg

1/2 cup semolina

1 tablespoon butter

1/4 cup cheese, grated

Salt and pepper to taste

METHOD

(1) Boil milk and water mixture with nutmeg powder.

(2) Add semolina gradually, stir constantly taking care to see that no lumps are formed. As the mixture starts to thicken, mix butter, grated cheese, salt and pepper. Continue stirring, till the mixture starts leaving the sides of the vessel. Take out on a greased plate. Spread and make it even with the back of a bowl. Allow to cool. It should be quarter inch in thickness.

(2) Cut out circles with a small round cutter of one inch diameter. Arrange these dots on a lightly greased baking tray.

Following are the five different suggestions for toppings :

(a) 1/2 cup carrot, grated; 1/2 cup cheese, grated; a big pinch mustard powder and little pepper powder. Mix all these ingredients and spread little on each dot.

(b) Put little grated cheese on each dot. Top it with a dot of tomato ketchup and a piece of capsicum.

(c) 1/2 cup cheese, grated; 1/2 cup green peas, boiled crushed, salt and pepper to taste. Mix together the above ingredients and arrange on each dot. Top it with a drop of either tomato ketchup or chilli sauce.

(d) 1/4 cup cheese, grated; 1/2 cup corn, boiled, crushed; salt; pepper to taste. Mix everything together and arrange on each piece. Dot with hot and sweet tomato sauce.

(e) 1/2 cup cheese sauce; 1/4 cup French beans and carrots, boiled, finely chopped; salt and pepper to taste. Mix everything together and arrange on each dot. Put a drop of tomato ketchup on top.

1. Cocktail appetizers on standing brinjal cat   p. 43
2. Vegetable mock pizza   p 36
3. Mini idlis   p. 41
4. Green peas tower   p 40
5. Pineapple punch   p. 32
6. Cool coconut drink   p. 32
7. Creamy cheese balls on reclining sweetlime cat   p. 37

GREEN PEAS TOWER (MAKES 20 TOWERS)

Towers are delicious but very filling.

INGREDIENTS (FOR THE VADAS)

1 cup potatoes, boiled and mashed

1/2 cup green peas, boiled and crushed

2 tablespoons thick sour curd

1/2 cup gram flour

2 tablespoons fresh coconut

2 tablespoons coriander leaves

1/4 teaspoon garam masala (see Pg. 287)

1 teaspoon anardana powder

1 teaspoon chilli-ginger paste

Sugar and salt to taste

Oil for deep frying

FOR THE GREEN PEAS TOWER

About 20 crisp puris each, 1" in diameter (see Pg. 126)

Sweet and sour chutney (see Pg. 125)

Green coriander chutney (see Pg. 126)

METHOD

(1) Combine all the vada ingredients in a plate and mix well. Make small flat vadas, (size of puris) with a hole in the centre. Deep fry in oil, till golden brown.

(2) Take the puris in plate. Apply little sweet and sour chutney on each. Put vadas over them and dot with green chutney. Repeat the process, thus forming towers.

TINY CHANNA SAMOSAS (MAKES 24 PIECES)

Crisp samosas - a favourite savoury snack of all Indians. They can be stuffed with varied fillings of your choice.

INGREDIENTS

FOR THE FILLING

2 tablespoons oil

1/2 cup cabbage, chopped

1/2 cup carrot, grated

1/2 cup green channa (Bengal green gram small variety), boiled

1/2 tablespoon ginger-chilli paste

Juice of 1/2 lemon

2 tablespoons coriander leaves

Salt to taste

FOR THE COVERING

1/2 cup flour

1/2 cup wheat flour

4 tablespoons oil

1/2 teaspoon salt

METHOD

FOR THE FILLING

Heat oil. Add all the vegetables, green grams and seasonings. Saute for five to seven minutes till soft. Remove from gas. Divide into 24 parts.

FOR THE COVERING

(1) Mix all the given ingredients and make a tough dough. Knead well and then divide into 12 equal sized balls.

(2) Roll each ball into three inches diameter. Cut in two. Stuff the above mixture in the centre. Fold into a triangle and bind the sides. Similarly make other samosas.

(3) Deep fry in oil till golden brown.

MINI IDLIS (MAKES 75 PIECES)

Mini idlis look like golden drops.

INGREDIENTS

FOR THE IDLIS

1 cup gram flour

1/2 cup semolina

3/4 cup sour curds

Salt to taste

2 teaspoons sugar

1-1/2 teaspoons green chilli-ginger paste

1 teaspoon soda

2 teaspoons fruit salt (readymade)

3/4 teaspoon citric acid

Green mango chutney

Fine green sev (see Pg. 127)

FOR THE MANGO CHUTNEY

1 bunch coriander leaves
(1-1/2 cups when chopped)

1 small green mango

1/2 teaspoon sugar

Salt to taste

3-4 green chillies

2 tablespoons dalia

METHOD

FOR THE IDLIS

(1)   Take gram flour and semolina in a vessel and soak them in sour curds. Keep covered for four to five hours.

(2)   Dilute dough with half cup of hot water and also add to it salt, sugar and green chilli-ginger paste.

(3)   Take mini idli moulds and grease them with oil. Put to heat. Meanwhile divide dough into two parts. To one half add soda, fruit salt and citric acid. Add little hot water over it and then beat the mixture. Take out the hot moulds and put one teaspoon of the mixture in each depression. Put in the cooker again and steamcook for five to seven minutes. Remove, apply oil on top. Make remaining idlis the same way using the remaining dough. Put a dot of green mango chutney on each idli and then top with green sev.

FOR THE MANGO CHUTNEY

Grind all the given ingredients together to a fine paste.

GOLDEN TOASTS (MAKES 16 TOASTS)

Bread and paneer toasts make ideal conversational pieces.

INGREDIENTS

8 slices bread, cut each into two

2 tablespoons butter

1 medium onion, chopped

4 green chillies, chopped

1/4 cup coriander leaves, chopped

1 medium tomato, chopped

Paneer from 1/2 litre milk (about 1/2 cup)

1/4 cup self raising flour

1/4 cup water

Salt to taste

Ghee for deep frying

METHOD

(1)   Melt butter and saute the onion till light pink. Add the chopped chillies, coriander and tomatoes. Saute for a while. When soft, add beaten paneer. Mix well.

(2)   Add flour and saute for another two minutes. Add water, salt and continue stirring till it collects like a ball in the vessel. Remove from gas. When still warm, apply evenly about a tablespoon of mixture on one side of all the bread pieces.

(3)   Deep fry in hot ghee on both sides till golden in colour. Serve hot.

CRISPY CURLS (MAKES 20 PIECES)

A snacky dish, can be served with any delicious dips, like orange cream dip and avocado dip.

INGREDIENTS

1-1/2 cup flour

1/2 teaspoon mustard powder

1/4 teaspoon pepper powder

Salt to taste

3 teaspoon ghee, melted

Oil for deep frying

METHOD

(1) Mix all the given ingredients and make a tough dough like puri. Knead well with little oil. Keep aside for at least 15 minutes.

(2) Break dough into 20 balls. Roll out each ball into thin rounds. Put three straight cuts, keeping the round still intact. Hold two opposite ends and twist without pressing the strips.

(3) Deep fry till light pink and crisp. Store in an airtight box.

ORANGE CREAM DIP (MAKES 1-1/4 CUP)

INGREDIENTS

1/2 cup paneer

1/4 cup orange juice

1 tablespoon lemon juice

2 tablespoons honey

1/4 cup fresh cream (top of cold milk)

Salt to taste

METHOD

(1) Prepare dip by mixing together the paneer, orange juice, lemon juice and honey in a mixer to get absolutely creamy consistency.

(2) Take out from the mixer jar and blend in cream and salt to taste. Cool in fridge, till serving time.

AVOCADO DIP (MAKES 1-1/2 CUPS)

INGREDIENTS

1 avocado

1/2 cup apple, chopped into tiny pieces

1 tablespoon fresh cream

1 tablespoon lemon juice

1 teaspoon powdered sugar

A dash powdered cinnamon and clove

Salt to taste

METHOD

(1) Split the avocado, remove stone and scoop out the pulp with a spoon, leaving enough pulp on the sides to keep it from falling apart. Mash the pulp with the spoon. It should make half cup.

(2) Add apple pieces, cream, lemon juice, sugar, salt and powdered cinnamon and clove. Mix well and then pile neatly back into the shell of the avocado to serve as a dip.

Note:

Dips can be served with potato wafers, banana wafers, cheese cracker biscuits or any other crisp biscuits.

COCKTAIL APPETIZERS

Cocktail appetizers are served as cocktails or pre-buffet accompaniments. They are served to whet the appetite before the main food is served. They are small, tasty and easy to eat, food pieces. Special care is taken to make them attractive, visually and tickle the palate. Appetizers are prepared in such a way that a guest can eat it in one or two bites. As they are served to be picked by cocktail sticks, they should be firm enough to hold on picks and should never drip.

Appetizers are the assortments of cooked, raw or pickled vegetables, cheese and fresh or canned fruits. In planning appetizers, avoid too many similar types. Give attention to the colour combinations of every food item. Even garnishes and the way of serving are equally important. One can select vegetables like cabbage or a big brinjal or fruits like grape fruit, sweet lime, orange as cushions to push cocktail sticks into them. Be sure that these cushions are not wobbly in the serving plate. With imagination one can make grapefruit reclining cat or a standing brinjal cat as cushions.

METHOD

FOR MAKING THE RECLINING SWEETLIME CAT

(1)   Select a sweetlime and a grape fruit. Cut off slices from both of them to have a firm base. Also cut off a slice from the sides where both will join, forming a neck of the cat. Join with toothpicks. Make curled tail out of a pipe cleaner or from curved brinjal stem.

(2)   Cut ears out of a carrot or from end pieces of lady fingers and fix them on the sweetlime head. Fix two eyes of red pumpkin seeds with pins. Mouth and whiskers are made out of small pieces of a red plastasin and 1-1/2 inches of broomstick. Cover neck joint with a red ribbon bow.

(3)   Put this reclining cat on a wooden board or a serving plate and use grapefruit body as a cushion to fix the cocktailpicks.

FOR THE STANDING BRINJAL CAT

(1)   Select one big oval and one small round brinjal. Remove their green parts.
(2)   Cut a slice out of the big brinjal to make a firm base.
(3)   Join two brinjals with toothpicks.
(4)   Make two ears by fixing about 1-1/2" pieces from two lady fingers.
(5)   Make two eyes by using red pumpkin seeds. Fix with pins.
(6)   Make mouth and whiskers with small pieces of plastasin and 2" pieces of broomstick. Tie ribbon as bow at the neck.
(7)   Make a tail out of a curled stem of a brinjal.
(8)   Use the body as cushion to fix cocktail-picks.

FRUITS AS COCKTAIL APPETIZERS ON PICKS

Seedless soft fruits are best for cocktails, as one can easily fix them on cocktail sticks. Black seedless green grapes, tinned pineapple segments, orange pieces, strawberries, melon pieces or scooped out melon balls and dates are frequently used as cocktail appetizers. Cheese cubes are good accompaniments with fruits.

VEGETABLES AS COCKTAIL APPETIZERS ON PICKS

INGREDIENTS

FOR THE PICKLED BABY ONIONS

10 baby onions

1 tablespoon salt

1 teaspoon glacial acetic acid

Red cochineal colour

FOR THE SPICY BABY POTATOES

10 baby potatoes

1 teaspoon butter

1 red chilli and 3 cloves garlic, ground

Salt to taste

1/2 teaspoon vinegar

FOR THE STUFFED MUSHROOMS

10 canned button mushrooms

1 tablespoon cheese, grated

1 tablespoon coriander leaves, chopped

1 tablespoon coconut, grated

FOR THE STUFFED MACARONI

10 big sized shell macaroni

2 tablespoons cheese, grated

1 teaspoon onion, grated

1/4 teaspoon red chilli powder

Salt to taste

FOR THE PICKLED VEGETABLES

10 pieces cauliflower

10 cubes carrots

10 cubes cucumber

3 cloves garlic

2 tablespoons salt

1 teaspoon chilli powder

1 tablespoon glacial acetic acid

FOR THE CARROT CURLS

1 carrot

METHOD

FOR THE PICKLED BABY ONIONS

Immerse the baby onions in enough water. Add salt, glacial acetic acid and red cochineal colour. Keep for two days in a bottle before using.

FOR THE SPICY BABY POTATOES

Boil the baby potatoes and peel them. Melt butter. Add the ground paste, salt and vinegar. Warm potatoes and spices on fast flame and serve hot.

FOR THE STUFFED MUSHROOMS

Remove stems from mushrooms. Stuff the hollow portion with a mixture of grated cheese, coriander leaves and grated coconut.

FOR THE STUFFED MACARONI

Boil the macaroni in salt water. Drain and cool. Stuff its hollow portion with a mixture of grated cheese, grated onion, salt to taste and red chilli powder. They can also be stuffed with a mixture of grated cheese and mayonnaise sauce.

FOR PICKLED VEGETABLES

Take all the above vegetables in a glass bottle. Fill water enough to immerse the vegetables. Add salt, chilli powder, and glacial acetic acid. Keep aside for two days before using.

FOR CARROT CURLS

Take out long thin slices with a parer. Roll up and fix a toothpick to hold. Chill in ice water to crisp.

Note:
To use carrot curls for garnishing salads and soups, remove toothpicks.

SALADS AND HORS D'OEUVRES

EGGLESS MAYONNAISE SAUCE (MAKES 1-1/2 CUPS)

A delicious creamy mayonnaise sauce, which can be easily mixed with many combinations of vegetable and fruit salads. As its basic ingredient is fresh cream, it is not advisable to keep for more than two days. It is better to use when fresh.

INGREDIENTS

200 grams fresh cream

2 teaspoons mustard powder

1/2 teaspoon salt

1/2 teaspoon pepper

3 tablespoons powdered sugar

1/4 cup (2 fl. ozs.) salad oil

3 teaspoons white vinegar

A few drops yellow colour

METHOD

(1) Take fresh cream in a vessel and to it add mustard powder, salt, pepper and sugar. Put this vessel over crushed ice and beat with an egg beater till little thick.

(2) Cradually add salad oil and beat further till it gets completely absorbed in the cream making a saucy consistency.

(3) Add and mix properly the vinegar and yellow colour. Pour in an airtight jar and store in the fridge.

MOCK MAYONNAISE SAUCE (MAKES 3/4 CUP)

Easy to make, tasty and can be preserved for a week in an airtight bottle in fridge.

INGREDIENTS

6 tablespoons milk powder

1/2 teaspoon mustard powder

1/2 teaspoon salt

2 teaspoons powdered sugar

1/2 teaspoon pepper

1/4 cup + 3 tablespoons (3 fl. ozs.) cold water

2 tablespoons white vinegar or lemon juice

6 tablespoons salad oil

METHOD

(1) Combine milk powder, mustard powder, salt, sugar and pepper in the jar of a mixer. Mix with a spoon.

(2) Add cold water and vinegar. Beat the mixture.

(3) Add salad oil, gradually beating all the time. Beat till the mixture has an even saucy consistency.

(4) Pour in an airtight bottle and store in fridge.

FANCY PINEAPPLE SALAD (10 SERVINGS)

The idea of shaping salad in an attractive pineapple shape. This can also be adapted for any other mayonnaise salad.

INGREDIENTS

FOR THE SALAD

4 medium sized potatoes, boiled

1 medium sized onion

2 rings canned pineapple

1 small capsicum

1/2 cup + 3 tablespoons (5 ozs.) mayonnaise sauce

Salt and pepper to taste

FOR THE TOPPING

4 big potatoes, boiled

Salt to taste

Mayonnaise sauce to bind

Few drops lemon, orange and green colours.

METHOD

(1) Cut the boiled potatoes, onion, pineapple and capsicum into small pieces.

(2) Mix in the mayonnaise sauce, salt and pepper.

(3) Arrange this salad in an oval shape on a serving plate (like a half pineapple).

(4) Take boiled potatoes given for topping and grate them. Mix in salt and mayonnaise and prepare a soft mixture which can be easily piped through a nozzle of a decorating bag.

(5) Take little portion of this mixture and evenly mix in few drops of green colour. Make four to five leaves (shaped like pineapple leaves) and put them in front of the oval shape. Arrange two small leaves on the opposite side.

(6) Divide the remaining potato mixture into three portions. Mix yellow and orange colours in two separate portions and keep the third portion colourless. Now fill all the three portions together side by side in a piping bag fitted with a big star nozzle. Make rows of star pattern diagonally on top of the oval shape. On completion, it will look like a half pineapple.

Note:

(a) Select potatoes which are not sticky.

(b) To mash potatoes, it is better to press them through a machine or a big 'sev' press.

(c) There should be no lumps in the potatoes, otherwise they will choke the nozzle.

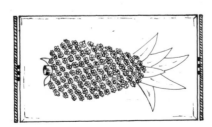
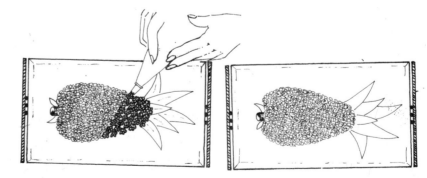

ORANGE AND NUTS COLESLAW (8 SERVINGS)

A cool and soft salad served to each guest in specially prepared orange baskets.

INGREDIENTS

FOR THE SALAD

2 cups cabbage, shredded

1 medium onion, sliced thin and long

2 carrots, grated

1 capsicum, cut into very thin long strips

2 oranges, remove segments

1/4 cup mayonnaise sauce

Salt, pepper and powdered sugar to taste

1/4 cup walnuts, chopped

Salad leaves to decorate

METHOD

FOR THE SALAD

(1) Mix together the prepared cabbage, onion, carrots, capsicums and orange segments and keep in the fridge

(2) Mix together the mayonnaise sauce, salt, pepper and sugar to taste. Keep in the fridge.

(3) Mix both the vegetables and mayonnaise together at the time of serving.

(4) Serve salad in individual orange baskets or serve in a bowl, decorated with orange segments, walnuts and salad leaves.

FOR THE ORANGE BASKET

(1) Select firm orange which can stand and does not wobble. Starting from the centre of the orange make two parallel cuts on the peel, reaching the opposite side at the centre. Do not cut the inside of the orange.

(2) Make another cut on the peel starting from one end of the handle, going round the orange, joining the opposite end of the handle. Do this on the other side also. Remove loose peel. Push a penknife under the handle and between the orange pieces and the peel. Then carefully remove all orange pieces leaving an empty basket.

(3) Make zigzag cuts on the edge with a scissor or cut scallops with a knife and attach a small red ribbon bow on top of the handle.

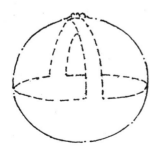  

FRENCH DRESSING (MAKES 1/2 CUP)

Easy to make common dressing, used in tossed salads.

INGREDIENTS	METHOD
1/4 cup salad oil	(1) Mix all the dry ingredients in salad oil
2 tablespoons powdered sugar	(2) Add vinegar and lemon juice. Mix very well.
1/2 teaspoon mustard powder	(3) Fill in a glass bottle and store in the fridge. Shake well everything before use.
3/4 teaspoon salt	
1/2 teaspoon pepper	
2 tablespoons white vinegar	
2 tablespoons lemon juice	

HAWAIIAN SUMMER SALAD (10-12 SERVINGS)

It is a delicious combination of crisp vegetables, fruits and nuts, lightly tossed with French dressing.

INGREDIENTS

2 cups white or red cabbage, finely shredded

1/2 cup corn, boiled

3/4 cup cucumber, chopped

1/2 cup red apple, chopped with skin

3 tablespoons onion, chopped

3 tablespoons green raw mango, peeled and chopped

1/4 cup walnuts, chopped

1/4 cup coconut, grated

1 cup French dressing

METHOD

FOR THE SALAD

(1) Prepare cabbage and cucumber. Wash them and drain off water. Take them with all the other prepared ingredients in a big bowl and keep in fridge till serving time.

(2) Toss everything lightly with French dressing. Fill in a red pumpkin bowl and serve decorated with white radish swans, red radish waterlilies and carrot daisies.

FOR THE RED PUMPKIN BOWL

(1) Select a firm oval shaped red pumpkin. Cut a thin slice from the side to make a base.

(2) Mark the shape of the bowl on the skin. Refer the given diagram. With a sharp pointed knife, cut the shape deep inside to open it out. Scoop out the pulp and keep only 1/2 inch of the skin.

(3) Decorate the edges with zigzag cuts.

(4) Now prepare the white radish swans in three different sizes, few red radish waterlilies, few watermelon skin leaves and carrot daisies. Fix them in position on the pumpkin bowl as shown in the photograph.

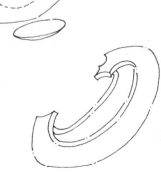 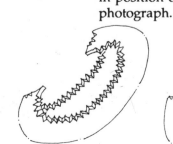 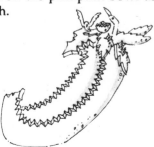

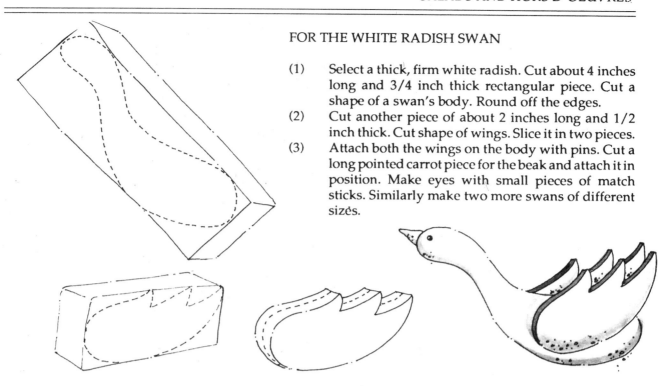

FOR THE WHITE RADISH SWAN

(1) Select a thick, firm white radish. Cut about 4 inches long and 3/4 inch thick rectangular piece. Cut a shape of a swan's body. Round off the edges.

(2) Cut another piece of about 2 inches long and 1/2 inch thick. Cut shape of wings. Slice it in two pieces.

(3) Attach both the wings on the body with pins. Cut a long pointed carrot piece for the beak and attach it in position. Make eyes with small pieces of match sticks. Similarly make two more swans of different sizes.

FOR THE RED RADISH WATERLILY

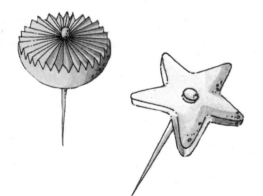

Cut it just like cucumber flower (see Pg. 125). Radish will open into two flowers. Pierce a pearl headed pin in the centre. This pin serves as a centre of the flower and at the same time helps in fixing the waterlily to the red pumpkin bowl. Similarly make few more lilies.

FOR THE CARROT DAISY

Cut round slices from a carrot. From each slice, cut out daisy shapes with a metal cutter. Make centres with pearl headed pins which will also help in fixing the daisy to the red pumpkin bowl.

FOR THE LEAVES

Cut a thick rectangular slice from a cucumber or a watermelon skin. Cut out the basic outline of the leaf. Then, cut the serrated edges. Make veins by removing thin small wedges from the centre.

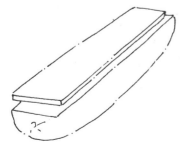 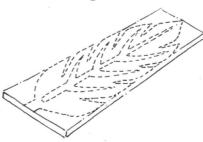

FRENCH RICE SALAD (8-10 SERVINGS)

A good flavoured rice mixed with vegetables and sweet and sour French dressing, can take place of salad as well as a pullao.

INGREDIENTS

3/4 cup long grained uncooked rice
1 teaspoon salt
1/2 cup French beans, chopped into small pieces
1/2 cup carrots, chopped into small pieces
1/2 cup green peas
3/4 cup French dressing
3 tablespoons onion, finely chopped
Salt to taste

METHOD

FOR THE SALAD

(1) Boil rice in one teaspoon salt water till tender but firm. Drain out extra water and cool or cook in a special rice cooker to get rice with separate grains.

(2) Boil French beans, carrots and peas in salt water. Drain and cool.

(3) Marinate these vegetables in half of the French dressing and keep aside for half an hour. Lightly squeeze out extra water.

(4) Add these vegetables, onions, salt to taste and remaining French dressing to the cooled rice. Mix everything well.

(5) Take any fancy shaped mould like heart, boat, hexagonal etc. Grease the inside with oil. Pack rice salad inside and level the top. Cool in fridge for an hour.

(6) Pass a knife all round the edge of the mould and then unmould on a serving plate.

(7) Decorate with salad leaves, fancy carrot and cucumber slices and seasoned wedges of tomatoes alternating with two way spring onion curls.

(8) To make seasoned tomato wedges, cut medium sized tomatoes into six equal wedges. Prepare mixture of salt, pepper and powdered sugar. Sprinkle over the surface of each tomato wedge.

FOR THE FANCY CARROT OR CUCUMBER SLICES

(1) Peel cucumber, cut lengthwise wedges at right angles very close to each other, about 1/8 inch. Cut all around at equal distance. Round off the edges of each wedge.

(2) Cut horizontal slices from top. Each slice will look like a flower.

FOR THE TWO WAY SPRING ONION CURLS

(1) Select and cut out the firm joint portion of about 2 inches from a spring onion. Remove broken layer.

(2) Starting from off centre of the onion piece, make very thin but deep cuts, going towards the open end. Repeat on the opposite side also. Keep it attached in the centre.

(3) Separate gently each cut portion with hand and then put in ice cold water for an hour. It will open out from both ends, like two flowers attached in the centre.

GOLDEN SALAD (4 SERVINGS)

Very attractive, colourful and juicy salad sure to be the star attraction at any party.

INGREDIENTS

2 tablespoons gelatine

1/4 cup sugar

1/4 teaspoon salt

3/4 cup canned pineapple syrup or juice

1/4 cup orange juice

1/4 cup vinegar

1 cup pineapple pieces

1/2 cup orange segments

1/2 cup carrots, grated

TO DECORATE :

Lettuce leaves

Capsicums

Fancy tomato wedges

Cucumber flowers.

METHOD

(1) Mix together gelatine, sugar and salt. Pour in pineapple syrup or juice and let it soak for five minutes. Place the vessel on slow heat and melt gelatine and sugar. Remove from heat and cool.

(2) Mix in orange juice and vinegar. Chill in fridge till semiset.

(3) Take out from fridge and fold in the pineapple and orange pieces and grated carrot. Pout this mixture into four rinsed fancy moulds. Put in fridge till firmly set.

(4) Unmould each one separately on serving plates and decorate with lettuce, capsicum, fancy tomato wedges and cucumber flowers, etc.

FOR THE FANCY TOMATO WEDGE

(1) Cut 8 wedges from a firm red tomato.
(2) From each wedge, separate thick skin from the pulp, keeping the base intact.
(3) Cut an inner petal in the thick skin. Push inner petal inside and pull out the outer petal.

FOR THE CUCUMBER FLOWER

See method and diagram on Pg. 125.

VEGETABLE JELLY-LOAF SALAD (10-12 SERVINGS)

A beautiful transparent salad showing vegetable pattern from inside and has a sweet and sour taste.

INGREDIENTS

1 packet lemon jelly crystals (85 grams) or

1 recipe lemon jelly (see Pg. 287)

1-3/4 cup hot water

1-1/2 tablespoons vinegar

1/4 teaspoon salt

10 French beans, cut long pieces, boiled in salt water

1/4 cup carrot slices

1/2 cup small pieces cauliflower, boiled in salt water

Few slices red radish

Few slices spring onions

METHOD

FOR THE SALAD

(1)   Melt jelly in hot water. Cool and add vinegar and salt. Pour a little of this mixture in a loaf tin to fill half inch of the base. Chill until set.

(2)   Arrange vegetables in a decorative pattern on the set jelly. First put three rows of long pieces of French beans, diagonally, leaving space in-between. Fill up gaps with carrot slices, cauliflower pieces. red radish slices, and spring onion slices.

(3)   Meanwhile chill remaining jelly till partially set. Spoon out some jelly over the arranged design.

(4)   Chop remaining vegetables and mix with remaining semiset jelly and pour in the loaf tin. Chill until firmly set.

(5)   Unmould on a square serving plate and garnish with vegetables, greens and dry onion lotus.

FOR THE DRY ONION LOTUS

(1)   Take small white onion. Peel and discard any damaged layer. Cut out extra roots at the base.

(2)   Pierce a penknife in the onion to cut a few layers of skin, keeping the centre intact. First make four right angle cuts. Then put two cuts in each quarter totally making 12 parts as petals.

(3)   Open out each petal gently with finger tips.

(4)   Add a few drops of red cochineal colour in ice cold water. Keep the onions in water for at least two hours to open out. Help the flower from time to time by spreading out petals on outer side.

(5)   Finally, the flower will open with a bud like centre and also take on the pink colour.

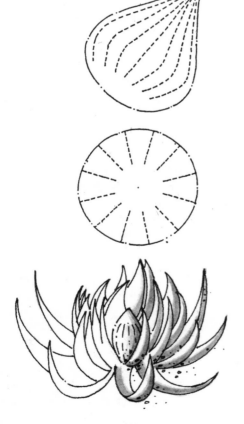

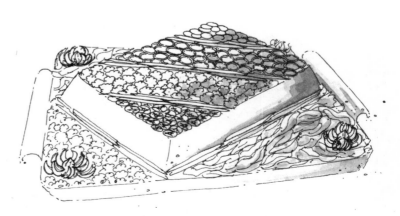

COOLING CURD TOWER SURROUNDED BY STUFFED CUCUMBER SLICES
(10-12 SERVINGS)

A delightful salad for a hot day !

INGREDIENTS

FOR STUFFING THE CUCUMBER

2 big cucumbers, about 8" long

1 cup cottage cheese, finely crumbled

2 tablespoons thick fresh cream
(from top of milk)

3 tablespoons desiccated coconut

Salt to taste

1 tablespoon lemon juice

1 tablespoon powdered sugar

Few drops yellow colour

FOR THE CURD TOWER

2 tablespoons gelatine

1/4 cup water

2 cups thick curd

1/2 cup cucumber, grated

Salt and pepper to taste

METHOD

FOR STUFFING THE CUCUMBER

(1)   Peel cucumber only if the skin is tough.

(2)   Carefully with the help of a penknife and back of a spoon, scoop out the entire soft seedy portion from the centre to make a hollow.

(3)   Prepare stuffing by properly mixing together the cottage cheese crumbs, fresh cream, coconut, salt, lemon juice and powdered sugar. Divide stuffing in two parts. Mix few drops of yellow colour in half of the mixture. Fill yellow stuffing in one cucumber and the white stuffing in the other cucumber. Chill cucumbers. Cut horizontal slices and keep them in fridge. Arrange around the salad mould at the time of serving.

FOR THE CURD TOWER

(1)   Soak gelatine in about quarter cup of water for five minutes and then melt on slow heat.

(2)   Add this melted gelatine in a mixture of curd, grated cucumber, salt and pepper. Mix evenly and pour in a tall wet jelly mould. Put in the fridge till firmly set.

(3)   Unmould on a serving plate. Keep in fridge till serving time. Decorate with stuffed cucumber slices.

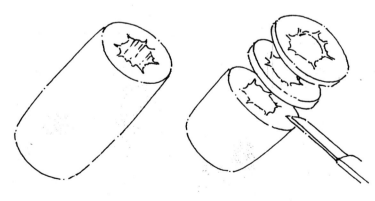

WHITE GRAM SALAD IN GARLIC VINAIGRETTE DRESSING (6 - 8 SERVINGS)

A delicious salad full of proteins, served in a watermelon bowl.

INGREDIENTS

FOR THE SALAD

2 cups white grams (chick peas), cooked

1/8 teaspoon soda bicarb

Salt to taste

1 medium sized onion, finely chopped

2 tablespoons coriander leaves, chopped

FOR THE VINAIGRETTE DRESSING

Salt and pepper to taste

2 teaspoons prepared mustard paste

1 - 1/2 tablespoons lemon juice

3 tablespoons refined oil or salad oil

3 cloves garlic, crushed

METHOD

FOR THE SALAD

(1)   Soak white grams overnight with one-eighth teaspoon of soda bicarb. Without changing water, pressure cook with one teaspoon of salt. Drain out extra water, and cool them.

(2)   Prepare the vinaigrette dressing by combining salt, pepper, mustard paste, lemon juice and oil in a bowl. Mix in crushed garlic.

(3)   Mix grams with chopped onions, coriander leaves, vinaigrette dressing and salt to taste.

(4)   Transfer the salad in a specially prepared water melon bowl.

FOR THE WATERMELON BOWL

(1)   Select a perfectly round watermelon with smooth dark green skin.

(2)   Cut off little portion of the skin to make a base for the bowl to stand.

(3)   Cut a shape of a bowl with two side handles. Scoop out entire red portion. Reduce thickness on the upper side of the bowl to 1 inch depth, by trimming some of the white portion.

(4)   Carve out design on the outer green skin to make it more decorative.

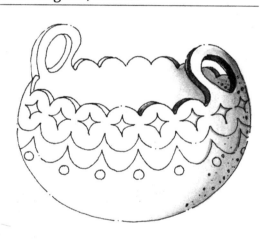

Spinach carrot raita in white pumpkin swan with
a.   Spring onion tree   p. 59
b.   Carrot rose   p. 246
c.   Bittergourd birds   p. 60
d.   Dry onion and carrot lotus   p. 60
e.   Carrot capsicum tree   p. 59

RAW MOONG DAL SALAD (6 SERVINGS)

A decorative and extremely nutritious salad of dal and vegetables.

INGREDIENTS

FOR THE SALAD

1/2 cup moong dal

(split green grams without skin)

1 cup cucumber, chopped

1/4 cup raw mango, chopped

Salt to taste

1/4 cup fresh coconut, grated

1 - 2 green chillies, finely chopped

1 tablespoon oil

1/4 teaspoon mustard seeds

TO DECORATE

Coriander leaves, chopped

Carrot and cucumber slices

Cucumber flowers stuffed with spicy curd

FOR THE SPICY CURD (Makes 1/2 cup)

1/4 cup thick fresh curd

1/4 cup thick fresh cream

1 teaspoon onion, grated

Salt to taste

A dash of pepper

METHOD

(1) Soak moong dal for three to four hours or till very soft. Drain off water.

(2) Peel and chop cucumber and raw mango into small pieces.

(3) Mix together the moong dal, cucumber, mango, salt, coconut and chillies. Transfer onto a serving plate.

(4) Heat oil and add mustard seeds. When they begin to splutter, pour over the salad.

(5) Sprinkle chopped coriander leaves on top of the salad and decorate with carrot and cucumber flowers stuffed with spicy curd.

FOR THE STUFFED CUCUMBER FLOWERS

(1) Make cucumber flowers as shown on Pg. 156

(2) Scoop out centre with a melon scooper. Stuff with a small quantity of spicy curd. Top with a piece of glazed cherry.

FOR THE SPICY CURD

Tie curd in a muslin cloth and drain off water. It should measure quarter cup. Mix the drained curd with cream, grated onion, salt and pepper. Chill in fridge before use.

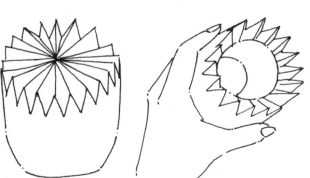

RED SESAME SEED SALAD IN WHITE PUMPKIN SHIKARA (8 - 10 SERVINGS)

A colourful salad in an attractive pumpkin boat.

INGREDIENTS

FOR THE SALAD

3 tablespoons sesame seeds

2 tablespoons poppy seeds

1 - 1/2 cups carrot, grated

1 - 1/2 cups beetroot, grated

1/4 cup coriander leaves, chopped

Salt to taste

2 tablespoons lemon juice

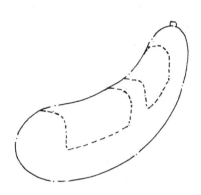

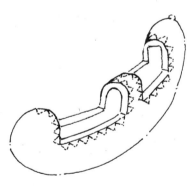

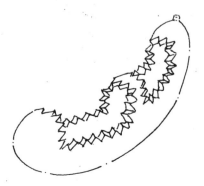

METHOD

FOR THE SALAD

(1)   Soak sesame seeds and poppy seeds for half an hour. Drain off water.

(2)   Mix together the grated carrot, beetroot, coriander leaves, chillies, the soaked sesame seeds, poppy seeds, salt and lemon juice.

(3)   Fill this salad in the white pumpkin shikara. Also place two to three carrot boatmen to make it look more attractive.

FOR THE WHITE PUMPKIN SHIKARA

(1)   Select a fresh white pumpkin resembling a boat shape. Put it in the correct position and cut off a slice at the bottom to make a base.

(2)   Keeping two-three inches roof (depending on the size of the pumpkin) in the centre of the pumpkin, cut out two slices from two sides as shown in the diagram.

(3)   Neatly scoop out the pulp from the centre and even under the roof leaving 1/4 inch wall on the sides and base. Take help of a spoon to scoop out.

(4)   Wash and dry pumpkin and then apply lemon juice on the inner side to avoid discolouration.

(5)   Now decorate edges by zigzag cuts.

(6)   Serve salad in this shikara with carrot boatmen.

FOR THE CARROT BOATMEN

(1)   Cut a thick, broad and 3 inches long slice from the carrot.

(2)   On one side cut half of head, neck, shoulder and hand. Turn the slice and repeat the same on the other side.

(3)   Cut out a half inch triangular shape from a carrot. Push one end of a toothpick in this triangle and the other in the hand of the boatman. Make 2 - 3 such boatmen and make them stand in the salad filled shikara.

SPINACH CARROT RAITA (10 SERVINGS)

A tasty Indian salad with a unique combination of raw spinach and carrot.

INGREDIENTS

1 tablespoon oil
1 teaspoon mustard seeds
1 cup spinach, finely chopped
3/4 cup carrot, grated
1 cup curd
Salt to taste
1 teaspoon powdered sugar
1 - 2 green chillies, finely chopped

METHOD

FOR THE SALAD

(1) Heat oil, add mustard seeds. When they stop spluttering, remove from heat.

(2) Now mix together spinach, carrot, curd and seasoning. Fill this salad in white pumpkin swan, surrounded by bitter gourd birds and many different flowers like carrot roses, dry onion and carrot lotus, carrot capsicum trees and spring onion trees.

FOR THE WHITE PUMPKIN SWAN

1) Select fresh green, white pumpkin with a swan like shape. Check if the skin is not bruised. Put it in the right position. Cut off a slice at the bottom to make a base.

(2) Carve a small beak shape out of a carrot or a red chilli and attach in position with a small toothpick.

(3) Pierce two heads of match sticks or cloves as two eyes.

(4) Cut off a thick slice from the round top to open pumpkin. Scoop out all the white soft pulp from inside leaving a half inch wall on all sides and base. Apply lemon juice inside to prevent discolouration.

(5) Cut out two wings from the skin of another pumpkin and attach with toothpicks on both sides.

(6) Cut out webbed feet out of the broad pumpkin slices and attach in the front of the swan.

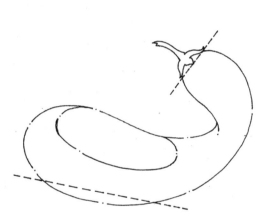

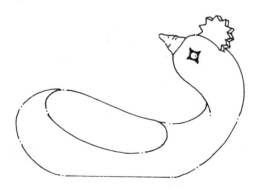

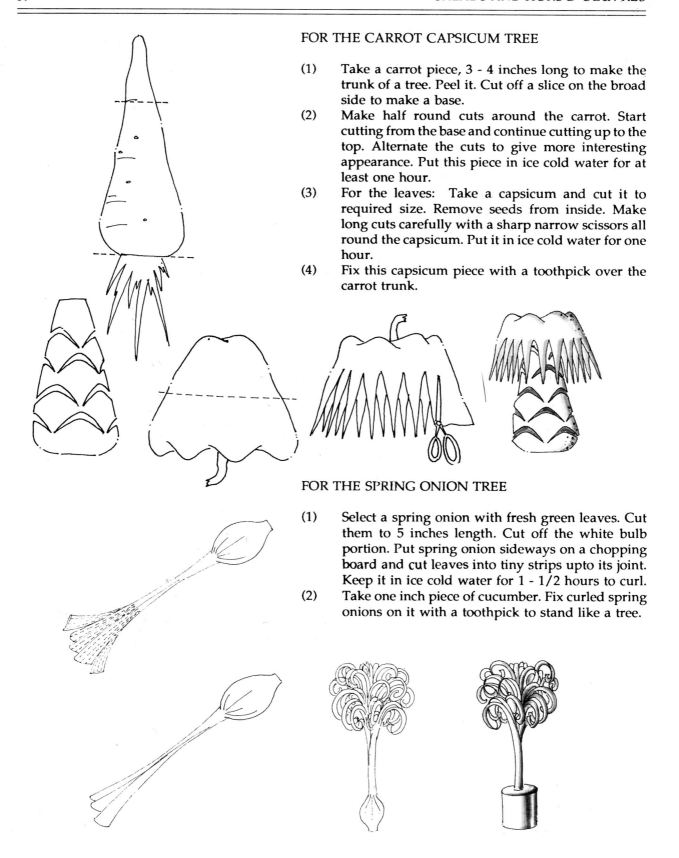

FOR THE CARROT CAPSICUM TREE

(1) Take a carrot piece, 3 - 4 inches long to make the trunk of a tree. Peel it. Cut off a slice on the broad side to make a base.

(2) Make half round cuts around the carrot. Start cutting from the base and continue cutting up to the top. Alternate the cuts to give more interesting appearance. Put this piece in ice cold water for at least one hour.

(3) For the leaves: Take a capsicum and cut it to required size. Remove seeds from inside. Make long cuts carefully with a sharp narrow scissors all round the capsicum. Put it in ice cold water for one hour.

(4) Fix this capsicum piece with a toothpick over the carrot trunk.

FOR THE SPRING ONION TREE

(1) Select a spring onion with fresh green leaves. Cut them to 5 inches length. Cut off the white bulb portion. Put spring onion sideways on a chopping board and cut leaves into tiny strips upto its joint. Keep it in ice cold water for 1 - 1/2 hours to curl.

(2) Take one inch piece of cucumber. Fix curled spring onions on it with a toothpick to stand like a tree.

FOR THE BITTER GOURD OR KANTOLA BIRD

(1)   Select three bitter gourds — one small round for the head, second almost double the size of the head, for the body and third for the wings.

(2)   Carve a very small beak out of carrot or use its stick end as beak. Pierce red pearly headed pins as eyes.

(3)   Attach head to the bigger bitter gourd with tooth-picks.

(4)   Push in two thick toothpicks as legs. If it does not balance than attach the third leg.

FOR THE CARROT ROSES
See Pg. 246.

FOR THE DRY ONION AND CARROT LOTUS

(1)   Select a medium sized onion. Peel and remove any damaged skin layer. Cut on both ends to make a base for two flowers. (each onion will make two flowers.)

(2)   Make big zigzag cuts with a penknife going right through the centre of the onion. It will open out into two parts.

(3)   Carefully separate atleast four outer layers of the onion. Discard the remaining centre part.

(4)   Rearrange these four layers alternately to make lotus flower.

(5)   Take a piece of a carrot and shape it to fit into the centre of the flower. Keep the top surface flat.

(6)   With a penknife, cut small wedges, about 1/8 inch apart at right angles to each other.

(7)   Put prepared carrot piece in the centre to complete onion lotus flower.

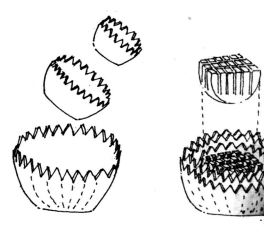

DELUXE TROPICAL FRUIT SALAD WITH (12 - 15 SERVINGS)
(A)   Special honey dressing
(B)   Low calorie orange dressing
(C)   Creamy cheese and ginger dressing

Highly decorative way of serving fruits for a banquet. Guests have the choice of three different dressings to choose from.

INGREDIENTS

FOR THE SALAD

1 big ready-to-eat papaya

5 chickoos

2 cups strawberries

3/4 kg. seedless grapes

3/4 kg. black grapes

Few glazed cherries

FOR THE SPECIAL HONEY DRESSING (makes 3/4 cup)

1/4 cup brown sugar

1/2 cup water

2 tablespoons honey

2 tablespoons lemon juice

2 tablespoons brown vinegar

2 tablespoons refined oil or salad oil

Salt and pepper to taste

FOR THE LOW CALORIE ORANGE DRESSING (makes 3/4 cup)

1 clove garlic, minced

1 tablespoon vinegar

3/4 cup orange juice

1/4 teaspoon red chilli powder

1 tablespoon sugar

1/2 teaspoon salt

1/8 teaspoon pepper

FOR THE CREAMY CHEESE AND GINGER DRESSING (makes 1 cup)

1/4 cup cheese, grated

1/4 cup orange juice

1 tablespoon ginger juice

1/2 cup cream

Salt and pepper to taste

METHOD

FOR THE SALAD

(1)   Select a ready to eat papaya with a very good shape. Peel and cut off a slice at the bottom to make a base. Also cut a hole in the centre of the base to remove some seeds. Place papaya in a plate and carve out five long windows as shown in the diagram. Clean seeds from inside of the papaya and also from the cut out pieces. Now position this papaya in the centre of a serving plate. Arrange the cut out pieces in front of the windows made in the papaya.
Cut out five small leaves out of green papaya skin, like carrot leaves (see Pg. 190). Fix all of them on top of the papaya neatly with a toothpick. Put one glazed cherry on top of the papaya.

(2)   Make stuffed chickoo flowers and arrange them between two long pieces of papaya and orange segments.

(3)   Fill strawberries inside the hollow of papaya.

(4)   Cut small bunches from both varieties of grapes and arrange them in the remaining empty place.

FOR THE SPECIAL HONEY DRESSING

(1)   Melt brown sugar in hot water. Cool it.

(2)   Add honey, lemon juice, vinegar, oil, salt and pepper. Shake vigorously to mix well.

FOR THE LOW CALORIE ORANGE FRUIT SALAD DRESSING

(1)   Mix garlic in vinegar and let it stand for an hour for the flavour to set in. Strain it.

(2)   Add orange juice, red chilli powder, sugar, salt and pepper to the vinegar. Shake well and keep in fridge till serving time.

FOR THE CREAMY CHEESE AND GINGER DRESSING

(1)   Blend grated cheese, orange juice and ginger juice in a mixer or with an egg beater.

(2)   Mix lightly the beaten cream and season with salt and pepper.

FOR THE STUFFED CHICKOO FLOWERS

(1)   Select five ready to eat chickoos. From each, cut out a hole from the stem end. Carefully remove seeds and white inedible portion. Now chickoos will have a hollow inside.

(2)   Prepare thick custard out of 90 ml. (3 fl. ozs.) of milk, 1 tablespoon custard powder and 1/2 tablespoon of sugar. Cool custard and stuff in the hollow portion of all the five chickoos.

(3)   Now peel the chickoos. Make zigzag cuts in the centre of the fruit just like cucumber flowers (see Pg. 152). The custard will also get divided into two parts. Each chickoo will make two flowers. Place half glazed cherry in the centre of each half.

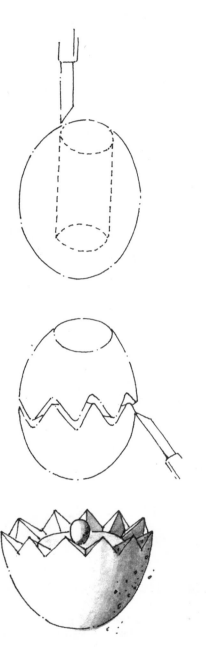

EXOTIC VEGETABLE - HORS-D' OEUVRE (20 SERVINGS)

An exotic salad decorated exquisitely with vegetable flowers, can be served as an hors-d'oeuvre at a buffet party.

INGREDIENTS

FOR THE MUSHROOM CHINESE STYLE

1 cup mushrooms (canned)

2 Kashmiri red chillies

3 cloves garlic

1 tablespoon vinegar

Salt to taste

A big pinch aji-no-moto

1 tablespoon oil

FOR THE PICKLED CARROTS

1 cup carrots' thick slices

1 tablespoon vinegar

1 tablespoon powdered sugar

Salt to taste

FOR THE BEETROOT SLICES IN BROWN VINAIGRETTE

12 slices beetroot, boiled

FOR BROWN VINAIGRETTE

3 tablespoons oil, refined or salad oil

1 - 1/2 tablespoons brown vinegar

2 teaspoons prepared mustard paste or powder

Salt and pepper to taste

2 teaspoons brown sugar

METHOD

Prepare red radish flowers, cucumber cherry lilies and spring onion chrysanthemum flowers according to the instructions. Arrange these flowers in an oval plate in such a way that it gets divided into three sections. Fill each section with specially prepared salads like: Mushrooms Chinese Style; Pickled thick carrot slices; Beetroot slices in brown vinaigrette.

FOR THE MUSHROOM CHINESE STYLE

(1)   Soak red chilli pieces and garlic in vinegar and little water for half an hour. Grind to a paste.

(20   Heat oil, add chilli-garlic paste. Fry for a minute. Then add the mushrooms and salt to taste. Toss for a few minutes and remove from gas. Serve hot or cold.

FOR THE PICKLED CARROTS

Mix all the ingredients together and keep for an hour. Remove slices from the liquid and arrange in the platter.

FOR THE BEETROOT SLICES IN BROWN VINAIGRETTE

(1)   Mix together all the ingredients for brown vinaigrette and keep for 15 minutes, for brown sugar to dissolve properly.

(2)   Take beetroot slices and dip each one in vinaigrette and arrange on the platter.

FOR THE RED RADISH FLOWER

(1)   Select a firm oval shaped red radish. Cut a slight base to make it stand.

(2)   Divide radish into 12 equal petals by piercing knife into the red skin only. Keep the base intact.

(3)   Separate red skin carefully by peeling it with a sharp narrow knife.

(4)   Immerse flower in ice cold water. Petals will open and will make a pretty flower.

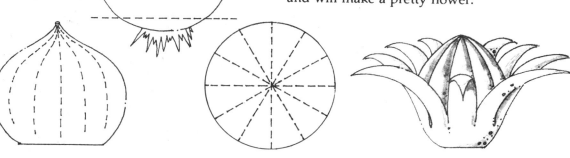

FOR THE CUCUMBER CHERRY LILY

(1)   Take about 2 - 1/2 inches piece of a cucumber. If the skin is tender, do not peel. Check if the piece stands properly.

(2)   Divide cucumber from the narrow end into four equal portions (if cucumber is thick, cut 5 portions) attached at the base.

(3)   Carefully open centre and separate seeded centre and remove it with a penknife. Now the piece will be hollow with four petals.

(4)   Hold each petal and cut serrated boarder by cutting straight and slant cuts.

(5)   In each petal cut out one inner petal. Push these small petals inside and gently pull the bigger petals outwards.

(6)   Put this lily in cold water for an hour or until petals open properly. Check the petals from time to time, pushing small petals inside and the outer ones outside to give a proper form.

(7)   Remove from water and fix a red glazed cherry in the centre or put a small red chilli flower (see Pg. 118)

FOR THE SPRING ONION CHRYSANTHEMUM

(1)   Cut out green leaves of spring onion and use the white bulb portion only. Select medium sized onion. Remove any damaged layer of skin.

(2)   Hold the onion upside down. From the base end, make very thin but deep cuts, going towards the open end of the onion. Do not forget to leave little attachment at the base.

(3)   Separate gently each petal with hand and then, put in ice cold water for 1 - 1/2 hours. It will open out into a pretty chrysanthemum flower.

Note:
One can make coloured onion chrysanthemums by adding a few drops of yellow or blue or red food colour in ice cold water. Onion will take colour as it opens.

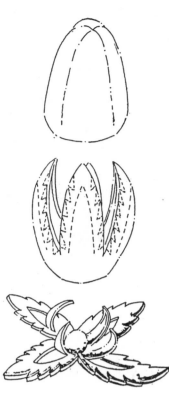

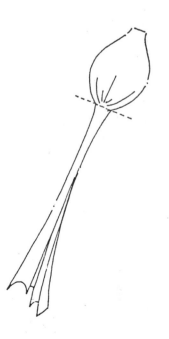

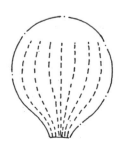

SWEET AND SOUR PINEAPPLE SALAD (6 SERVINGS)

Ideal salad to make when pineapples are in season

INGREDIENTS

FOR THE SALAD

1 cup fresh or canned pineapple pieces

1/4 cup sugar

Juice of 1/2 lemon

1/2 cup water

1/2 cup spaghetti, cooked

1/4 cup carrots, chopped and boiled

1/2 cup pieces of thick coconut cream

FOR THE SWEET AND SOUR DRESSING

1/2 cup liquid from cooked pineapple or syrup from the can

Juice of 1/2 lemon in case of canned pineapple

Salt and pepper to taste

2 teaspoons corn flour

2 teaspoons fresh cream

METHOD

(1) Pressure cook the fresh pineapple pieces with sugar, lemon juice and water. Drain out liquid and cool pineapple pieces.

(2) Prepare the sweet and sour dressing by mixing together the pineapple syrup, salt, pepper and corn flour. Heat on gas and mix well till thick. Cool and mix in fresh cream.

(3) Toss spaghetti, grapes, carrots and coconut pieces with the dressings.

(4) Serve in a specially prepared pineapple bird.

FOR THE PINEAPPLE BIRD

(1) Select a ready-to-eat pineapple with a good crown of leaves. Trim off any brown leaves. Pull out six leaves from the centre of the leaves to make side wings of the bird.

(2) Position pineapple on a flat board in such a way that the crown of leaves point upwards. Cut a base to make it stand firmly.

(3) Cut out a slice from the top in such a way that there is one inch space in the front and half inch on the opposite side.

(4) Scoop out the pulp from inside keeping a side wall and base of 1/4 inch thickness.

(5) Select a red radish of medium size to make the head. Trim off its, roots, keeping pointed little portion as a beak. Insert two cloves as eyes. Cut out zigzag comb from a slice of carrot and fix on the head. Take about 3 inches long tapered clean piece of carrot and fix head on it with two toothpicks. Finally, fix firmly this neck on the pineapple with two toothpicks in the one inch area of the front.

(6) To finish, insert three leaves on the sides as wings.

VITAMIN SALAD IN GUAVA BOATS (6 SERVINGS)

A vitamin packed nutritious salad.

INGREDIENTS	METHOD
FOR THE SALAD	**FOR THE SALAD**

INGREDIENTS

FOR THE SALAD

1 tablespoon oil

1/2 cup raw papaya pieces

1/2 cup carrot pieces

1/2 cup guava pieces
(preferably pink variety)

1/2 cup cucumber pieces

1/2 cup bedana pomegranate (soft seeded)

Salt to taste

2 tablespoons lemon juice

1/2 cup coriander leaves, chopped

FOR THE STEWED GUAVA BOATS

3 guavas - big sized (preferably pink variety)

1/4 cup sugar

1/2 teaspoon salt

1 tablespoon lemon juice

METHOD

FOR THE SALAD

(1) Heat oil and add pieces of raw papaya and carrot. Stir well and keep for a few minutes, till they are soft but crisp. Remove from heat and cool.

(2) Mix together the guava, cucumber, pomegranate, salt, lemon juice and coriander leaves.

(3) Serve individually in stewed guava boats.

FOR THE STEWED GUAVA BOATS

(1) Cut all the guavas into halves, lengthwise. Put them in a broad vessel.

(2) Add enough water to immerse them. Also add sugar, salt and lemon juice. Put on the gas and cook for 10 minutes.

(3) Remove from gas and cool. Scoop out the seed portion from the centre with a spoon so that each half will have enough hollow to stuff in the vitamin salad. Tuck in two small carrot leaves on top with tiny sprig of coriander leaf in the centre. Method for carrot leaves (see Pg. 190)

1. Hawaiian summer salad in red pumpkin bowl with -
a. White radish swan   p. 49
b. Red radish water lily   p. 49
c. Carrot daisy   p. 49
d. Leaves   p. 49

2. Exotic vegetable salad hors' d'oeuvre with -
e. Cucumber cherry lily   p. 64
f. Spring onion chrysanthemum   p. 64
g. Red radish flower   p. 63

MEAL ON A PLATTER WITH FIFTY FIFTY DRESSING (12 - 15 SERVINGS)

A sumptuous salad which gives ample scope for creativity.

INGREDIENTS

8 paneer eggs

Few drops yellow colour

2 cup mixture of hara channa (Bengal green grams) and Kabuli chana (cheekpeas)

A pinch soda bicarb

6 red radish, cut into flowers

1 cup white radish slices

2 medium tomatoes, sliced

1 cucumber, sliced

About 20 French beans

2 medium firm-red tomatoes

Salt to taste

3/4 cup French dressing

3/4 cup mayonnaise dressing

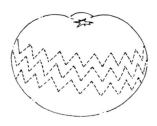

METHOD

(1)   For paneer eggs — Take 1 - 1/2 cups of paneer. Mix it with 1/2 teaspoon of salt and beat it with hands to make a smooth paste. If too soft to handle then chill for an hour in fridge. Divide this paneer into 1/3 and 2/3 parts. To 1/3 part, add few drops of yellow colour. Mix and make four balls. Wash hands and then divide the remaining 2/3 portion in four parts. Use each portion to cover the yellow ball. Form into egg shapes. Put in a plate and chill them in fridge. Then cut all four eggs into two, thus making eight halves.

(2)   Soak grams overnight and boil them with salt and a pinch of soda bicarb in pressure cooker. Drain off water.

(3)   The red radish flowers (see Pg. 63).

(4)   Cut slices of white radish, tomatoes and cucumbers.

(5)   String French beans and boil in salt water.

(6)   To prepare tomato rings — Cut 1/4 inch zigzag pattern slices out of two firm red tomatoes. Remove pulp from the centre.

(7)   Pass bunch of French beans through these tomato rings. Make four such bunches.

(8)   Prepare **fifty-fifty dressing** by mixing french dressing and mayonnaise sauce. Beat well to make a smooth consistency. Fill in the bowl. Keep this bowl in the centre. of a square serving plate.

(9)   **Arrange French beans - tomato ring bunches across the tray dividing it into four sections. Fill up each section with paneer egg halves, green and white grams, sliced tomatoes, cucumber slices red radish lilies and white radish slices.**

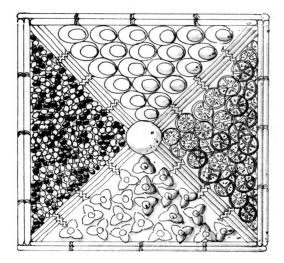

SOUPS

CHINESE SWEET CORN SOUP (6 SERVINGS)

Most popular Chinese vegetarian soup which can be served with few pieces of carrots and cabbage floating on top.

INGREDIENTS

3 cups stock (out of small cabbage, few French beans, 1 carrot, 1 onion, 1 potato)

2 tablespoons oil

1 can cream style sweet corn (400 grams)

Corns from 1 corn cob, boiled

Salt to taste

1/2 tablespoon aji-no-moto

1 tablespoon sago

2 tablespoons corn flour

Soya sauce, chilli sauce and green chillies in vinegar

METHOD

(1) Cut vegetables for stock into big pieces. Cook them in pressure cooker with three cups of water. Reserve the stock.

(2) Heat oil. Add sweet corns from can and the boiled corns. Saute for a few minutes. Add stock and boil. Also add salt, aji-no-moto and washed sago.

(3) Blend corn flour in little water and add to the boiling soup. Simmer soup for 15 minutes.

(4) Serve each serving of soup with quarter teaspoon of green chillies in vinegar, three to four drops of soya sauce and two drops of chilli sauce.

INDIAN CURRY CORN SOUP (6 SERVINGS)

Spicy as usual to suit the Indian palate.

INGREDIENTS

1 can cream style sweet corn (400 grams)

2 tablespoons butter

1 small onion, chopped

1 - 1/2 tablespoons flour

1 tablespoon curry powder

3 cups stock (out of few French beans,

1 carrot, 1 onion, tomatoes and beetroot)

Salt to taste

1 teaspoon red chilli powder

METHOD

(1) Cut vegetables for stock into big pieces and pressure cook with three cups of water. Strain water as stock.

(2) Boil red chilli powder in quarter cup of water and Strain. Keep aside.

(3) Melt butter and saute the chopped onion very light brown. Stir in flour and curry powder. Stir for a few minutes. Add cream style corn. Saute for few more minutes. Now add stock, red chilli water and salt to taste. Simmer for 15 minutes.

WHITE PUMPKIN SOUP (6 SERVINGS)

A good, healthy and creamy soup.

INGREDIENTS

1/2 kg. white pumpkin

1 onion

1 cup white sauce

Salt and pepper to taste

1/2 cup cheese, grated

METHOD

(1) Peel and cut white pumpkin and onion into big pieces. Add two cups water and pressure cook. Cool and blend in an electric blender.

(2) Mix together the white sauce and white pumpkin puree. Add salt and pepper to taste. Adjust consistency by adding water. Boil soup for 15 minutes. Strain soup again through a fine sieve.

(3) Serve hot with grated cheese.

Note :

(a) Cream of cauliflower or cream of leek soups are made in the same way as pumpkin soup.

(b) White sauce is made out of 2 tablespoons butter, 1 - 1/2 tablespoons flour and 1 cup milk.

CREAM OF ASPARAGUS SOUP (6 SERVINGS)

A delicious soup delicately flavoured with spices.

INGREDIENTS

2 tablespoons butter

1 onion, chopped

1 small can asparagus or 250 gram fresh asparagus

1 - 1/2 tablespoons flour

3 cups stock (out of 1 each of carrot, onion, potato)

2 tablespoons butter

1 onion, chopped

1 small can asparagus or 250 grams fresh asparagus

METHOD

(1) Cut vegetables for stock into big pieces and pressure cook with three cups of water. Strain water as stock.

(2) Melt butter and saute the onion for four to five minutes. Then add chopped asparagus. Cover pan and cook for five more minutes. Sprinkle flour and stir until smooth. Pour in stock and mix well. Add bay leaf and mace. Season with salt and pepper. Bring to a boil and simmer for ten to fifteen minutes.

(3) Remove bay leaf and mace. Put soup through a fine moulie or into an electric blender. Reheat soup by adding milk. Adjust seasoning to taste.

(4) Serve hot with bread croutons.

Note :

Cream of mushroom soup is made in the same way.

MINESTRONE SOUP (6 SERVINGS)

Excellent combination of vegetables and macaroni in a soup, but very filling.

INGREDIENTS

FOR THE STOCK

10 - 12 french beans

2 potatoes

4 tomatoes

1 small piece cabbage

2 carrots

VEGETABLES FOR THE SOUP

5 french beans

2 small carrots

1 small tomato

1/4 cup green peas

1 onion

2 tablespoons butter

2 tablespoons tomato ketchup

1 cup macaroni, boiled

8 tablespoons cheese, grated

2 tablespoons corn flour

2 tablespoons barley, uncooked

METHOD

(1) Cut vegetables for stock into big pieces. Cook in a pressure cooker with four cups for water. Strain water as stock. Cook barley in cooker with a little water.

(2) Cut vegetables given for soup into small pieces.

(3) Heat butter and saute the vegetables for a few minutes. Pour the stock and boil till vegetables are cooked.

(4) Add macaroni and barley. Boil.

(5) Blend corn flour in a little cold water and add to the boiling soup. Add salt to taste.

(6) Mix in tomato ketchup and cheese. Give a boil and serve hot.

CREAM OF SPINACH SOUP (6 SERVINGS)

A nutritious spinach soup, laced with fresh cream.

INGREDIENTS

4 cups stock (out of 2 onions and 2 potatoes)

2 bunches spinach

1 tablespoon butter

1 onion, chopped

100 grams fresh cream

Salt and pepper to taste

1 - 1/2 tablespoons corn flour

1 - 1/2 cups milk

METHOD

(1) Cut vegetables for stock into big pieces. Pressure cook with four cups of water. Strain water as stock.

(2) Wash spinach and grind to a fine paste.

(3) Heat butter and saute the onions till soft.

(4) Mix spinach paste and saute further. When soft and cooked, mix salt, pepper, stock and boil.

(5) Strain the soup and put again on gas. Blend corn flour in milk and add to the soup. Simmer for ten minutes. Serve laced with fresh cream in each bowl.

LENTIL MULLIGATAWNY SOUP (6 SERVINGS)

A lentil soup delicately flavoured with spices.

INGREDIENTS

1/4 cup lentils

1 - 1/2 tablespoons rice

1 large tomato

1 carrot

2 cloves garlic, flaked

1 onion

1 small piece ginger

1 small piece cinnamon

A few curry leaves

1/2 coconut, extract milk

1/2 lemon

1 tablespoon cummin seeds

1 tablespoon coriander seeds

Salt to taste

METHOD

(1) Wash lentils and rice. Pour three cups of water and boil until they are cooked.

(2) Cut tomato, carrot, garlic, onion and ginger into small pieces. Add to the boiling soup. Also mix the curry leaves and the cinnamon piece. Simmer till the vegetables are tender. Add more water if required.

(3) Roast cummin and coriander seeds and powder them. Add to the soup. Blend in an electric blender. Put it back on the gas. Add coconut milk, salt to taste and lemon juice. Simmer for a few minutes and serve hot with a slice of lemon in each bowl.

CHEESE SOUP (6 SERVINGS)

A very rich soup, quick and easy to make.

INGREDIENTS

2 tablespoons butter

1 small onion, finely chopped

1 tablespoon flour

2 - 1/2 cups milk

1 - 1/4 cups water

1/2 cup cheese, grated

Pepper, salt and sugar to taste

1 - 1/2 tablespoons tomato ketchup

METHOD

(1) Melt the butter and saute the onion till soft.

(2) Stir in flour, when it bubbles, pour milk and water. Stir constantly till evenly mixed. Boil it.

(3) Add grated cheese, salt, pepper, sugar and tomato ketchup. Give one boil and serve hot with bread croutons.

VEGETABLE SOUP (FOR 6 SERVINGS)

A light and delicious soup.

INGREDIENTS

1 onion

2 potatoes

1 carrot

1/2 head celery, (optional)

2 tomatoes

2 tablespoons butter

1 - 1/2 tablespoons flour

Salt, pepper to taste

Juice of 1/2 lemon

1/2 cup green peas, boiled

METHOD

(1) Cut vegetables in convenient sized pieces. Melt butter and saute vegetables for a few minutes.

(2) Pour water about two cups and simmer till the vegetables are tender. Make puree in an electric blender. Put it back on the gas.

(3) Blend flour in water and add to the boiling soup. Mix in lemon juice.

(4) Serve hot soup with green peas floating in each bowl.

WHITE PUMPKIN AND MOONG DAL SOUP (6 - 8 SERVINGS)

A nutritious soup topped with colourful floats.

INGREDIENTS

1 tablespoon butter

1 onion, chopped

1/2 cup moong dal, soaked for two hours

1/2 kg. white pumpkin, chopped with skin

1 cup milk

Salt and pepper to taste

6 - 8 teaspoons cheese, grated

METHOD

(1) Melt butter and lightly saute the onion. Add the soaked moong dal and pumpkin pieces. Remove from gas. Add a cup of water and pressure cook.

(2) Make a fine puree in an electric blender.

(3) Season with salt and pepper. Add water to adjust the consistency.

(4) Boil the soup once again.

(5) Serve topped with one teaspoon of grated cheese in each soup bowl.

Note :

You can also serve a brown bread float in each bowl. Cut a circle out of a slice of brown bread. Decorate it with a border made out of a mixture of mashed potatoes, salt, pepper and little milk. Decorate with a piece of cherry in the centre.

ALMOND SOUP (6 SERVINGS)

An unusual combination of nuts and vegetables for a soup.

INGREDIENTS	METHOD
4 cups vegetable stock (out of a small cabbage, 1 tomato, 1 carrot, 1 potato, 1 onion, a few French beans)	(1) Cut vegetable for stock into big pieces. Pressure cook with four cups of water. Strain water as stock.
1 cup almonds	(2) Blanch almonds. Cut them into pieces. Mix with milk and blend in the mixer.
3/4 cup milk	(3) Mix together the almond milk, stock, salt and pepper. Boil it.
Salt and pepper to taste	(4) Blend corn flour in water and add to the soup. Stir till thick, like a soup. Add a few drops of essence before serving. Serve with a few thin slivers of almonds.
3 tablespoons corn flour	
A few drops almond essence (optional)	

CREAM OF TOMATO SOUP (6 SERVINGS)

Most favourite soup for both, children and grown-ups !

INGREDIENTS	METHOD
1 kg. tomatoes	(1) Cut all the vegetables into small pieces and cook in the pressure cooker with two cups of water. Make puree with an electric blender.
1 carrot	(2) Mix together the white sauce, tomato puree and seasonings. Boil for a few minutes.
1 onion	(3) Strain the soup through a fine strainer. Serve hot with little fresh cream in each bowl.
2 - 3 cloves garlic	
Small piece beetroot	**Note :**
1 cup white sauce*	White sauce is made out of 2 tablespoons of butter, 1 - 1/2 tablespoons of flour and 1 cup of milk.
Salt, pepper and sugar to taste	
For topping	
Little fresh cream	

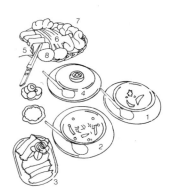

1. Coconut soup   p. 76
2. Minestrone soup   p. 71
3. Angel's fingers   p. 78
4. White pumpkin and moong dal soup   p. 73
5. Brown bread   p. 79
6. Garlic bread   p. 80
7. Buttermilk rolls   p. 81
8. Rice bread   p. 81

COCONUT SOUP (4 SERVINGS)

An appetising soup of a beautiful purplish - pink colour, served cold.

INGREDIENTS

10 cocums, new if possible

4 cups water

1 coconut

1 spring curry leaves

6 - 8 cloves garlic

Salt to taste

1 tablespoon oil

1 teaspoon mustard seeds

METHOD

(1) Boil cocums with one cup of water. Drain and reserve the water.

(2) Extract milk from the coconut with three cups of water.

(3) Make a paste of curry leaves, coriander leaves and garlic. Add a little water and extract the juice as masala water.

(4) Mix together the cocum water, coconut milk and masala water. Add salt to taste.

(5) Now heat the oil and splutter the mustard seeds in it. Add to the soup. Mix well and serve cold.

WHITE SOUP (6 SERVINGS)

A simple soup with herbal flavour.

INGREDIENTS

1 potato, chopped

1 medium turnip, chopped

1 cup cabbage, chopped

1 medium onion, chopped

1 leek head (optional)

1 bay leaf

1 - 2 cloves

Salt and pepper to taste

6 teaspoons cheese, grated

1/2 cup milk

METHOD

(1) Pressure cook all the vegetables and spices with one cup of water.

(2) Remove bay leaves and cloves. Make puree in an electric blender and sieve.

(3) Boil soup with salt and pepper.

(4) Add hot milk just before serving.

(5) Soup can be served with one teaspoon of grated cheese in each bowl.

ACCOMPANIMENTS TO SOUPS

CHEESE FIGURES (MAKES 6 PIECES)

Quick to make cheesy titbits.

INGREDIENTS

6 slices bread

4 tablespoons cheese, grated

3 tablespoons butter

Few glazed cherries

METHOD

(1) Cut out different figures of bread with bread cutters.
(2) Dip one side of each figure in melted butter.
(3) Top these figures with grated cheese.
(4) Decorate with slices of glazed cherries.
(5) Arrange these figures in a greased baking tray. Bake at 200ºC. for 15 to 20 minutes till they are crisp.

CHEESE SHAPES (6 SERVINGS)

Crispy snack. Good to eat with many soups.

INGREDIENTS

5 tablespoons corn flour

4 tablespoons cheese, grated

1/2 teaspoon mustard powder

1/2 teaspoon baking powder

1 tablespoon butter, melted

METHOD

(1) Mix together all the above ingredients well and make a dough. Use milk if required.
(2) Give different shapes like twisted straws, sticks, etc. or by cutters.
(3) Deep fry in ghee. They should be light brown in colour.

POTATO STICKS (MAKES ABOUT 20 PIECES)

Soft and juicy sticks.

INGREDIENTS

2 potatoes, boiled, mashed

2 tablespoons butter, melted

1/3 cup flour

Salt and pepper to taste

1/4 teaspoon cummin or shahjeera

METHOD

(1) Mix all the above ingredients together and make a soft dough.
(2) Roll into small sticks and arrange on a greased baking tray.
(3) Bake at 200ºC till light brown in colour. Turn sides of sticks while baking.

BREAD STICKS (MAKES 20 STICKS)

Very crisp sticks, can be made in advance and stored.

INGREDIENTS	METHOD
1/2 teaspoon salt	(1) Melt salt and sugar in lukewarm water.
1 teaspoon sugar	(2) Mix yeast and caraway seeds in flour. Make a soft dough with prepared water. Knead with margarine. Put this dough in an oiled vessel. Cover with a wet cloth. Keep aside for 1 - 1/2 hours or till the dough is double in size.
1 - 1/2 teaspoons yeast	
1/2 teaspoon caraway seeds	
2 cups flour	
1 tablespoon margarine or butter	(3) Knead dough again. Take little dough and roll out into thin stick. Similarly make the other sticks and arrange them on greased baking tray. Cover with wet cloth and keep aside for about half an hour.
	(4) Heat oven to 250°C. Bake the sticks for 10 minutes. Then reduce temperature to 100°C. Turn sides of sticks and bake further for 20 to 30 minutes till sticks are crisp.

ANGEL'S FINGERS (MAKES 20 - 25 PIECES)

Very unusual accompaniment to soup in taste and appearance.

INGREDIENTS	METHOD
3/4 cup flour	(1) Combine together the flour, cheese, water, salt and oil. Knead well to form a pliable dough. Keep aside for half an hour.
3 tablespoons cheese, grated	
Water to bind	
1/4 teaspoon salt	(2) Peel the boiled potatoes and cut into long chips. Sprinkle little salt and red chilli powder on them.
1 tablespoon oil	
3 medium sized potatoes, boiled	(3) Knead dough again and make 10 to 12 balls. Roll them into thin circles. Cut each one into two. Put one potato chip in each half of the circle. Apply water on edges. Roll into long shape. Press sides and cut tiny fringes. Deep fry on medium gas till little brown in colour.
1 teaspoon red chilli powder	
Ghee for frying	
To decorate	
Potato rose	(4) Serve in a plate with potato rose and capsicum leaves. Make a mixture with mashed potato, salt, little milk and yellow colour.
Capsicum leaves	

Note:
Method of making a rose is similar to marzipan rose. (see Pg. 227)

SALLY LUNNS (6 SERVINGS)

A sweet bread made into a fancy shape.

INGREDIENTS

1 tablespoon butter

1/2 teaspoon sugar

Milk as required

1 - 1/2 teaspoons yeast

2 cup flour

1/2 teaspoon salt

Sugar glaze

METHOD

(1) Melt butter in a vessel. Mix in sugar, milk, yeast and quarter cup of flour (out of 2 cups). Make an even batter. Cover and keep aside for 10 minutes till mixture is frothy.

(2) Mix salt in the remaining flour. Make a soft dough with the above prepared mixture. Use more milk to make a right consistency dough.

(3) Knead dough for a few minutes and form into a ball.

(4) Grease a round jelly tin 6" deep and 4" diametre, with ghee. Put the dough in it. cover it with a wet cloth. Keep aside till it becomes double in size for about 1 - 12 hours.

(5) Heat oven to 250°C. Put Sally Lunns for baking in the centre of the oven. Bake for 25 minutes till the crust becomes dark brown.

(6) Remove from oven and unmould on wire rack. Cool. Apply sugar glaze when bread is still warm.

(7) For sugar glaze take equal quantity of sugar and water in a small vessel. Heat on gas and give one boil. Remove from gas.

BROWN BREAD (MAKES 8 ROLLS)

Simple to look and easy to digest.

INGREDIENTS

1/2 tablespoon brown sugar

1/2 teaspoon salt

Few drops caramel colour

1 cup wheat flour

1 cup flour

1 - 1/2 teaspoons yeast

1 tablespoon refined oil

Ghee to glaze

METHOD

(1) Dissolve brown sugar, salt and colour in luke warm water.

(2) Combine the two flours and mix in yeast and oil.

(3) Make a soft dough with the above prepared water. Take more water if required.

(4) Knead for a few minutes.

(5) Put dough in an oiled vessel. Cover with a wet cloth. Keep aside for 1 - 1/2 hours or till double in size.

(6) Knead dough again. Make eight balls. Arrange them in an greased baking tray. Cover with a wet cloth and keep aside till double in size.

(7) Heat oven to 250°C. bake the breads till light brown in colour, about 20 minutes. Remove from the oven. Cool them on cloth or wire rack. Grease them with ghee when hot.

GARLIC BREAD (6 SERVINGS)

A very soft bread with garlic flavour.

INGREDIENTS

1/2 teaspoon sugar

3/4 teaspoon salt

1/2 cup + 3 tablespoons (5 fl. ozs.) lukewarm water

1 - 1/2 teaspoons fresh yeast

2 cups flour

1 tablespoon butter

6 cloves garlic, mashed

Ghee to glaze

METHOD

(1) Melt sugar and salt in lukewarm water.

(2) Mix fresh yeast in flour and make a soft dough with the above prepared water.

(3) Knead dough for a few minutes. Keep it in an oiled vessel. Cover with wet cloth and keep aside for one and a half hours or till double in size.

(4) Knead dough with butter and garlic. Make one big oval ball on a greased tray. Cover with a wet cloth till double in size.

(5) Heat oven to 250°C. Bake the bread for 20 to 25 minutes till light brown on top. Remove from oven and cool on wire rack. Apply ghee as glaze. Cut into slices and serve.

POTATO ROLLS (MAKES 8 ROLLS)

Each roll can be of a different shape -— a knot, a twist, a flower, a shell, etc.

INGREDIENTS

2 teaspoons sugar

1/3 cup lukewarm milk

1 teaspoon salt

1 - 1/2 teaspoons fresh yeast

1/2 cup boiled potatoes, mashed

2 cups flour

1 - 1/2 tablespoons vanaspati ghee

METHOD

(1) Melt sugar in lukewarm milk.

(2) Mix salt, yeast and mashed potatoes in flour.

(3) Make a soft dough with the milk mixture. Use more milk if required.

(4) Knead with ghee. Put dough in an oiled vessel. Cover with a wet cloth till double in size.

(5) Knead dough again. Divide into eight balls. Roll each ball into different shapes. Arrange them on a greased baking tray. Cover with an oiled plastic sheet till double in size.

(6) Heat oven to 250°C. Bake potato rolls for 15 to 20 minutes till light brown on top.

(7) Remove from oven, cool on wire rack and apply ghee as glaze.

BUTTERMILK ROLLS (MAKES 8 ROLLS)

Shaping and method of making is the same as for potato rolls, but texture and the taste are different.

INGREDIENTS

1 teaspoon sugar

1/2 cup thick buttermilk

1 teaspoon salt

1 - 1/2 teaspoons fresh yeast

2 cups flour

1 - 1/2 tablespoons vanaspati ghee

METHOD

(1) Melt sugar in lukewarm buttermilk.

(2) Mix salt and yeast in the flour.

(3) Make soft dough with the above prepared buttermilk. Use more water if required.

(4) Knead with ghee. Put dough in an oiled vessel. Cover with wet cloth till double in size.

(5) Knead dough again. Divide into eight balls. Roll each ball into different shapes. Arrange them on a greased baking tray. Cover with an oiled plastic sheet till double in size.

(6) Heat oven to 250°C. Bake rolls for 15 to 20 minutes till light brown on top.

(7) Remove from oven. Cool on wire rack and apply ghee as blaze.

RICE BREAD (MAKES 8 ROLLS)

A bread made without butter, yet soft and tasty.

INGREDIENTS

1/2 teaspoon salt

2 cups flour

1/4 cup cooked rice

1 - 1/2 teaspoon fresh yeast

1/2 cup water

Ghee to glaze

METHOD

(1) Mix salt and flour together. Make a well in the centre. Put rice in it. Pour warm water on the rice. Melt fresh yeast in it, without much disturbing the flour. Cover and keep for half an hour.

(2) Make a soft dough. Use water as required.

(3) Knead dough for a few minutes. Put dough in an oiled vessel. Cover with a wet cloth and keep aside till double in size.

(4) Reknead dough and make about eight oval shaped balls. Arrange them on a greased tray. Cover with a wet cloth. Keep till double in size.

(5) Heat oven to 250°C. Bake rice bread till light brown in colour, about 15 to 20 minutes. Take them out and cool on wire rack. Apply ghee as a glaze.

CHELSEA CHEESE RING (6 SERVINGS)

Extremely good blend of cheese in a fancy shaped bread.

INGREDIENTS

3 cups flour

1/2 cup cheese, grated

1 - 1/2 teaspoons mustard powder

3/4 teaspoon salt

3/4 teaspoon pepper

1/2 teaspoon sugar

1 - 1/2 teaspoons fresh yeast

1/2 cup water

1 - 1/2 tablespoons butter

Ghee to glaze

METHOD

(1) Take flour, half of the cheese, mustard powder, salt and pepper in a shallow dish.

(2) Melt sugar and fresh yeast in lukewarm water. Add to the flour mixture and make a soft dough. Take more water if required.

(3) Knead dough with butter. Keep in an oiled vessel covered with a wet cloth till double in size.

(4) Knead dough again. Make a ball and roll out into a 9" x 11" rectangle. Apply milk all over. Sprinkle remaining cheese on it. Roll out the longest side like a Swiss roll. Seal edges. Cut into 12 equal sized slices. Arrange these slices, cut side down in a greased round cake tin of 8 - 1/2 inches in diametre. Cover with oiled plastic bag till double in size.

(5) Heat oven to 250°C. and bake bread till light brown on top for about 20 to 30 minutes.

(6) Remove from heat. Cool for a while and turn out on a wire rack. Apply ghee on top for glaze.

PERSIAN NAN (6 SERVINGS)

A good bread served with soups or with meals to substitute chappatis.

INGREDIENTS

2 cups flour

1/2 teaspoon salt

1/2 cup lukewarm water

2 teaspoons sugar

1 teaspoon fresh yeast

1 tablespoon vanaspati ghee

1 tablespoon semolina

Milk as required

1/2 teaspoon sesame seeds

1/2 teaspoon poppy seeds

METHOD

(1) Combine flour and salt in a shallow dish. Make a well in the centre. Mix lukewarm water, sugar and yeast in the well. Cover and keep for 10 minutes. The mixture will become frothy.

(2) Make a soft dough with more water. Knead with ghee.

(3) Leave dough in an oiled vessel, covered with a wet cloth till double in size.

(4) Knead dough again and make a ball. Roll out to about 10 inches in diameter. Apply ghee and then sprinkle semolina over it. Fold and make into a ball again. Roll this ball to about six inches to seven inches round. Apply milk all over the top surface. Sprinkle the mixture of sesame seeds and poppy seeds.

(5) Leave to rise again on a greased baking tray, covered with oiled plastic sheet till double in size.

(6) Heat oven to 250°C. Bake Persian nan till golden brown in colour, about 20 minutes.

(7) Remove and cool on wire rack.

INDIAN CURRIES AND VEGETABLE DISHES

HYDERABADI CURRY (6 - 8 SERVINGS)

A delicious curry with a rich taste of nuts.

INGREDIENTS

FOR THE GRINDING MASALA

1/4 cup (60 grams) almonds

1/4 cup (60 grams) cashew nuts

30 grams (1 oz.) peanuts

30 grams (1 oz.) roasted grams (dalia)

1/2 cup coconut, grated

1 tablespoon coriander seeds

1 tablespoon sesame seeds

1 tablespoon cummin seeds

1 tablespoon poppy seeds

10 cloves garlic

1 piece cinnamon

1 medium sized onion

6 - 8 green chillies

1 inch piece ginger

FOR THE CURRY

1/2 cup ghee

5 - 6 curry leaves

1/4 teaspoon turmeric powder

Salt to taste

1 tablespoon onions, fried golden brown

2 cups coconut milk

1/2 kg. tomatoes, make puree

Juice from 1/2 lemon

1 tablespoon tomato ketchup

1/2 kg. potatoes, boiled

1 cup green peas, boiled

2 carrots, cut into small pieces, boiled

METHOD

(1) Grind all the ingredients for masala together in water to make a fine paste.

(2) Take ghee in a thick pan. Saute the ground masala, curry leaves, turmeric powder and salt.

(3) Mix in the golden fried onions and coconut milk. When it starts to boil, add tomato puree, lemon juice and tomato ketchup.

(4) Simmer for 15 minutes. Mix in the boiled potatoes, peas and carrots. Serve hot.

KOFTA BHAJI (6 - 8 SERVINGS)

Dal balls in spicy tomato gravy.

INGREDIENTS

FOR THE KOFTAS

1 cup moong dal (split green gram without skin)

1 large onion, finely chopped 5 - 6 cloves garlic, finely chopped

3 slices bread, soaked in water and mashed

1 - 1/2 teaspoon chilli-ginger paste

1 - 1/4 teaspoon turmeric powder

Salt to taste

Ghee for frying

FOR THE GRAVY

1/2 cup ghee

2 large onions, sliced

3 - 4 cloves garlic, chopped

1/2 kg. tomatoes, make puree

1/2 bunch coriander leaves, chopped

1 teaspoon red chilli powder

1 tablespoon chilli-ginger paste

1/2 teaspoon garam masala (see pg. 287)

METHOD

FOR THE KOFTAS

(1)   Soak moong dal for an hour, cook till soft but dry.
(2)   Mix in all the ingredients. Make lemon sized balls of the mixture.
(3)   Fry them till golden brown in ghee.

FOR THE GRAVY

(1)   Saute onions till golden brown in half cup ghee.
(2)   Add the chopped garlic and saute.
(3)   Mix together all the ingredients and about one cup of water.
(4)   Simmer for 15 minutes. Add the koftas, few minutes before serving.

MATAR PANEER MAKHANWALA (6 - 8 SERVINGS)

A very creamy rich curry.

INGREDIENTS

400 grams cooking paneer (see Pg. 16)

3 onions, chopped

2 tablespoons butter

3 green chillies, chopped

2 tablespoons flour

1 - 1/2 cups milk

200 grams fresh cream

1/2 cup tomato ketchup

Salt to taste

2 teaspoons chilli powder

1 cup green peas, boiled

A few coriander leaves, chopped

METHOD

(1) Cut paneer into small cubes. Heat about two and a half cups of water with a teaspoon of salt. Soak paneer pieces for five minutes and then drain them.

(2) Saute onions in butter till transparent. Add the chopped green chillies. Fry them. Then add flour and stir for a few more minutes. Pour in milk, mix well and stir continuously till thick. Now mix in fresh cream, water. and tomato ketchup Give one boil. Lastly mix in the peas, paneer and chopped coriander leaves.

VEGETABLE MALAI KOFTA CURRY (6 - 8 SERVINGS)

Soft vegetable koftas in delicious Mughlai gravy.

INGREDIENTS

FOR THE KOFTAS

1/2 cup French beans, chopped, boiled

1/2 cup carrots, chopped, boiled

1/2 cup cauliflower, chopped, boiled

2 medium potatoes, boiled

2 tablespoons butter

1/4 teaspoon dry ginger powder

1/2 teaspoon white pepper powder

1/4 teaspoon rock salt powder

2 tablespoons gram flour

Salt to taste

Oil for deep frying

FOR THE GRAVY

1/2 cup oil

3 - 4 cardamoms

3 - 4 cloves

3 - 4 pieces cinnamon

3 Kashmiri chillies, soaked in water and ground to a paste

1 big onion, boiled, ground

4 cloves garlic and 1 inch ginger, ground

1 teaspoon turmeric powder

2 tablespoons curd

2 tablespoons poppy seeds, soaked in water and ground to a paste

Salt to taste

1 tablespoon cummin powder

1/2 teaspoon white pepper powder

1/2 teaspoon coriander cummin powder

1/4 teaspoon dry ginger powder

1 cup khoya

METHOD

(1) For koftas, mash the boiled vegetables and mix with gram flour and salt.

(2) Heat butter and add all the spices. Saute for a minute. Add prepared vegetables and mix well. Remove from gas and cool. Make balls and deep fry in oil.

(3) Heat oil, add cardamoms, cloves and cinnamon. Saute. Add paste of red chillies, onions, garlic-ginger and turmeric powder. Saute till oil separates. Add curd and poppy seed paste. Saute. Add salt, cummin powder, pepper powder, dry ginger powder and coriander - cummin powder. Saute. Then add khoya. Saute. Add little water to make the right consistency gravy. Give a boil and add koftas at the time of serving.

GOAN GREEN CURRY (6 - 8 SERVINGS)

An unusual curry with a very tasty green gravy.

INGREDIENTS

FOR THE GRINDING MASALA

2 cups coriander leaves, chopped

10 green chillies

5 - 6 cashewnuts

1 medium sized onion

2 tablespoons poppy seeds

1 tablespoon sesame seeds

1 inch piece ginger.

FOR THE CURRY

1/2 kg. lady fingers, cut into 1/2 inch pieces

Ghee to fry

2 tablespoons gram flour

1 cup thin coconut milk

1/2 cup thick coconut milk

6 cocums

Salt to taste

1 cup green peas, boiled

Few coriander leaves to garnish

METHOD

(1)   Take ghee in a pan and fry the lady fingers. Remove and keep aside.

(2)   Remove extra ghee keeping half cup of ghee in the pan. Fry the ground masala paste. Dissolve gram flour in thin coconut milk. Add to the masala.

(3)   Boil cocums in little water and take out extract. Add this to the boiling gravy. Add salt to taste. At the time of serving mix in thick coconut milk, green peas and lady fingers. Garnish with coriander leaves.

VEGETABLE MAKHANWALA (8 - 10 SERVINGS)

A very likeable curry for any buffet party.

INGREDIENTS

1/4 kg. French beans

1/4 kg. carrots

1/4 kg. cauliflower

1/4 kg. potatoes

1/4 cup ghee, melted

1 big onion, chopped

1 tablespoon cummin seeds

3 tomatoes, peeled, chopped or 1/2 can tomato puree (450 grams)

1 tablespoon red chilli powder

Salt to taste

Sugar in case of canned tomato puree only

3 tablespoons fresh cream (from top of milk)

3 tablespoon butter

A pinch red edible colour

1/4 kg. paneer made from 1/2 litre milk (optional)

METHOD

(1)   Cut French beans, carrots, cauliflower and potatoes into small pieces and boil them. Keep the stock.

(2)   Heat ghee in a vessel. Saute the chopped onions and cummin seeds till light brown. Add tomato pieces or puree and fry for a few more minutes till ghee separates.

(3)   Add boiled vegetables with its stocks, salt and chilli powder. Boil them. Add sugar in case of canned tomato puree.

(4)   Add fresh cream, butter, colour and fried paneer pieces. Give one boil and serve.

KASHMIRI BRINJAL KORMA (6 - 8 SERVINGS)

Soft brinjal curry in curds and spices.

INGREDIENTS

4 cups small pieces brinjal, without skin (take big soft variety of Bharta brinjals)

2 tablespoons oil

1 teaspoon cummin seeds

1/2 cup onions, chopped

10 cloves garlic, chopped

1/4 teaspoon turmeric powder

2 teaspoons red chilli powder

1 cup curd beaten

1/4 cup coriander leaves

2 tablespoons vinegar

2 tablespoons sugar

Salt to taste

Oil for deep frying

METHOD

(1)   Deep fry all the brinjal pieces.

(2)   Take two tablespoons of oil in a vessel and heat it. Add cummin seeds and splutter them. When they turn brown, add onions and garlic. Saute till they are soft. Add turmeric and chilli powder. Saute for half a minute. Mix in fried brinjal pieces, beaten curds, chopped coriander leaves, vinegar, sugar and salt to taste. Simmer for a few minutes and serve hot.

AMRUT CURRY (8 - 10 SERVINGS)

A very spicy curry, good for people who love pungent flavours.

INGREDIENTS

FOR THE GRINDING MASALA
10 green chillies

2 teaspoons red chilli powder

1 piece ginger

1 teaspoon garam masala (see Pg. 287)

4 tablespoons coriander-cummin powder

2 tablespoons sesame seeds

1 tablespoon turmeric powder

2 tablespoons poppy seeds, soaked in 1/4 cup water for 15 minutes

FOR THE CURRY
1/2 cup ghee

2 onions, chopped

3 tomatoes, chopped into small pieces

1/4 cup mixture of currants and cashewnuts

1/2 cup curds

12 medium sized potatoes, boiled and cut into two or

3/4 kg. very small potatoes, boiled

1 cup green peas

Few coriander leaves, chopped

METHOD

Take half cup of ghee in a thick bottom vessel and heat. Saute onions in ghee till brown. Add the ground masala paste and saute till it emanates a good aroma and ghee separates. Add tomato pieces, cashewnuts and currants. Saute further till tomatoes become pulpy and gets evenly mixed with the masalas. Add the beaten curds and about one cup of water. Boil for a few minutes. Add potatoes, green peas and salt to taste. Simmer for 10 minutes and garnish with coriander leaves before serving.

WHITE BEAN CURRY (6 - 8 SERVINGS)

A creamy white curry with beans and vegetables

INGREDIENTS

1/2 kg. double beans (fresh), take out beans from pods **or**

1 cup haricot beans

1/2 cup ghee

2 big onions, chopped

6 cloves garlic, chopped

2 tablespoons ground almonds

1/2 teaspoon garam masala (see Pg. 287)

1/2 teaspoon cardamom powder

1/4 teaspoon black pepper powder

1 tablespoon chilli ginger paste

3 potatoes, chopped

2 medium tomatoes, chopped

400 grams cauliflower, chopped

1 big carrot, chopped

1 cup milk

1 cup coconut milk

1/4 teaspoon saffron

1 cup curd

Salt to taste

Pinch of soda

METHOD

(1) If using haricot beans, soak them overnight and pressure cook them with a little salt and a big pinch of soda bicarb.

(2) Heat ghee and saute onions and garlic till light brown in colour. Add all the dry ingredients like ground almonds, garam masala, cardamom powder, black pepper powder and also the chilli ginger paste. Saute for a minute. Add all the vegetables and fry for a few more minutes.

(3) Add milk and coconut milk. Cover and cook till vegetables are done.

(4) Dissolve the saffron in curds and add to the vegetables. Also add the salt to taste. Simmer curry till the gravy is thick.

MIXED PULSES CURRY WITH METHI KOFTAS (10 SERVINGS)

Protein-rich curry with methi balls.

INGREDIENTS

FOR THE KOFTAS

1 cup semolina

1/2 cup fenugreek leaves (methi)

1 teaspoon chilli-ginger paste

3/4 cup curd

A pinch asafoetida

A pinch soda bicarb

Salt to taste

1 teaspoon sugar

2 tablespoons oil

FOR THE GRINDING MASALA

1/2 cup coconut, grated

10 black peppercorns

10 cloves garlic

1 medium onion

5 green chillies

1 inch ginger piece

FOR THE CURRY

1/4 kg. sprouted channa (Bengal grams), boiled

1/4 kg. sprouted moong (green grams), boiled

1/4 kg. sprouted muth (moth beans), boiled

1/2 coconut extract milk (2 cups)

Salt to taste

2 tablespoons ghee

METHOD

(1) Mix all the ingredients given for the koftas and make small balls. Arrange them in a colander and steam them for 15 minutes. Keep aside.

(2) Heat ghee and fry the ground masala paste. Add coconut milk and all the sprouted and boiled pulses and salt to taste. Simmer for 10 minutes. Add koftas and simmer for another five minutes.

1. Kofta bhaji   p. 84
2. Matar paneer makhanwala   p. 85
3. Mixed pulses curry with methi kofta   p. 92
4. Goan green curry   p. 87
5. Aro dal   p. 96
6. Carrot champa flowers   p. 102

GREEN CORN CURRY (6 - 8 SERVINGS)

A versatile green gravy of corns. Can also be prepared with peas or mixed vegetables.

INGREDIENTS

FOR THE CURRY

6 corn cobs, take out corns and boil in salt water (2 cups corns).

Reserve 1 - 1/2 cups stock.

1/2 coconut - extract milk (1 - 1/2 cups)

4 tablespoons ghee

Salt to taste

FOR THE GRINDING MASALA

1 big onion

6 cloves garlic

Few curry leaves

3/4 cup coriander leaves, chopped

1 piece cinnamon

2 - 3 cloves

2 tablespoons poppy seeds

1 tablespoon coriander seeds

5 green chillies

METHOD

(1) Heat ghee in a pan. Saute the ground masala paste till ghee separates and aroma emanates.
(2) Pour corn stock, stir and boil gravy.
(3) Add corns and simmer till gravy is nice and thick.
(4) Now pour coconut milk. Give a boil and serve hot.

ALU MATAR CURRY (6 - 8 SERVINGS)

A simple combination of potatoes and peas with little spicy tomato gravy.

INGREDIENTS

1/2 cup oil

3 - 4 cardamoms

1 tablespoon thin shreds ginger

1 onion, boiled, ground to a paste

8 cloves garlic, ground

3 - 4 Kashmiri chillies, soaked in water and ground to a paste

1 - 1/2 tablespoons poppy seeds

1/4 teaspoon rock salt powder

1 teaspoon cummin powder

1/2 teaspoon white pepper powder

2 cups tomato juice

1 teaspoon turmeric powder

Salt to taste

1/2 kg. green peas, boiled

1/2 kg. potatoes, boiled, cubed

METHOD

Heat oil and first saute the cardamom and ginger shreds. Add onion paste and fry till light brown. Add red chilli paste, poppy seed paste, rock salt powder, cummin powder and pepper powder. Fry until oil separates. Add tomato juice, turmeric and salt. Fry until oil separates. Add peas and potatoes. Mix well. Add little water to make required gravy consistency.

GARLIC BUTTERMILK (MAKES 3 CUPS)

A good accompaniment to a spicy pullao.

INGREDIENTS

1 - 1/2 cups fresh curd

1 - 1/2 cups water

Salt to taste

2 tablespoons ghee

1 tablespoon cummin seeds

5 cloves garlic, crushed

2 green chillies, split

METHOD

(1)   Beat curd and add water. Beat till even and frothy. Add salt to taste.

(2)   Heat ghee in a small vessel. Add cummin seeds, crushed garlic and green chillies. When cummin turns brown, pour over buttermilk. Serve at room temperature.

ARO DAL (6 - 8 SERVINGS)

Simple and delicious dal good to serve with pullaos and parathas.

INGREDIENTS	METHOD
1/2 cup lentil (masoor dal)	(1) Wash both dals and soak in water for an hour. Add turmeric, half of the green chillies, ginger, half of the garlic and salt. Boil on medium gas till cooked.
1/2 cup moong dal (split green grams without skin)	
1/2 teaspoon turmeric powder	(2) Add the chopped tomato.
4 green chillies, chopped	(3) Temper with ghee, cummin, remaining garlic, chilli and curry leaves.
1/2 inch ginger, cut into pieces	(4) Give one boil and remove.
8 - 10 cloves garlic, chopped	
Salt to taste	
1 tomato, chopped	
1 tablespoon ghee	
1 teaspoon cummin seeds	
Few curry leaves	

MAHARANI DAL (8 - 10 SERVINGS)

A Mughlai dal good to serve with any pullao.

INGREDIENTS	METHOD
1/2 cup kidney beans (rajma)	(1) Soak rajma, urad and channa dal for four hours. Pressure cook. Remove in a thick vessel and continue to simmer for another half an hour. The mixture should become extremely soft.
1/2 cup black gram (whole urad)	
1/2 cup split Bengal gram (channa dal)	
3 tablespoons oil	(2) Heat oil in another thick vessel. Add the chopped onions, chillies, tomatoes and ginger. Saute for a few minutes till soft. Add turmeric, red chilli powder and colour. Saute for a few more minutes.
1 big onion, chopped	
4 green chillies, chopped	
2 big tomatoes, chopped	
1 - 1/2 inch ginger, crushed	(3) Pour dal mixture. Add salt to taste. Give a boil. Before removing from the gas, add fresh cream and butter.
1/2 teaspoon turmeric powder	
2 teaspoons red chilli powder	
Little red colour	(4) Serve hot. Sprinkle chopped coriander leaves on top before serving.
Salt to taste	
2 tablespoons fresh cream (from top of milk)	
2 tablespoons butter	
Few coriander leaves to garnish	

VEGETARIAN EGG CURRY (6 - 8 SERVINGS)

Floating halves of vegetarian eggs in tomato gravy.

INGREDIENTS

FOR THE EGG YOLK

1/4 cup moong dal (split green grams without skin)

1 pinch turmeric powder

Few drops lemon juice

Little salt

FOR THE EGG WHITE

Paneer out of 1 litre milk (see Pg. 16)

1 tablespoon corn flour

1/4 teaspoon salt

Ghee to fry eggs

FOR THE GRAVY

2 tablespoons oil

1 big onion, chopped

1/2 kg. tomatoes, make puree

1 tablespoon chilli-ginger paste

Salt to taste

1/2 teaspoon turmeric powder

2 tablespoons ghati masala (see Pg. 288)

1 cup green peas, boiled

1/2 cup curds, beaten

Few coriander leaves, to garnish

METHOD

(1) Wash moong dal and soak in a cup of water for one hour. Boil dal with salt and turmeric powder. Cook till soft and dry. Remove from gas and cool. Mix lemon juice and make small balls and keep aside.

(2) Make paneer out of one litre milk. Add corn flour and salt. Knead till very soft. Divide into same number of balls as dal balls. Make a cup shape of each portion and put dal yolk in the centre. Cover paneer and make smooth oval shape. Heat ghee and fry these mock eggs till light brown.

(3) Heat oil and fry the onion light brown. Pour tomato juice and all masalas and green peas. Boil and put in the beaten curds.

(4) Cut vegetarian eggs into halves and put them in gravy while serving. Garnish with coriander leaves.

METHI—BANANA SABJI (6 SERVINGS)

A unique combination of sweet bananas and bitter fenugreek leaves in a dry vegetable dish.

INGREDIENTS

6 bananas (Rajali banana)

1 dozen tiny bunches fenugreek leaves (methi) (1 cup)

3 teaspoons sugar

2 tablespoons oil

Oil and asafoetida for seasoning

Salt and turmeric to taste

Coriander leaves to garnish

METHOD

(1) Clean and wash fenugreek leaves and chop them fine.

(2) Make thin slices of banana and mildly heat them on tava (griddle) with little oil around them.

(3) Heat oil. Add asafoetida. After a minute add banana slices. Spread the chopped fenugreek leaves and spices over it. Within five minutes, fenugreek will stick to bananas. Turn banana pieces and cook for few more minutes.

(4) Garnish with coriander leaves before serving.

Note:

(a) Any other variety of banana can be used, provided they are not fully ripe.

(b) A little sugar masks the bitter taste of fenugreek, without affecting its health-promoting virtues.

KADHI (6 - 8 SERVINGS)

A sweet and sour curry with curd as a main ingredient.

INGREDIENTS

FOR THE KADHI

2 cups curd (plain or sour)

6 tablespoons (split gram flour) channa flour

1 tablespoon chilli-ginger paste

1 - 1/2 tablespoons salt

2 tablespoons sugar

1/4 teaspoon asafoetida

3 cups water

Few coriander leaves

2 tablespoons coconut grated

TO TEMPER

1 tablespoon ghee

1 teaspoon cummin seeds

1 teaspoon mustard seeds

1/2 teaspoon fenugreek seeds

Few curry leaves

1 - 2 sticks cinnamon

3 - 4 cloves

FOR THE PAKODAS

1/2 cup wheat flour

1/2 cup split gram flour

1/4 teaspoon soda bicarb

A pinch asafoetida

Salt to taste

1 tablespoon hot oil

Oil for deep frying

METHOD

(1) Combine together all the kadhi ingredients and beat well with an egg-beater. Add three cups of water and beat.

(2) Prepare tempering by heating together all the ingredients in a small vessel except curry leaves. When mustard seeds stop spluttering, remove from gas, hold vessel over kadhi and add curry leaves. After half a minute pour tempering into the kadhi.

(3) Now put the kadhi vessel on the gas and let it boil. Stir often to avoid formation of lumps.

(4) Serve hot with coriander leaves and fresh coconut sprinkled over it.

Variations:

(1) 1/2 cup pieces of lady fingers or radish can be added to kadhi while boiling.

(2) At the time of serving, pakodas too can be added to kadhi.

FOR THE PAKODAS

(1) Mix all ingredients together and make a soft consistency batter with water. Mix well and beat mixture for two minutes.

(2) Heat oil and fry small pakodas till golden brown.

(3) Add pakodas to kadhi only at the time of serving.

PANEER CORN KORMA (6 - 8 SERVINGS)

Excellent paneer curry with creamy corn gravy.

INGREDIENTS

FOR THE CURRY

200 grams paneer, cubed

3 tablespoons oil

2 large onions, thinly sliced

3 - 4 whole cardamoms

2 tomatoes, chopped

1 cup curd

1 teaspoon red chilli powder

1/4 teaspoon turmeric powder

Salt to taste

1 can cream style sweet corn (400 grams)

2 tablespoons coriander leaves, chopped

FOR THE ROASTING (LIGHTLY) & GRINDING

1/4 cup fresh coconut, grated

2 teaspoons poppy seeds

6 - 8 cashewnuts

5 green chillies

METHOD

(1) Heat oil and saute small pieces of paneer cubes till light brown. Keep them aside.

(2) Saute thinly sliced onion to golden brown. Drain oil and cool. Crush them.

(3) Now in the remaining oil, add slightly opened cardamoms, quickly followed by ground masala paste, crushed onions, chopped tomatoes, beaten curd, red chilli powder, turmeric and salt. Stir often till oil separates.

(4) Now add paneer cubes, corns from the can and a glass full of water. Mix and simmer for 10 minutes. Sprinkle chopped coriander at the time of serving.

KHATA CURRY (10 - 12 SERVINGS)

A mixed vegetable curry without the use of oil.

INGREDIENTS

6 corn cobs, cut into 2 inch pieces

400 grams suran (yam), peel, cut big pieces

500 grams potatoes, peel, cut big pieces

12 - 15 long pieces patara stems (stems of colocassia leaves)

250 grams lady fingers, cut long pieces (optional)

3 Rajali bananas, cut 4 pieces of each banana with skin

250 grams cucumber, peel, cut long pieces

2 tablespoons gram flour

1 - 1/2 cups thin coconut milk

1 cup thick coconut milk

2 tablespoons jaggery

3 tablespoons tamarind extract

1 tablespoon chilli-ginger paste

1 tablespoon red chilli powder

1/2 teaspoon turmeric powder

Salt to taste

METHOD

(1) Pressure cook suran and corn pieces in salt and turmeric water for two whistles only. Remove in a big vessel and put on the gas for further cooking.

(2) Add potato pieces and patara stems. Add water as required and boil further. When they are half cooked, add lady fingers, bananas and cucumber pieces. Now cook everything well.

(3) Blend gram flour in thin coconut milk. Add it to the curry. Mix all masalas, jaggery and tamarind. Boil further. Finally add thick coconut milk. Mix well and remove from gas.

CARROT CHAMPA FLOWER

(1)   Cut out about 2 inches piece from a fresh carrot. Trim it to a cone shape with smooth round top.

(2)   Starting from the narrow end, cut out first set of three round petals attached on the narrow end. Trim each one to a pointed shape.

(3)   Cut out three inner petals, alternating the first three by inserting knife at right angle from top to the depth of only 1/2 inch. Trim each one to a pointed shape by removing sides.

(4)   Now a small triangular portion will remain in the centre. Carefully cut out the centre, leaving a small hollow.

(5)   Insert a stick in the narrow end to make a stem. Cover the stick by passing it through a tubelike spring onion leaf.

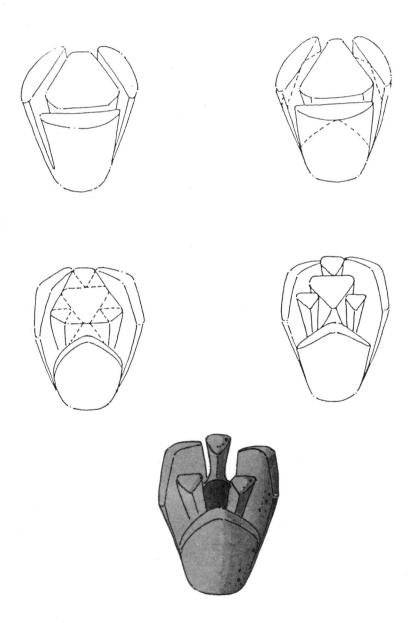

INDIAN BREADS — PURIS AND PARATHAS

RAW BANANA PARATHAS (MAKES 10 PARATHAS)

Excellent paratha recipe for strict vegetarians.

INGREDIENTS

FOR THE STUFFING

3 raw banana - three sided, thick skin variety

1 tablespoon chilli-ginger paste

Juice of 1 lemon

2 teaspoon sugar

Salt to taste

2 tablespoons coriander leaves

2 tablespoons fresh coconut, grated

FOR THE COVERING

1-1/2 cups wheat flour

1/2 cup semolina, fine variety

3 tablespoons oil

Salt to taste

METHOD

(1) Pressure cook bananas with skin. Remove skin and mash them well. Add all the ingredients given for stuffing. Divide into 10 balls.

(2) Make dough out of wheat flour, semolina, oil and salt with water. Cover and keep for at least 15 minutes. Take little more oil and knead the dough well. Divide into 10 balls.

(3) Roll out each ball to about four inches in diametre. Put a tablespoons of the stuffing in the centre and cover it. Roll out again to six inches diametre paratha.

(4) Shallow fry these parathas in oil or ghee. Repeat the process with the remaining dough and stuffing.

PUNJABI ROTIS (MAKES 12 ROTIS)

Thick rotis, soft like bread with spicy layer in between.

INGREDIENTS

1 cup flour

1 cup wheat flour

1/2 cup curd

1 teaspoon salt

1 teaspoon sugar

1 tablespoon yeast

1 tablespoon ghee

Ghee for shallow frying

FOR THE GRINDING MASALA PASTE

2 tablespoons aniseeds, powdered

2 tablespoons chaat masala (see Pg. 286)

1 teaspoon chilli-ginger paste

METHOD

(1) Sift flour and wheat flour together.

(2) Add curd, salt, sugar and yeast. Make a soft dough with water. Knead well with ghee and keep in an oiled vessel, covered with wet cloth for 1-1/2 hours.

(3) Mix all spices together and make fine paste with water.

(4) Now knead the dough again and make small balls. Roll out each ball into a round of about four inches diameter. Apply prepared paste over each and fold them. Again roll out and shallow fry them on medium gas with ghee.

DAL PARATHAS (MAKES 10 PARATHAS)

Mildly flavoured soft parathas.

INGREDIENTS

1/2 cup channa dal (spilt Bengal gram)

1/2 cup tur dal (split red gram)

Salt to taste

2 teaspoons red chilli powder

1 teaspoon cummin powder

1-1/2 cup wheat flour

2 tablespoons ghee

Salt to taste

METHOD

(1) Cook both dals in cooker with little water. Mash them. Add salt, red chilli powder and cummin powder.

(2) Make paratha dough with wheat flour, salt and ghee. Make parathas, stuffing the dal mixture (just like raw banana paratha). Shallow fry in ghee.

Note:

If dal mixture is loose, heat on gas till dry.

PAPAYA PARATHAS (MAKES 10 PARATHAS)

Very spicy parathas.

INGREDIENTS

FOR THE STUFFING

1 small raw papaya, grated (1 cup)

2 teaspoons pomegranate seeds, ground

Salt to taste

2 teaspoon red chilli powder

1/2 teaspoon garam masala (see Pg. 287)

1 teaspoon chilli-ginger paste

1/2 cup coriander leaves, chopped

FOR THE DOUGH

1-1/2 cups wheat flour

1/2 cup gram flour

2 tablespoons oil

Salt to taste

1/2 teaspoon turmeric powder

Oil for shallow frying

METHOD

(1) For stuffing — mix all the given ingredients together and divide into 10 portions.

(2) Make dough out of wheat flour, gram flour, salt, turmeric powder and oil. Knead with water and little oil and divide into 20 balls. Roll each ball to six inches diametre. Evenly spread one portion of stuffing on one rolled out ball. Cover with another. Seal edges and shallow fry in oil. Repeat with remaining dough and stuffing.

Note:

One can make parathas out of grated carrot in the same way.

MUGHLAI PARATHAS (MAKES 15 PARATHAS)

Plain and crisp parathas, good to eat with spicy curries.

INGREDIENTS

1/4 cup semolina

1-1/2 cups wheat flour

1-1/2 cups flour

3/4 cup oil

1/2 cup milk

Salt to taste

Oil for shallow frying

METHOD

(1) Combine semolina, wheat flour and flour. Mix oil and salt properly in flour mixture. Make dough (like puri) with water. Knead well (slightly tight). Cover and keep for atleast half an hour.

(2) Make 15 balls. Roll out a ball, apply oil on its surface. Pleat it and make a circular roll. Press and roll out again. Pat paratha with hands before placing on tawa (griddle).

(3) Heat tawa and shallow fry paratha in oil. Pat again the ready hot paratha before serving. Make all parathas the same way.

CAULIFLOWER AND PANEER PARATHAS (MAKES 12 PARATHAS)

These square stuffed parathas when served hot, are excellent to eat with curd !

INGREDIENTS

FOR THE STUFFING

1 cup paneer, crumbled

1 cup cauliflower, finely chopped

1 tablespoon butter

1/2 teaspoon cummin seeds

1 tablespoon green chillies, chopped

1/4 cup onions, chopped

1/2 teaspoon turmeric powder

2 teaspoons chaat masala (see Pg. 286)

Salt to taste

FOR THE PARATHA DOUGH

2 cups flour

1/4 cup ghee

Salt to taste

Ghee for shallow frying

METHOD

(1) Melt butter and add cummin, chillies and onions. Saute for a few minutes till soft. Add turmeric and chaat masala. Saute for half a minute. Then add paneer crumbs, cauliflower pieces and salt to taste. Mix everything very well. Cover and cook on slow heat till cauliflower is soft. Divide into 12 portions.

(2) Make dough out of flour, ghee and salt. Knead well. Divide into 12 balls. Roll each ball into six inches diametre rounds. Spread stuffing in the centre, in square shape. Wet the edges, fold, stick and roll lightly again to make square parathas. Shallow fry in ghee. Serve hot.

BHAAT NA THEPLA (12 THEPLAS)

A good way of using leftover rice.

INGREDIENTS

1/2 cup gram flour

1/2 cup wheat flour

1/2 cup rice flour

1/4 cup onions, grated

3/4 cup cooked rice, slightly mashed

2 tablespoons coriander leaves

1 tablespoon chilli-ginger paste

1/4 teaspoon turmeric powder

Salt to taste

A pinch asafoetida

1 tablespoon sugar

1/2 cup curd

3 tablespoons oil

1/2 tablespoon red chilli powder

Oil for shallow frying

METHOD

(1) Mix all the given ingredients well. Add just enough water to make dough. Divide into 12 balls.

(2) Roll thepla to six inches diametre rounds and shallow fry in oil. Serve hot or cold.

1. Vangi bhat   p. 120
2. Spiced rice   p. 115
3. Potato kofta biryani   3a. Potato kofta   p. 118
4. Garlic buttermilk   p. 95
5. Radish puris   p. 108
6. Punjabi rotis   p. 103
7. Cauliflower and paneer paratha   p. 105
8. Chhunda   p. 285
9. Hot mango pickle   p. 284

MILK PURIS (15 PURIS)

Very unusual way of preparing dough with milk, which makes the puris soft and juicy.

INGREDIENTS	METHOD
1 cup milk	(1) Boil milk. Add flour and salt to it.
1-1/2 cups flour	(2) Stir vigourously with a rolling pin and mix well.
1/2 teaspoon salt	(3) Stir till the flour is cooked and dry. Remove from the gas and cool. Divide dough into 15 portions and make balls. Roll each ball with little dry flour into three inches diametre and deep fry in ghee till light pink in colour.

ALU PURIS (15-20 PURIS)

Excellent with any spicy vegetable.

INGREDIENTS	METHOD
1-1/2 cups wheat flour	Make dough by mixing all the given ingredients. Use water, if necessary. Divide into 20 balls. Roll them with little dry flour into three inches diametre and deep fry in ghee.
1-1/2 cups flour	
2 tablespoons oil	
2 potatoes, boiled, mashed	
3 cloves garlic, finely mashed	
1/2 bunch coriander leaves	
1/2 cup curd	
Salt to taste	
Ghee for deep frying	

RADISH PURIS (15-20 PURIS)

A typical taste of radish makes it very appetizing.

INGREDIENTS	METHOD
1 cup rice flour	Mix everything together and make a dough. Make thick puris with little dry flour (just like alu puris) and deep fry in oil. Serve hot.
1 cup wheat flour	
1/2 cup curd	
1 onion, grated	
1 white radish, grated (1/3 cup)	
1 tablespoon green chilli-ginger paste	
Salt to taste	
1/2 teaspoon turmeric powder	
2 tablespoons oil	
Oil for deep frying	

URAD DAL PURIS (10 PURIS)

They can be served with meal or as a snack, with sweet and sour date chutney.

INGREDIENTS

1 cup urad dal

3/4 cup flour

3/4 cup wheat flour

2 tablespoons ghee

2 tablespoons oil

1/3 teaspoon asafoetida

1 teaspoon red chilli powder

Juice of 1 lemon

1 teaspoon chilli-ginger paste

Little salt for the dough

Salt to taste

METHOD

(1) Soak urad dal for six hours. Grind to a paste.
(2) Make dough like puris (slightly tight) with flour, wheat flour, ghee and salt. Divide into 10 balls. Put oil in a vessel to heat. Add dal and fry on medium gas till cooked. Remove from the gas and cool. Add all the spices and mix well. Divide into 10 balls. Put oil in a vessel to heat. Add dal and fry on medium gas till cooked. Remove from the gas and cool. Add all the spices and mix well. Divide into 10 balls.
(3) Make puris by stuffing urad dal mixture in the dough balls, roll out and deep fry in oil over medium gas till light pink and crisp.

CREAMY BESAN PARATHAS

Soft and delicious parathas can be served with any vegetable curry.

INGREDIENTS

FOR THE DOUGH

2 cups wheat flour

1 cup flour

1/4 cup ghee, melted

1/2 teaspoon salt

FOR THE STUFFING

1 cup mint leaves, chopped

1 cup coriander leaves, chopped

6 green chillies

2 tablespoons oil

1 teaspoon cummin seeds

1/4 cup onions, chopped

1/4 teaspoon turmeric powder

1 cup gram flour

1 cup curd

1 cup water

Salt to taste

Ghee for shallow frying

METHOD

(1) Make a soft paratha dough with given ingredients.
(2) Make fine paste out of mint, coriander and green chillies.
(3) Heat oil, add cummin seeds. When brown, add onion and saute them till light brown. Add paste and turmeric.
(4) Mix together gram flour, curd and water evenly. Pour over onion. Add salt to taste. Stir continuously to avoid formation of lumps. Cook the mixture till it leaves the sides of the vessel and is fairly thick. Allow to cool. Make 15 balls.
(5) Roll out each dough ball. Stuff in the creamy besan ball. Cover and roll again into thick paratha. Take little flour for easy rolling. Repeat the process.
(6) Shallow fry in little ghee.

TOASTER NAAN (MAKES 12 PIECES)

A naan made easily at home in a toaster.

INGREDIENTS

1 teaspoon sugar

1/2 teaspoon salt

1 teaspoon yeast

2 cups flour

3 tablespoons curd

2 tablespoons ghee

2 tablespoons butter

METHOD

(1)   Melt sugar and salt in half a cup of lukewarm water.

(2)   Mix yeast in the flour. Then mix in curd and make a soft dough with prepared water. Knead well with ghee. Keep this dough in an oiled vessel, covered with a wet cloth. Leave aside till double in size.

(3)   Reknead dough and make 12 balls.

(4)   Roll out each ball on a floured board to fit into a toaster (like a bread slice).

(5)   First, roast these rolled out naans lightly on griddle (tawa). Then at the time of serving insert each into the toaster and toast. Two layers will separate. Remove and serve hot with a little butter on top.

DOODHI-BAJARI NA THEPLA (12 THEPLAS)

Soft and spicy millet flour rotis.

INGREDIENTS

1 cup millet (bajari) flour

1 cup wheat flour

1 cup white pumpkin with skin, grated

Curd as required

1/4 teaspoon turmeric

Salt to taste

1/2 lemon sized jaggery

1 teaspoon cummin seeds

1 tablespoon chilli ginger paste

1 tablespoon sesame

1 tablespoon red chilli powder

A big pinch asafoetida

2 tablespoons oil

Oil for shallow frying

METHOD

Mix all the given ingredients well except curd. Add curd as required to make the dough. Divide into 12 balls. Roll each into six inches diametre rounds and shallow fry in oil. Serve hot or cold.

INDIAN PULLAOS

SPINACH PULLAO WITH PANEER (10 -12 SERVINGS)

Taste of spinach blends very well with rice making the dish nutritious and tasty.

INGREDIENTS

FOR THE PANEER

1/2 litre milk

1/2 lemon or 1/4 teaspoon citric acid

1 teaspoon flour

2 tablespoons coriander leaves, chopped

1 green chilli, finely chopped

1/2 teaspoon salt

Ghee to fry

FOR THE PULLAO

2 cups rice

1 tablespoon cummin seeds

1 tablespoon ghee

Salt to taste

1 big onion, chopped

1 big bunch spinach (ground to a paste)

4 green chillies, chopped

1 inch ginger piece, chopped

Few cashewnuts, fried

METHOD

(1) To prepare paneer, boil milk. Add lemon juice drop by drop or citric acid pinch by pinch till the milk separates and the colour of its water become greenish. Remove from heat and cool. Then tie in a thin cloth till water drains out completely. Now mix flour, coriander leaves, salt and chillies. Mix well. Make a flat ball and wrap in the cloth. Put weight on it and leave aside for half an hour. Open the cloth and cut small pieces. Heat ghee and fry these pieces till golden brown.

(2) Wash rice and soak in water for half an hour. Heat ghee in a flat vessel. Add cummin seeds and onions. Fry onions till brown. Add spinach paste, chopped green chillies, ginger and salt. Stir for some time. Then add the required water to cook the rice. When water begins to boil, add rice and cook. When almost cooked add paneer pieces. Cover and keep till the water is absorbed. Serve hot. Garnish with fried cashewnuts.

BABY ONIONS PULLAO (10 — 12 SERVINGS)

A simple pullao which can be served with any spicy curry.

INGREDIENTS

2 cups long grained rice

3 tablespoons ghee

1 heaped teaspoon onion, chopped

3-4 dry red chillies

4 cloves

2 sticks cinnamon

Salt to taste

20 small onions or baby onions

METHOD

(1) Soak rice in cold water for 10 minutes. Drain off water.

(2) Heat ghee and saute the cummin seeds, chopped onions and red chillies for a few minutes. Add the cloves, cinnamon and rice. Saute a little longer. Add enough hot water to cook rice. Add salt to taste. Cook rice till partially done.

(3) Parboil the peeled baby onions for 10 minutes, drain and add to the rice. Cover the pan and simmer gently till done. Serve hot.

Note :

For extra flavour, add equal quantity of coconut milk instead of water to cook rice.

GREEN PEAS PULLAO (10 - 12 SERVINGS)

A simple pullao with green peas which can blend well with any spicy curry.

INGREDIENTS

2 cups rice

1 cup peas

1/4 cup oil or ghee

1 teaspoon cummin seeds

3-4 cinnamon

3-4 cloves

3-4 cardamoms

1/4 cup cashewnut pieces

1 big onion, boiled and ground

1 inch piece ginger, ground

8 cloves garlic, ground

1 teaspoon white pepper powder

1/2 teaspoon aji-no-moto

Salt to taste

METHOD

(1) Wash rice and soak in water for half an hour.

(2) Heat oil or ghee. Add cummin, cinnamon, cloves cardamoms and cashewnut pieces. Saute for a minute. Add onion paste, ginger paste, garlic paste, aji-no-moto and white pepper powder. Saute for two minutes.

(3) Add green peas and rice, saute for another two minutes. Pour about three cups of hot water and salt to taste. Cover and cook till rice and peas are done.

VITAMIN KHICHADI (10 - 12 SERVINGS)

Pullao with spicy pulses.

INGREDIENTS

2 cups rice

1/4 cup oil

6 cardamoms

1-2 pieces cinnamon

2-3 bay leaves

1 big onion, sliced

1/4 cup masoor (lentil)

1/4 cup urad (black gram)

1/4 cup small variety gram

A big pinch soda bicarb

Salt to taste

FOR THE GRINDING MASALA

2 medium onions

1 cup coconut, grated

1 big tomato

2 green chillies

1 teaspoon aniseeds

1 teaspoon poppy seeds

1/2 inch ginger piece

1-2 pieces cinnamon

1-2 cardamoms

METHOD

(1) Heat half of the oil. Saute for a minute the cardamoms, cinnamon and bay leaves. Add sliced onion and saute till light brown. Add the washed rice and saute for a few more minutes. Add sufficient hot water and salt to taste. Cook till done.

(2) Soak masoor, black grams and grams overnight. Pressure cook with half teaspoon salt and a big pinch of soda bicarb.

(3) Heat remaining oil and saute the ground paste till you get a good aroma and oil separates. Add one cup of water and salt to taste. Give a boil. Add cooked pulses and simmer for 10 minutes. Keep the gravy thick.

(4) Roughly mix in cooked rice and spicy pulses together to make vitamin khichadi.

VEGETABLE LAYERED KHICHADI (10 - 12 SERVINGS)

An ideal combination of dal, rice and vegetables, in one dish. The aroma of all three, blends extremely well. It tastes good with 'kadhi' or garlic buttermilk.

INGREDIENTS

2 cups rice

1-1/2 cups tur dal (split red gram)

1/2 cup moong dal (split green gram without skin

6 medium sized potatoes

10 very small onions

6 small brinjals or 10 padvals

1/4 cup ghee

4-5 cloves

1-2 pieces cinnamon

3-4 cardamoms

1/4 teaspoon turmeric powder

Salt to taste

1 cup coriander leaves, chopped

1/2 cup fresh coconut, grated

1 tablespoon sugar

1/4 teaspoon asafoetida

1/2 teaspoon red chilli powder

1 tablespoon chilli ginger paste

METHOD

(1) Wash rice and dals separately

(2) Take a big and thick vessel. Heat ghee and put in cloves, cinnamon and cardamoms. After a minute, add dal, a big pinch of turmeric powder and salt sufficient for dals. Mix well and add two cups of hot water. Cover and allow to simmer till dals are semicooked.

(3) Combine coriander leaves, coconut, salt, sugar, asafoetida, turmeric, red chilli powder and chilli-ginger paste in a big plate. mix well.

(4) Prepare vegetables. Peel and cut potatoes into four. Peel onions. If big, cut into two pieces. In case of brinjals, put two slits to stuff in spices and in case of padvals, peel and put a slit to stuff in spices.

(5) Stuff the prepared spices in either brinjals or padvals. Mix remaining spices with potato and onion pieces.

(6) Arrange all the vegetables with spices over semi-cooked dal. Add warm water as required to cook vegetables. Cover and cook further.

(7) When vegetables are semi cooked, evenly spread the rice over them. Add salt to taste and enough warm water to cook the rice. Cover and cook till done and all the water has evaporated. This way the vegetable khichadi roughly makes three layers.

BROWN RICE (10 - 12 SERVINGS)

A simple but delicious pullao, to be served with spicy dals or curries.

INGREDIENTS

2 cups rice

4 tablespoons ghee

4 onions, chopped

1 tablespoon brown sugar

5 cardamoms

5 cloves

5 peppercorns

2 cinnamon sticks

Salt to taste

1/4 cup cashewnuts, fried

METHOD

(1) Heat ghee in a large pan. Add onions and saute till brown. Add brown sugar and all the spices and stir for few minutes. Pour in sufficient hot water to cook the rice. Stir and bring to a boil, twice. Put in the rice and salt.

(2) Stir well, cover the pan and allow to boil. Lower heat and simmer till water has absorbed. If rice is not done, add a little more hot water. Serve hot garnished with fried cashewnuts.

SPICED RICE (10 - 12 SERVINGS)

Easy to make spicy pullao.

INGREDIENTS

2 cups rice

1/2 cup oil

2 tablespoons coriander seeds

1/2 teaspoon cummin seeds

8 black peppercorns

1/2 teaspoon fenugreek seeds

8 red Kashmiri chillies

1/4 cup tamarind

1/4 cup jaggery

1/2 cup coconut, grated

1/2 teaspoon mustard seeds

1/4 cup peanuts

A few curry leaves

METHOD

(1) In a teaspoonful of oil fry the coriander seeds, cummin seeds, peppercorns, fenugreek seeds and chillies until brown. Pound to a fine powder.

(2) Cook rice till each grain is separate. Allow to cool. Dissolve the tamarind and jaggery in one cup of water. Place the above mixture on the fire. When thick, remove from the gas. Extract liquid. Mix with pounded spices, cooled rice and grated coconut. Mix everything well.

(3) In a separate pan, heat the remaining oil. Add mustard seeds. When they stop spluttering, add peanuts and curry leaves. Cook for few minutes, add the spiced rice and keep on a low fire for 15 minutes. Serve hot.

VEGETABLE PULLAO (10 - 12 SERVINGS)

An ideal pullao for picnics. Tastes good, hot as well as cold.

INGREDIENTS

FOR THE GRINDING MASALA

1 teaspoon cummin seeds

4-5 cloves garlic, flaked

2 tablespoons coriander seeds

2 inch dry coconut piece

2 inch ginger piece

2-3 green chillies

4-5 red chillies

FOR THE PULLAO

3/4 cup ghee

3-4 medium sized onions, chopped

2 cups rice

Salt to taste

1/2 coconut, extract milk (2 cups)

4 tomatoes, cut into small pieces

1/2 cup carrots, diced, boiled

1 cup green peas, boiled

1 capsicum, chopped into small pieces

Little saffron

3 tablespoons curd

METHOD

Heat ghee in a vessel and saute the onions. Add the ground paste and rice. Saute. Add salt to taste. When it gives out a good aroma, pour in coconut milk and the required amount of water to cook rice. When it begins to boil, add tomato pieces. Cover and cook on high flame. When the rice is almost cooked and very little water is left, mix carrots, peas, capsicum and saffron mixed in curd. Reduce temperature, cover, put little water on the lid and cook till rice is cooked and water has been absorbed.

BROKEN WHEAT PULLAO (10 SERVINGS)

An unusual and nutritious pullao with broken wheat and mixed vegetables.

INGREDIENTS

2 cups broken wheat

1-1/2 cups sour curd

1-1/2 cup water

3/4 cup carrots, grated

1/2 cup coconut, grated

1/2 cup onion, chopped

1 teaspoon chilli-ginger paste

Salt to taste

METHOD

(1) Roast the broken wheat lightly for five to six minutes. Remove from heat.
(2) Add beaten curd and water. Mix well and cover vessel. Keep aside for at least half an hour.
(3) Now mix in vegetables, chilli-ginger paste and salt.
(4) Pressure cook till done. Serve hot with curd or kadhi (see Pg. 99).

GREEN AND WHITE RING PULLAO (10 - 12 SERVINGS)

A very decorative and tasty pullao.

INGREDIENTS

FOR THE WHITE PULLAO

FOR THE GRINDING MASALA

1/2 cup coconut, grated

1 small onion

5-6 cloves garlic, flaked

2-3 green chillies

1/2 inch ginger piece

1 tablespoon poppy seeds

1 teaspoon cummin seeds

1 cup rice

2 tablespoon curd

Salt to taste

1/2 cup corns, boiled

2 tablespoons ghee

FOR THE GREEN PULLAO

FOR THE GRINDING MASALA

1/2 cup coriander leaves

1/2 cup spinach leaves

2-3 green chillies

1/2 inch ginger piece

5-6 cloves garlic, flaked

1 cup rice

2 tablespoons curd

Salt to taste

2 tablespoons ghee

1/2 cup green peas, boiled

METHOD

FOR THE WHITE PULLAO

(1)   Heat ghee and saute the ground masala paste. Add the washed rice and saute for a few more minutes. Add about two cups of hot water and salt to taste. Cook till done. Mix in curd and corn just before removing from the gas.

FOR THE GREEN PULLAO

(1)   Heat ghee and saute the ground masala paste. Add washed rice and saute for a few more minutes. Add about two cups of hot water and salt to taste. Cook till done. Add boiled green peas and curd. Mix and remove from the gas.

TO SET THE PULLAO

Take a ring mould and grease it with oil. First layer the mould with white pullao and level it. Over it make a layer of green pullao. Cover with a foil and bake at 200°C for 20 minutes. Unmould hot pullao on a serving plate.

POTATO AND GREEN PEA BIRYANI (10 - 12 SERVINGS)

Very delicious Mughlai pullao.

INGREDIENTS

2 cups rice

2 onions, sliced

3/4 cup ghee

6-8 cardamoms

6-8 cloves

A few sticks cinnamon

A few bay leaves

8-10 black peppercorns

6 cloves garlic, chopped

2 green chillies, chopped

1/2 inch ginger, crushed

Salt to taste

3 big potatoes, peel and cut big pieces

1/2 cup green peas

1 big tomato, cut into pieces

3 tablespoons fresh coconut

Little yellow colour or saffron

1/2 cup milk

1/2 cup onions, sliced, golden fried

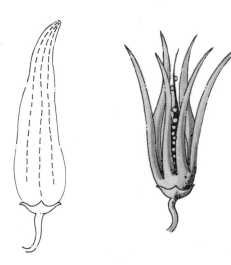

METHOD

(1)   Fry the sliced onions in a little ghee till golden brown. Add half of the cardamoms, cloves, cinnamon, bay leaves and black pepper. Also add garlic, green chillies and ginger. Fry for a minutes. Then add one and a half cups of water, and salt to taste. Give one boil. Now mix in potato pieces, green peas and tomatoes. Cover and cook till done and little gravy remains. Mix in grated coconut.

(2)   Heat about two tablespoons ghee. Add the remaining cardamoms, cloves, cinnamon, pepper and bay leaves. Add about three cups of water. Add rice which has been washed and soaked for half an hour. Add salt to taste. Boil for about 12 minutes till rice is almost done. Drain in a colander, reserving the water.

(3)   Now take a thick vessel. Spread half of the rice. Cover with potatoes and green peas with gravy. Spread remaining rice over it. Sprinkle about quarter cup of rice water.

(4)   Mix yellow colour or saffron in milk and evenly pour over rice.

(5)   Cover vessel with a wet cloth and also with a lid. Put on slow gas for 10 to 15 minutes.

(6)   Heat remaining ghee and pour over biryani.

(7)   Garnish biryani with golden fried slices of onions (See Pg. 283) and green chilli flower tucked in the centre.

Note:

In case the rice sticks to the base, put 'tava' or an iron girdle on the gas, under the biryani vessel.

FOR THE GREEN CHILLI FLOWER

(1)   Select a fresh green, straight and little broad chilli.

(2)   Starting from the pointed end slit chilli with a sharp knife upto its stem end, leaving about quarter inch as a petal attachment. Cut only the skin without disturbing the seeds inside.

(3)   Depending on the size of the chilli, make four to five such cuts to make as many petals. Separate each petal carefully from the seed stalk in the centre.

(4)   Put chilli flower in ice cold water. It will open in about one to two hours.

POTATO KOFTA BIRYANI (10 - 12 SERVINGS)

A pullao to serve with flair.

INGREDIENTS

2 cups rice

FOR THE KOFTAS

4 medium sized potatoes

1 teaspoon red chilli powder

1/4 teaspoon turmeric powder

Salt to taste

1/2 teaspoon chilli-ginger paste

2 teaspoons lemon juice

2 tablespoons gram flour

Little coriander leaves, chopped

Ghee for deep frying

FOR THE GRAVY

1/2 cup ghee

2 onions, chopped

1 teaspoon chilli-ginger paste

4-5 sticks cinnamon

4-5 cloves

3-4 red chillies

1/4 teaspoon cardamom powder

1/4 kg. tomatoes, chopped

1/2 cup green peas, boiled

1/4 teaspoon garam masala (see Pg. 287)

Salt to taste

1/2 cup coriander leaves, chopped

1/2 cup coconut, grated

1/2 cup curd

1/4 cashewnuts, fried

METHOD

(1) Wash rice and soak in water for 15 minutes.

(2) Boil potatoes. Peel and mash them. Add red chilli powder, turmeric powder, salt to taste, little green chilli-ginger paste and lemon juice. Also mix in gram flour and coriander leaves. Mix everything well and make small balls. Heat ghee and fry these koftas till golden brown.

(3) Cook rice with salt. It should be well cooked, but firm.

(4) Heat ghee in a pan. Saute onions till brown. When almost brown, saute green chilli-ginger paste, cinnamon, cloves, red chillies and powdered cardamom. Then mix in tomatoes, green peas, salt and garam masala. When tomatoes become soft, add coriander leaves, coconut and curd. Also add the koftas and fried cashewnuts. Remove from heat.

(5) Take a vessel. Apply ghee all over. Spread half of the rice. Pour kofta curry over it. Cover and put on slow gas for 20-30 minutes and serve hot, **or**
Take a baking dish and arrange biryani the same way. Cover the dish with aluminium foil and bake at 200ºC for 20 minutes till thoroughly warmed.

VANGI BHAAT (10 - 12 SERVINGS)

A pleasantly spiced pullao with specially prepared black masala.

INGREDIENTS

2 cups rice

1/4 cup oil

1 teaspoon mustard seeds

1/4 teaspoon asafoetida

Few curry leaves

2 tablespoons cashewnuts

2 tablespoons peanuts

1/4 kg. long brinjals, cut into small pieces

Salt to taste

5 teaspoons black masala (see Pg. 289)

2 tablespoons coconut, grated

3 tablespoons fresh cream

METHOD

(1) Heat oil and add mustard seeds. When they splutter, add asafoetida and curry leaves. After a minute add cashewnuts and peanuts. Saute a little then add soaked rice. Saute for a few more minutes.

(2) Add brinjal pieces and salt. Pour warm water enough to cook rice. Cover and cook. When almost cooked, add black masala, fresh coconut and cream. Stir lightly and serve hot.

INDIAN SAVOURIES

GREEN PEAS DAHI VADAS (MAKES 30 PIECES)

If you want to impress your guests, make these soft and double coloured dahi vadas.

INGREDIENTS

1-1/4 cup urad dal (split black gram)

1/4 teaspoon soda bicarb

Salt to taste

3 tablespoons oil

2 cups green peas, pounded

4 medium sized potatoes, boiled, mashed

3 tablespoons coconut , grated

3 tablespoons coriander leaves, chopped

Juice of 1/2 lemon

1/2 teaspoon garam masala (see Pg. 287)

1 tablespoon chilli ginger paste

3 cups curd, beaten

Red chilli powder to sprinkle

Few coriander leaves to garnish

100 grams fine potato straws

METHOD

(1) Soak urad dal overnight. Next day grind to a fine paste. mix in asafoetida, pinch of soda bicarb and little salt. Keep aside.

(2) Heat oil in a pan. When hot, add the pounded peas. Put a pinch of soda bicarb. Fry and stir often till peas are cooked. Remove from heat and cool. Add the mashed potatoes, grated coconut, chopped coriander leaves, lemon juice, salt, garam masala and chilli ginger paste. Mix everything well and make lemon sized balls.

(3) Now take each ball, dip in the urad dal batter and deep fry in oil till light brown in colour.

(4) Put these vadas in thin buttermilk for three minutes. Remove, squeeze and arrange on a serving plate. Pour beaten curd on them. Sprinkle salt, red chilli powder, coriander leaves and fine potato straws.

CORN BOMBS (MAKES 10 BOMBS)

Golden corn croquettes are excellent for any party. One can also use green peas instead of corns.

INGREDIENTS

FOR THE COVERING

6 big potatoes

4 tablespoons gram flour

Salt to taste

1-1/2 tablespoons lemon juice

1 tablespoon chilli ginger paste

FOR THE CORN STUFFING

corns from 4 corn cobs, (1-1/4 cups)

1/4 cup coconut, grated

1/2 cup coriander leaves, chopped

Salt, sugar to taste

1-1/2 tablespoons lemon juice

1-1/2 teaspoons chilli ginger paste

FOR THE BOMB

3/4 cup crushed vermicelli

Oil for deep frying

METHOD

(1) Boil potatoes and mash well. To it add salt, juice of lemon, chilli ginger paste and gram flour. Mix well and divide into 10 equal sized balls.

(2) To the boiled corns, mix in the grated coconut, chopped coriander leaves, salt, sugar to taste, lemon juice, chilli ginger paste. Divided into 10 parts.

(3) Take little oil on your fingers and make flat puris out of potato balls. Put one part of corn mixture in each centre and bind the open edges together. Make an oval shape. Roll them in vermicelli and deep fry. They will have a golden colour. Remove on paper. Serve hot with chutney.

VEGETABLES STUFFED RING (10 SERVINGS)

This unique dish has an Indian taste but set in western style.

INGREDIENTS

2 carrots, grated

1/2 cup breadcrumbs

FOR THE POTATO COVERING

8 big potatoes, boiled, mashed

1/4 cup sagodana

1 tablespoon peanuts, pounded

Salt to taste

2 tablespoons lemon juice

1 tablespoon chilli ginger paste

FOR THE PEA STUFFING

1-1/2 cups green peas, pounded

2 tablespoons oil

A pinch asafoetida

A pinch soda bicarb

1 tablespoons lemon juice

2 teaspoons chilli ginger paste

Salt to taste

1-1/2 tablespoons coriander leaves, chopped

1-1/2 tablespoons fresh coconut, grated

1/4 teaspoon garam masala (see Pg. 287)

METHOD

(1) Spread grated carrot at the bottom of a greased ring mould of eight inches diameter. Sprinkle breadcrumbs all over.

(2) Take two-third part of the mashed potatoes. Soak sagodana in water for five to 10 minutes and drain them. Mix with the above potatoes. Add the ground peanuts, salt, 2 tablespoons lemon juice and chilli-ginger paste. Mix well. Now press a little of this mixture at the bottom and sides of the ring mould. Keep aside little of this mixture for covering.

(3) Take two tablespoons of oil and asafoetida in a pan and heat it. When hot, add the pounded peas. Add soda bicarb. Saute, stir often till cooked. Remove from gas and cool. Add one-third part of the mashed potatoes and all the seasoning. Mix well. Stuff this mixture in the ring mould.

(4) Bake in the oven at 200°c for 20 to 25 minutes. Remove and cool slightly. Unmound on a serving plate. Serve with chutney or tomato ketchup.

BREAD PAKODAS (MAKES 36 PIECES)

A quick recipe of pakodas, where bread pieces taste like paneer.

INGREDIENTS

1 cup gram flour

1 cup millet flour

1 cup curd

2 onions, chopped

1 teaspoon dried anardana (pomegranate seeds), ground

2 teaspoons chilli ginger paste

1/2 cup roasted peanuts, ground

2 tablespoons coriander leaves, chopped

Salt to taste

6 slices bread

Oil for deep frying

METHOD

(1) Combine together the two flours, three-fourth cup curd, chopped onions, pomegranate powder, chilli ginger paste, peanuts, coriander leaves and salt to taste. Add extra water to make a thick batter.

(2) Make buttermilk out of the remaining quarter cup of curds and one cup of water. Cut each slice of bread into six pieces. Soak them in buttermilk for a minute. Squeeze them and put in batter. Do six pieces at a time. Coat with batter and deep fry in oil till brown. Serve hot with ketchup.

BREAD CANAPES WITH PANEER, PEAS AND NUTS FILLING (MAKES 12 PIECES)

A sizzling snack with spicy filling for tea party.

INGREDIENTS

FOR THE CANAPES

12 slices, bread

12 pastry tins

Butter as required

FOR THE FILLING

1/2 cup cooking paneer, small pieces (see Pg. 16)

1/4 cup cashewnuts

Ghee to fry paneer pieces

2 tablespoons oil

2 medium sized onions

1 teaspoon cummin seeds, roasted, ground

1/4 teaspoon garam masala (see Pg. 287)

1 teaspoon chilli ginger paste

6 cloves garlic, mashed

1 tablespoon currants

Salt to taste

1/2 cup green peas

4 teaspoons curd

1/2 cup coriander leaves, chopped

1 teaspoon curry powder (see Pg. 287)

METHOD

FOR THE CANAPES

Lavishly grease the pastry tins with butter. Take bread slices and cut them to the size of the pastry tin. Wet slices on both sides and press in the tin. Apply little more butter on top. Heat the oven to 150ºC. Crisp these prepared tins in the oven. This will take about 25 minutes to crisp them light brown. Remove from the oven and cool.

FOR THE FILLING

(1)   Cut paneer into small pieces. Deep fry till golden brown in ghee. Fry cashewnuts till light brown. Keep aside.

(2)   Heat little oil in a pan and fry the chopped onions till brown. Add cummin, garam masala, chilli ginger paste, garlic and currants. Saute. Add paneer and cashewnuts. Add salt, peas, curd, coriander leaves and curry powder. Put on the fire and cook till dry.

(3)   Fill the canapes with this mixture just before serving and sprinkle each canape with chopped coriander leaves.

CORN HANDWA (MAKES 8 SLICES)

A decorative cake with a novel idea for a tea party.

INGREDIENTS

1/2 cup carrots

1/2 cup French beans

1 big capsicum

5 slices bread

1 cup milk

400 grams potatoes, boiled, mashed

Corns from 6 corn cobs, boiled in salt water (2 cups)

Salt, sugar to taste

METHOD

(1)   Cut carrots, French beans and capsicums into small pieces. Boil them in salt water and drain.

(2)   Soak bread slices in milk. When soft, make pulp.

(3)   Now mix together the mashed potatoes, bread pulp, half of the boiled corns and all the boiled vegetables. Add salt, sugar, chilli ginger paste and garam masala. Mix everything well. Divide into two parts.

1 tablespoon chilli ginger paste

1/4 teaspoon garam masala (see Pg. 287)

1 tablespoon oil

1/2 cup breadcrumbs

1/4 cup tomato ketchup

TO DECORATE

1/4 cup tomato ketchup

2 teaspoons corn flour

1 small carrot.

Few boiled corns

(4) Apply oil inside a vessel. Sprinkle breadcrumbs. Spread one part of the above mixture. Pour tomato ketchup over it. Again spread breadcrumbs and the remaining vegetable mixture. Level it and sprinkle breadcrumbs.

(5) Heat oven to moderate 200°C. temperature. Bake handwa till top crust become light brown. Remove handwa, cool for few minutes and then invert on a serving plate.

(6) To decorate, mix tomato ketchup and corn flour. Heat on gas, stir constantly till thick. Remove from gas and cool. Fill in an icing syringe with a star nozzle. Decorate handwa with slices of carrot, corns and tomato ketchup icing.

MOONG DAL ROLLS (ABOUT 24 ROLLS)

Two coloured rolls, sliced and mildly tempered with mustard and sesame seeds.

INGREDIENTS

FOR THE STUFFING

3 tablespoons oil

1 cup corns, grated

Salt and sugar to taste

1 - 1/2 teaspoons chilli ginger paste

1 cup milk

1/2 cup coconut, grated

1/2 cup coriander leaves, chopped

1 big potato, boiled, mashed

Juice of 1 lemon

FOR THE COVERING

2 cups moong dal (split green grams without skin)

1/2 cup carrots, French beans, chopped

1/4 teaspoon turmeric powder

Salt to taste

2 teaspoons chilli ginger paste

3/4 cup sour curd

1 cup water

TO TEMPER

2 tablespoons oil

1 teaspoon mustard seeds

1 tablespoon sesame seeds

METHOD

FOR THE STUFFING

(1) Heat oil and add the grated corns. Add salt, sugar and chilli ginger paste. Stir often. When it changes colour, add milk and mix well. Cook further till milk is absorbed and corns are cooked.

(2) Remove from gas, transfer out in a shallow plate and cool. Mix in coconut, coriander leaves and mashed potatoes. Divide into four portions. Roll out into long balls and keep ready.

FOR THE COVERING

(1) Soak moong dal for four to five hours. Make a fine paste and put in a thick vessel.

(2) Add all the spices and one cup of water. Mix everything very well.

(3) Put on the gas and stir continuously till the mixture is thick. Add carrots and French beans. Stir the mixture till it leaves the sides of the vessel. Remove immediately into a shallow plate. Divide into four parts. Spread out each part and put stuffing in the centre. Cover and make a roll. Smoothen out with oily fingers.

(4) Cool rolls and then cut them into half inch thick slices. Arrange in a serving plate.

(5) Temper with spluttered mustard seeds and sesame seeds in oil. Sprinkle evenly on all pieces.

Note:
To get crisp moong dal rolls, one can shallow fry slices with little oil.

CHAATS

A chaat is a combination of several items mixed with different chutneys, sometimes curd and sprinkled with crisp sev like vermicelli and specially prepared chaat masala. It makes a very interesting chatpata (sweet sour and hot) snack, excellent for a tea party.

SONTH PAPADI CHAAT (10 SERVINGS)

INGREDIENTS

FOR THE PAPADI

1/2 cup wheat flour
1/2 cup flour
1/4 teaspoon salt
2 tablespoons melted ghee

FOR THE SWEET AND SOUR CHUTNEY

1/2 kg. dates
150 grams tamarind
100 grams jaggery
1/2 teaspoon salt
1/2 teaspoon black pepper powder
1 teaspoon roasted cummin seeds, powdered
2 teaspoons red chilli powder

FOR THE CHAAT

1 - 1/2 cups curd, beaten with 1/2 teaspoon salt
2 medium sized potatoes, boiled, diced
1/2 cup Kabuli chana (chickpeas), boiled in salt water
10 - 12 teaspoons chaat masala (see Pg. 286)
Few coriander leaves, chopped

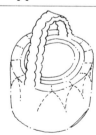

METHOD

FOR THE PAPADI

Combine all papadi ingredients together and make dough like puri (slightly tight). Divide into big balls and roll out thinly. Cut into very small diamond pieces and deep fry in oil till crisp and light brown in colour.

FOR THE SWEET AND SOUR CHUTNEY

(1)   Remove seeds from dates and tamarind. Wash them and put in a vessel. Add water enough to cover them.
(2)   Add jaggery and all other spices.
(3)   Pressure cook. Cool and strain to a thick paste. Adjust consistency with water and use as required.

Note:
Chutney can be preserved in fridge for a week.

TO ASSEMBLE PAPADI CHAAT

In each bowl put a few pieces of papadi, potaatoes pieces and channas. Pour over the beaten curd evenly. On top, add sweet and sour chutney. Sprinkle chaat masala and coriander leaves. For special occasions, you may serve beaten curd and 'sweet and sour chutney' in cucumber flower baskets.

FOR THE CUCUMBER FLOWER BASKET

(1)   Select a thick, about 8 inches long cucumber. Cut horizontally in the centre. This will make two flower baskets.
(2)   Put two parallel cuts, piercing right inside to make a handle. Cut from the sides to separate handles. Scoop out the pulp from underneath the handle and the seeds from the handle and seeds from the inside of the cucumber, making a hollow to fill in the chutney.
(3)   Separate skin with a sharp knife at right angles from all around the sides of the basket, keeping it attached at the base. Put vertical cuts of about half inch broad to make petals. Shape each petal.
(4)   Make inner two more circles of petals, alternating the first one. Put basket in ice cold water for an hour to open out.

CRISP PALAK CHAAT (FOR 8 SERVINGS)

INGREDIENTS

FOR THE PALAK BHAJIA

18 palak leaves (spinach)

1/2 cup flour

1/2 cup gram flour

A pinch of soda bicarb

1/2 teaspoon salt

FOR THE CHAAT

1 - 1/2 cup curd beaten with 1/4 teaspoon salt 3/4 cup sweet and sour chutney (see Pg. 129)

8 teaspoons chaat masala (see Pg. 286)

METHOD

FOR THE PALAK BHAJIA

(1) Trim thick veins of palak leaves and wash them.
(2) Prepare a thin batter of flour, gram flour, soda bicarb and salt.
(3) Dip each palak leaf in the batter and deep fry in oil till crisp.

TO ASSEMBLE CRISP PALAK CHAAT

Take three palak bhajias in each plate, pour curd and sweet and sour chutney evenly on top. Sprinkle chaat masala and coriander leaves.

PURI POTATO CHAAT (4 - 6 SERVINGS)

INGREDIENTS

FOR THE PURIS (Makes 24 pieces)

1/2 cup flour

1/2 cup wheat flour

1/2 teaspoon salt

2 tablespoons oil

Oil for deep frying

FOR THE GREEN CHUTNEY (Makes 1/4 cup)

3/4 cup coriander leaves, chopped

2 cloves garlic

1 green chilli

1/4 teaspoon salt

1/2 lemon

1 tablespoon dalia

1 tablespoon fresh coconut

FOR THE CHAAT

2 medium sized potatoes, boiled

4 teaspoons chaat masala (see Pg. 286)

2 tablespoons coriander leaves, finely chopped

1 cup thick curd, beaten with 1/4 teaspoon salt

Sweet and sour chutney (see Pg. 125)

METHOD

FOR THE PURIS

Mix all the given ingredients and make a slightly tight dough. Knead well. Break into small balls and roll out into one inch tiny circles. Prick holes in each with a fork. Deep fry in oil till crisp and light brown in colour.

FOR THE GREEN CHUTNEY

Combine all the given ingredients and grind to a fine paste. Make the chutney semi liquid by adding quarter cup of water for easy spreading.

Note:

This chutney is commonly served with many other snacks. It can be filled and served in a papaya flower bowl.

TO ASSEMBLE PURI POTATO CHAAT

(1) Chop the boiled potatoes into thin small slices. Sprinkle chaat masala and chopped coriander leaves. Mix evenly so that each piece is coated with the masala and coriander.
(2) Take each puri and dip in beaten curds. Arrange them in a serving plate. Top each one with potato pieces and dot with sweet and sour chutney and green chutney. Serve immediately before it turns soggy.

FOR THE PAPAYA FLOWER BOWL

Method for carving is the same as cucumber flower basket (see Pg. 125). Make papaya flower bowl without handle. For drawing see Pg. 127

GREEN CHANNA CHAAT (8 - 10 SERVINGS)

INGREDIENTS

FOR THE SEV

1 cup gram flour
A pinch turmeric powder
1/4 teaspoon soda bicarb
Salt to taste
1 tablespoon hot oil
Oil for frying

FOR THE COCUM CHUTNEY (Makes 1/2 cup)

10 new cocums
1 lemon sized jaggery
1/4 teaspoon cummin seeds, roasted and powdered
A pinch salt
1/4 teaspoon black pepper powder
1 cup water

FOR THE CHAAT

2 - 1/2 cups green channa (green Bengal grams) boiled in salt water.
2 medium sized onions, finely chopped
4 medium sized potatoes, chopped
1 big tomato, chopped
2 cucumbers, chopped
2 tablespoons oil
4 tablespoons chaat masala (see Pg. 286)
Chopped coriander leaves and green chillies to garnish

METHOD

FOR THE SEV

(1)   Make a very soft dough (consistency like cake icing) by mixing all ingredients with water.

(2)   Heat oil. Sev is made with a cookie press machine with changeable plates having different sizes of holes. Make sev direcly in hot oil with a plate having fine holes. Fry till very light pink and crisp. Take out on an absorbent paper. Lightly crush while using.

Note:

Green sev is made by adding quarter cup very fine paste of spinach to the dough.

FOR THE COCUM CHUTNEY

Boil all the given ingredients together till cocums are cooked. Cool and make a fine paste. Adjust consistency with water.

TO ASSEMBLE GREEN CHANNA CHAAT

(1)   Heat oil. Add boiled channa and two tablespoons chaat masala. Mix evenly and remove from the gas.

(2)   Take channa in a serving plate. Spread potatoes, onions, tomatoes, cucumber pieces over it. Pour cocum chutney, evenly. Sprinkle remaining chaat masala, sev and chopped coriander leaves and green chillies.

PAPAYA FLOWER BOWL

MOONG AND CORN CHAAT (6 - 8 SERVINGS)

INGREDIENTS

FOR THE MASALA CORN

1 cup corns, boiled, crushed

1 tablespoon oil

Juice from half lemon

1 teaspoon chilli ginger paste

1 teaspoon sugar

Salt to taste

FOR THE RICE SEV

1 cup rice flour

1/2 teaspoon salt

1/4 teaspoon pepper powder

2 tablespoons sour curd

1 tablespoon cream (top of the milk)

Oil for deep frying

FOR THE CHAAT

1 cup moong, sprouted, boiled in salt water

1 cup potatoes, boiled, chopped

1/2 cup onions, chopped

1 - 1/2 cups fresh curd,

beaten with 1/2 teaspoon salt

Chaat masala to taste (see Pg. 286)

Coriander leaves to garnish

Sweet and sour chutney to taste (see Pg. 125)

Green chutney to taste (see Pg. 126)

Puri out of one recipe, crushed (see Pg. 126)

METHOD

FOR THE MASALA CORN

Heat oil, add crushed corn and all the spices. Mix well and remove from gas.

FOR THE RICE SEV

Make a soft dough, like cake icing. Fill into a sev machine and press them over hot oil. Fry sev till pink and crisp. Crush to small pieces.

TO ASSEMBLE MOONG AND CORN CHAAT

First take the crushed puris in a plate. Put moong, masala corn, potatoes and onions on top. Cover with beaten curd. Sprinkle chaat masala, sweet and sour chutney and green chutney. Finally garnish with rice sev and coriander leaves.

BHAJI PANEER GOTA (ABOUT 25 PIECES)

Delicious and nutritious balls — a sure hit for any party.

INGREDIENTS

1 cup gram flour

1 cup paneer

1/2 cup fenugreek leaves (methi leaves,) chopped

1/2 cup spinach, chopped

1 banana, mashed

METHOD

(1) Mash paneer to a smooth paste.

(2) Mix together all the given ingredients in the gram flour together with the paneer paste. Add sufficient water to make a thick batter. Beat well for a few minutes. Cover and keep for at least half an hour. Drop a teaspoonful of batter into the hot oil and deep fry till golden brown.

1/4 teaspoon turmeric powder

1/2 tablespoon chilli ginger paste

1 teaspoon red chilli powder

A pinch asafoetida

1/4 teaspoon soda bicarb

Salt to taste

1 tablespoon hot oil

Oil for deep frying

Serve hot with 'Dahiwali hari chutney' (green chutney in curd)

Note :

For chutney see Pg. 126 Mix one given recipe of green chutney with quarter cup beaten fresh curd.

SURAN PATRA (10 - 12 SERVINGS)

Colocassia leaves spirals, layered with spicy yam paste.

INGREDIENTS

FOR THE SURAN PASTE

12 medium sized colocassia leaves (patra)

1 - 1/2 cups suran (yam) boiled, mashed

1 - 1/2 cups potatoes, boiled, mashed

1/2 cup coconut, grated

1/4 cup coriander leaves, chopped

Juice of 1 lemon

Salt to taste

Sugar to taste

1 teaspoon chilli ginger paste

FOR THE GRAM FLOUR PASTE

1 - 1/2 cups gram flour

1 teaspoon red chilli powder

1/4 teaspoon turmeric powder

2 tablespoons sesame seeds

A big pinch asafoetida

2 tablespoons tamarind pulp

2 tablespoons jaggery

1 teaspoon chilli ginger paste

Salt to taste

TO TEMPER

1 tablespoon oil

1 tablespoon mustard seeds

1 tablespoon sesame seeds

TO DECORATE

Coriander leaves, chopped

Little coconut, grated

METHOD

(1) Trim stem of leaves and wash them.

(2) Prepare suran paste by combining all the given ingredients. Divide into six parts.

(3) Prepare gram flour paste by mixing together all the given ingredients. Divide into six parts.

(4) Take on a big leaf and over it, apply gram flour paste. Put second leaf over it and apply paste once again. Then fold sides and apply paste. Take one portion of the suran paste and spread on the partly folded leaves. Then make a roll. Prepare remaining rolls in the same way. Arrange them in a greased plate and steam them. When rolls are warm, cut into slices. Arrange in a plate. Splutter sesame seeds and mustard seeds in hot oil and pour over the slices. Sprinkle coriander leaves and grated coconut. Serve with green chutney.

CARROT BONDA (MAKES 30 PIECES)

Hot carrot balls accompanied with spicy curd for a quick evening snack.

INGREDIENTS

FOR THE BONDA

1 cup carrot, grated

1 cup white pumpkin, grated

1/4 cup onion, grated

1/4 cup coriander leaves, chopped

3/4 cup coarse wheat flour

3/4 cup gram flour

1 tablespoon chilli ginger paste

A big pinch asafoetida

1/4 teaspoon turmeric

2 teaspoons red chilli powder

1/2 teaspoon ajwain

A big pinch soda bicarb

Salt to taste

Sour curd to bind

FOR THE SPICY CURD

1 cup fresh curd, beaten

1 green chilli, finely crushed

1/4 inch ginger, finely chopped

Salt to taste

2 teaspoons sugar

1 tablespoon oil

1/2 teaspoon mustard seeds

METHOD

FOR THE BONDA

Mix together all the given ingredients. Add curd just enough to bind. Make flat round bondas and deep fry in oil till golden brown. Serve hot with tomato ketchup or serve cold with spicy curd.

FOR THE SPICY CURD

Heat oil and splutter the mustard seeds. Add to the curd. Then add other spices and mix well.

TO SERVE

Cover top of each bonda with the spicy curd and arrange them on a serving plate. Sprinkle chopped coriander leaves.

BAJRI NA VADA (MAKES 20 - 25 PIECES)

Excellent snack for picnics and tours. They can be stored for 2 - 3 days.

INGREDIENTS

2 cups coarse millet flour (bajri)

2 cups coarse wheat flour

1/2 cup moong dal flour

1 - 1/2 tablespoons chilli ginger paste

2 teaspoons red chilli powder

METHOD

(1) Mix together all the ingredients. Add curd just enough to bind. Keep aside for about an hour.
(2) At the time of preparation, add hot oil and mix well.

1/4 teaspoon asafoetida

2 tablespoons sesame seeds

1 - 1/2 teaspoons ajwain

3 tablespoons jaggery

1/4 teaspoon soda bicarb

Salt to taste

2 tablespoons hot oil

Curd to bind

Oil for deep frying

(3) Now wet your hands and take about two tablespoons of this mixture. Make a flat round and deep fry in hot oil. Repeat. First let the vadas fry over high flame. When they begin to rise, reduce heat to medium. Fry till golden brown and remove on an absorbent paper. Serve them hot or cold.

TRICOLOUR DHOKLA (10 - 12 SERVINGS)

A traditional tricoloured, steamed Gujarati snack, made for special occasions.

INGREDIENTS

FOR THE WHITE LAYER

1 - 1/2 cups rice

1/2 cup urad dal (split black gram)

Salt to taste

A pinch asafoetida

1/2 teaspoon soda bicarb

2 tablespoons oil

1/2 cup thick sour buttermilk

FOR THE GREEN LAYER

1 cup coriander leaves, chopped

1/4 cup fresh coconut, grated

1 tablespoon roasted Bengal gram (dalia)

3 green chillies

Salt to taste

Juice of one small lemon

FOR THE YELLOW LAYER

1 cup channa dal (split Bengal gram)

1 cup moong dal with skin (split green gram with skin)

1 tablespoon chilli ginger paste

Salt to taste

1/4 teaspoon turmeric powder

1/2 cup thick sour buttermilk

METHOD

FOR THE WHITE LAYER

(1) Wash rice and urad dal together and then dry on cloth. (Sunlight is not necessary.) Make a coarse powder in the grinder.

(2) Mix all ingredients in a big vessel. Add little hot water to the ground mixture to make a medium thick batter. Beat with hand for a few minutes to make it light and fluffy. Transfer this into a big vessel and cover with a tight lid. Put in a warm place for 10 -12 hours to ferment.

FOR THE GREEN LAYER

Mix all the ingredients and make a fine chutney in a grinder. At the time of making dhokla, mix in half a cup of white dhokla mixture and two drops of green colour.

FOR THE YELLOW LAYER

Soak both the dals separately for four to five hours. Remove skin of moong dal as much as possible. Then grind to a paste. Mix both pastes with other ingredients. Beat mixture with hand to make it light and fluffy. Then cover with a tight lid and keep in a warm place for four to five hours to ferment.

1 teaspoon sugar

A pinch asafoetida

1/2 teaspoon soda bicarb

3 tablespoons oil

FOR PREPARING THE DHOKLAS

1/4 cup oil

1/4 cup water

1/4 teaspoon citric acid

Fruit salt as required

1/2 teaspoon soda bicarb

TO TEMPER

2 tablespoons oil

1 teaspoon mustard seeds

1 teaspoon sesame seeds

FOR THE DHOKLAS

(1) Combine oil, water and citric acid in small vessel. Heat mixture. When it starts boiling, remove from gas and add half teaspoon soda bicarb. It will bubble. Stir with a spoon and pour half into white fermented batter and half into yellow fermented batter. Mix well.

(2) Take a vessel, big enough to hold eight inches diametre deep plate. Put about two cups of water in it and a metal ring in the centre to put the plate on. Cover with a tight lid and boil water. Meanwhile grease plate with oil and put on the ring to preheat.

(3) Now divide yellow batter into two parts. To one part add half teaspoon fruit salt. Beat very well and pour into a hot greased deep plate. Cover lid and steam the dhokla for five mintes till it is half cooked.

(4) Remove plate and pour half of the green mixture. Spread evenly all over. Put it back to steam for two minutes.

(5) Divide white batter in two parts. Mix quarter teaspoon of fruit salt and beat well. Pour over the green layer. Steam for another three to four minutes till done.

Insert a sharp knife in the steamed dhokla. If it comes out clean, then the dhokla is ready.

(6) Remove plate and apply one tablespoon of oil all over and allow to cool. Then cut into pieces. Prepare second plate the same way. Take out dhoklas in a serving plate.

(7) Prepare tempering and sprinkle all over dhoklas. Garnish with coriander leaves and fresh grated coconut.

TO TEMPER

Heat oil in a small vessel. Add mustard seeds, when they begin to splutter, add sesame seeds and cover with a lid. Remove from the gas as they stop spluttering. Immediately pour over dhoklas.

1. Cucumber baskets with curd and sweet and sour chutney   p. 125
2. Papaya flower bowl with green chutney   p. 127
3. Moong dal rolls   p. 124
4. Suran patra   p. 129
5. Bread pakodas   p. 122
6. Crisp palak chaat   p. 126
7. Carrot bonda   p. 130
8. Golden creamy drink   p. 35

INDIAN SWEETS

PINEAPPLE BARFI (10 - 12 PIECES)

A light sweet with pineapple flavour.

INGREDIENTS

1 cup khoya

1 cup paneer

1/3 cup pineapple, chopped

1/2 cup powdered sugar

Silver varakh (foil) for decoration

Butterpaper cups

METHOD

(1) Break khoya into small crumbs and warm on slow heat. Remove from gas when little ghee separates. Cool.

(2) Take paneer in a vessel and warm on slow heat and stir constantly till little dry. Remove from gas and cool.

(3) Mix together the khoya, paneer and powdered sugar. Rub well and prepare a soft mixture.

(4) One can give different shapes, e.g.
(a) Spread half of the mixture in a plate. Sprinkle pineapple pieces and cover them with remaining mixture. Pat and bind everything well. Spread silver varakh on top. Cut into diamond shaped pieces.
(b) Make lemon sized balls. In each, stuff a pineapple piece. Roll into a smooth ball. Put little silver varakh on top and serve them in butterpaper cups.
(c) One can make oval shapes instead of round by stuffing big pineapple pieces inside.

MALAI HALWA (6 SERVINGS)

A halwa with a pure taste of cream.

INGREDIENTS

1 litre milk

150 grams (5 ozs.) sugar

2 tablespoons curd, beaten

1 cup cream (from top of milk)

1/4 teaspoon cardamom powder

Few pistachios and almonds, sliced

METHOD

(1) Combine milk, sugar and curd together. Cook on slow heat, stirring constantly until milk curdles. Cook till the mixture is dry.

(2) Add cream gradually. Keep stirring until well blended and the liquid is absorbed.

(3) Mix cardamom powder. Remove in a glass serving dish and garnish with slices of almonds and pistachios.

CORN HALWA (MAKES 15 PIECES)

A koprapak (coconut sweet) with a corny taste.

INGREDIENTS

1/2 cup pure ghee

3/4 cup coconut, grated

1 cup paste of corn, (grate 6 corns, add a little water if needed and grind to a paste)

Little saffron

Little milk to dissolve saffron

3/4 cup sugar

1/4 cup water

1/2 teaspoon cardamom, powdered

Few silver varakh (foil)

METHOD

(1) Take one-third of the ghee and fry the grated coconut.

(2) When light brown in colour, remove in a plate. In the same pan take the remaining ghee and fry the corn paste. Fry on slow heat till light brown. Now ·mix in fried coconut.

(3) Dissolve saffron in a little milk.

(4) Boil sugar and water till the syrup is of one and a half thread consistency.* Remove and pour into the coconut and corn mixture. Mix in saffron and cardamom. Mix everything well and stir till ghee separates.

(5) Take out halwa in a plate. Level it and spread silver varakh. Cool and cut into pieces.

Note:
Put a drop of thick syrup in a bowl of water. If it does not dissolve immediately, the syrup is of one and half thread consistency.

SHAHI TUKDE (10 SERVINGS)

A mughlai way of making a delicious sweet out of bread.

INGREDIENTS

10 slices bread

Ghee for frying

3/4 litre milk

3/4 cup sugar

1/2 teaspoon cardamom powder

Little saffron, mixed with yellow colour

About 1/4 cup cream (from top of the milk)

Few almonds and pistachios, sliced

METHOD

(1) Remove crust from bread slices. Deep fry in ghee till golden brown.

(2) Heat milk. Add sugar, cardamom and saffron with yellow colour.

(3) Take a broad vessel and spread the bread slices. Pour over the milk enough to cover them. Simmer on gas. Milk will be absorbed by bread slices. Keep turning sides of bread slices. Remove slices on a serving plate when they have absorbed maximum milk. Pour some extra milk around these slices in the serving plate. Allow shahi tukde to cool. Add cream on top and sprinkle slices of almonds and pistachios.

CREAM DROPS (6 SERVINGS)

Colourful balls floating in thick milk.

INGREDIENTS

1/2 cup khoya, crumbled

1 tablespoon powdered sugar

1/2 teaspoon milk masala powder (see Pg. 288)

1/2 cup desiccated coconut

2 tablespoons pure ghee

1/2 cup semolina

1 - 1/2 litres milk

1 cup sugar

Few drops red and green colour

1/4 teaspoon cardamom powder

Few almonds, sliced

METHOD

(1) Take khoya crumbs in a vessel and warm on a slow heat. Stir constantly till khoya is soft and little ghee separates. Remove and cool. Mix powdered sugar and milk masala. Roll into very small balls - about 25.

(2) Roast the desiccated coconut on slow heat till crisp. Remove and cool.

(3) Melt ghee and fry semolina till light. Add half cup milk and mix. Also mix in half cup of the sugar and another half cup milk. Stir well and when dry, mix in coconut. Mix well till it leaves the sides of the vessel. Remove from heat and cool. Divide into two parts. To one part add red colour and to the second part add green colour.

(4) Make smooth balls of the above mixture and in each, stuff in the khoya balls.

(5) Meanwhile scald milk - till it is little thick. Add remaining sugar and boil for a few more minutes.

(6) Add prepared cream drops in milk and boil for three minutes more. Mix cardamom powder. Remove from gas and transfer in a serving bowl. Cool at room temperature. Sprinkle slices of almonds.

CARROT SANDESH BOAT (MAKES ABOUT 18 - 20 PIECES)

A traditional Bengali sweet served in carrot boats.

INGREDIENTS

250 grams carrots

1/2 cup paneer

1/2 cup powdered sugar

1/2 cup sugar

2 teaspoons milk masala powder (see Pg. 288)

METHOD

(1) Cut carrots into two inch pieces. Cut each piece lengthwise into two. Scoop the centre of each piece making a boat shape.

(2) Take half cup sugar and carrot boats in a vessel. Add water enough to cover these pieces. Put on the gas and boil for 15 minutes till carrot boats are cooked. Drain boats from the syrup and cool on a strainer.

(3) Take paneer and powdered sugar in a shallow dish and beat well. Make small long balls of this sandesh and stuff them in the boats, sprinkle milk masala powder on top.

CARROT GULAB JAMUNS (MAKES 40 PIECES)

Golden carrot gulab jamuns are nutritious and sumptuous.

INGREDIENTS

250 grams carrots (preferably red Delhi variety)

125 grams plain khoya

125 gulab jamun khoya

6 teaspoons corn flour

Few pistachios and sugar crystals

Ghee for frying

250 grams (9 ozs.) sugar

1 - 1/4 cups water

Few drops rose essence or cardamom powder

METHOD

(1) Grate carrots. Put them in a vessel, cover. Cook in a pressure cooker (without pressure) for 20 minutes. Squeeze out extra water. Mash and grind to a pulpy mixture.

(2) Break both varieties of khoya into crumbs. Add carrot pulp and corn flour. Mix everything well and make a smooth dough.

(3) Form into 40 small balls. In each ball stuff a crystal of sugar and a pistachio. Form into smooth round balls.

(4) Fry these balls in ghee on medium heat till golden brown in colour.

(5) When the balls are being fried, combine sugar and water in a vessel. Boil for a few minutes till little sticky. Remove from gas. Add either rose essence or cardamom powder.

(6) Put the fried gulab jamuns in sugar syrup. Serve them after they are well soaked for at least two hours.

DATE AND NUT SLICES (MAKES 20 PIECES)

An unusual sweet with a combination of dates and nuts-ideal for the winter.

INGREDIENTS

1 packet seedless black dates (400 grams)

2 tablespoons fresh cream (from top of milk)

3/4 cup pistachios, cashewnuts, almonds, combined

10 Marie biscuits or any plain biscuits, powdered

METHOD

(1) Separate dates. Take them in a thick vessel and put on slow gas. Add cream and warm mixture for 10 minutes. Try to mash dates when they start to warm.

(2) Add biscuit powder, (keeping aside two tablespoons) and nuts. Mix well and remove from gas.

(3) Take an aluminium foil. sprinkle the remaining biscuit powder and place the prepared mixture on it. Roll mixture into a long smooth cylindrical shape. Cover snugly in the same foil. Leave in fridge for four to five hours. Before serving, remove and cut into 1/2 inch thick slices.

VERMICELLI PANEER LADDOO (MAKES 25 PIECES)

Paneer balls stuffed with vermicelli and coated with coconut.

INGREDIENTS

2 cups paneer

3/4 cup powdered sugar for paneer

Little saffron or a few drops yellow colour

3/4 cup vermicelli

3/4 cup milk

1 tablespoon ghee

1/2 cup sugar for vermicelli

1/4 cup fresh coconut, grated

A few almonds, chopped

1/2 teaspoon cardamom powder

3 to 4 tablespoons desiccated coconut

METHOD

(1) Take paneer, powdered sugar and dissolved saffron in a shallow dish. Knead well till smooth. Divide into 25 balls.

(2) Heat ghee. Add the crushed vermicelli and fresh coconut. Fry till light pink in colour. Add milk, chopped almonds and cardamom powder. When milk starts to evaporate, add sugar. Stir well till mixture leaves the sides of the vessel. Remove from the gas and cool. Divide into 25 portions.

(3) Stuff each vermicelli ball into the paneer portion. Roll each ball in desiccated coconut.

DATES AND PANEER LADDOO (MAKES 15 PIECES)

Attractive date balls with soft paneer inside.

INGREDIENTS

1 tablespoon cream (from top of milk)

1 packet seedless black dates (400 grams)

3 tablespoons dry coconut, finely grated or desiccated coconut

1 - 1/2 cups paneer

1/2 cup powdered sugar

1/2 teaspoon cardamom powder

METHOD

(1) Melt cream in a thick vessel. Add dates. Stir and keep mashing the dates till they are pulpy. Add and mix half of the grated dry coconut. Remove from gas and cool. Divide into 15 portions.

(2) Take paneer, sugar and cardamom in a shallow dish and mash very well to a fine paste. Make 15 balls.

(3) Take one portion of date and flatten it on your palm. Put one ball of paneer in the centre and cover it, making a ball. Similarly make other balls. Roll each one in grated coconut. Keep in fridge till serving time.

PANEER MAKAI KI KHEER (6 - 8 SERVINGS)

A typical Indian dessert served with puris on special occasions.

INGREDIENTS

1 litre milk

3/4 cup fresh corns, grated

1 cup sugar

1/2 cup cooking paneer, cubed

2 tablespoons almonds and pistachios, chopped

1/4 teaspoon powdered cardamom

METHOD

Mix together milk and grated corn. Put on the gas to cook. Stir often. After 15 minutes, add sugar, add sugar and paneer pieces. Simmer for another 15 minutes. Add almonds and pistachios when kheer consistency (fairly thick) is reached. Mix in cardamom powder and remove from gas. Serve either at room temperature or cool in a fridge.

SEMOLINA COCONUT DELIGHT (MAKES 25 PIECES)

A delicious coconut and semolina sweet for festivals.

INGREDIENTS

FOR THE STUFFING

3/4 cup coconut, grated

1/2 cup sugar

1/4 teaspoon cardamom powder

3 almonds, blanched and finely chopped

1 teaspoon poppy seeds

A little saffron

30 ml. (1 fl. oz.) water from coconut or plain water

FOR THE COVERING

150 ml. (5 fl. ozs.) milk

150 ml. (5 fl. ozs.) water

4 tablespoons sugar

2 pinches nutmeg powder

1/4 teaspoon cardamom powder

1/2 cup semolina

1 tablespoon butter

Silver varakh (foil) for decoration

METHOD

FOR THE STUFFING

Mix all the ingredients and keep aside for half an hour. Then put on the slow gas and cook, stirring continuously till sugar dissolves. Now allow the mixture to simmer till it becomes sticky. Take out in a plate and allow it to cool. Divide into 25 portions.

FOR THE COVERING

(1)   Warm mixture of milk, water, sugar, nutmeg and cardamom. Gradually add semolina and stir continuously till it starts to thicken. Add butter and mix well. Heat further till mixture leaves the sides of the vessel. Remove from the gas and cool. Divide into 25 portions.

(2)   Roll each portion of semolina into two inches rounds and put in the one portion of stuffing. Cover and make a flat ball. Repeat the process.

(3)   Deep fry these balls in ghee till golden brown. Remove, cool and decorate with silver varakh.

Note:

One can also add quarter cup of grated carrot to the boiling milk.

MOONG DAL AND SEMOLINA SHEERA (6 SERVINGS)

Excellent sweet dish to be served with other main dishes.

INGREDIENTS

1 cup moong dal (split green gram without skin)

1/2 to 3/4 cup ghee

1/2 cup fine semolina

1/2 cup khoya, crumbled

2 cups milk

1 - 1/2 cups sugar

1/2 teaspoon cardamom powder

Little saffron

Almonds and pistachios for decoration

METHOD

(1) Soak moong dal for four to five hours. Grind to a fine paste.

(2) Heat ghee, add moong dal paste and semolina. Roast, stirring constantly to break all lumps. Roast till light pink in colour, good aroma emanates and ghee separates. Add khoya. Mix well and roast for another five minutes.

(3) Warm milk and add to the moong dal mixture. Allow the milk to be absorbed. Add sugar, saffron and cardamom powder. Mix well. Stir till mixture leaves the sides of the vessel and little ghee separates. Remove from the gas and transfer into a serving dish. Decorate with almonds and pistachios.

KESAR MALAI PEDA (MAKES 24 PIECES)

Creamy soft 'n' sweet balls with saffron flavour.

INGREDIENTS

1 litre milk

150 grams sugar

1/4 teaspoon citric acid

1 teaspoon corn flour, dissolved in little cold water

1/4 teaspoon saffron, dissolved in little milk

1/4 teaspoon cardamom powder

Few pistachios for decoration

METHOD

(1) Boil milk in a thick vessel till it is reduced to half its quantity. Add sugar and boil for another five to seven minutes. Keep stirring.

(2) Melt citric acid in two teaspoons of water and add little by little to the boiling milk. The milk will start curdling. Add the dissolved corn flour and keep stirring till almost dry. Add saffron and cardamom powder. Mixture should collect like a soft ball. Remove from gas and cool Make round balls, slightly flattened while the mixture is still warm. Decorate with sliced pistachios.

1. Corn halwa   p. 135
2. Cream drops   p. 136
3. Date and paneer ladoo   p. 138
4. Carrot sandesh boat   p. 136
5. Pineapple barfi   p. 134

MEXICAN DISHES

The backbone of Mexican cuisine consists of maize, beans and chillies. Many spices and herbs like oregano, wild mint, celery, black sage, bay leaves, coriander, cummin, anise, cloves, etc. are used with great imagination to enhance taste of Mexican food. This is the main reason of its popularity in India where people enjoy spicy, crisp novelties. It also provides great scope for preparing vegetarian varieties.

TACO

It is a crisp fried corn tortilla shell to hold fillings, topped with shredded cabbage, spring onions, lettuce, etc. and varieties of Salsas (sauces) and grated cheese. Taco can be served as one of the main dishes on a buffet table or as a snack at tea party.

TORTILLAS

They are like thick chappatis made of either wheat flour or maize flour. Various kinds of fillings can be put in and folded before eating.

TOSTADOS AND TOSTADAS

Tostados are the crisp fried tortillas. Toppings are spread over and eaten. Tostadas are the pieces of tortillas usually about quarter of the whole round. They are eaten as crisps, often dipped in some sauce before meal with drinks or as snacks.

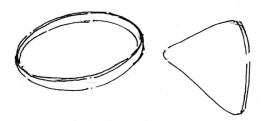

MEXICAN CURRY (8 - 10 SERVINGS)

Mixed vegetables and bean curry to be served with Mexican rice.

INGREDIENTS

100 grams green peas

100 grams carrots, cut into long strips

150 grams French beans, cut into long strips

250 grams cauliflower, cut into small pieces

1 - 1/2 cups stock

1/2 cup kidney beans (rajma)

3 tablespoons oil

2 onions, sliced

2 green chillies, chopped

3 - 4 dry red chillies

4 tablespoons tomato ketchup

2 tablespoons chilli sauce

Salt and pepper to taste

2 tablespoons vinegar

METHOD

(1) Boil green peas, carrots, French beans and cauliflower in salt water, drain and reserve the stock.

(2) Soak kidney beans for five to six hours, cook them in salt water, drain and grind to a paste.

(3) Heat oil in deep pan. Fry onions, till light brown. Then fry green chillies and red chillies. Pour vegetable stock and boil. Add the boiled vegetables and boil for five to seven minutes. Mix rajma paste and spices. Simmer for 10 minutes. Serve hot with Mexican rice.

MEXICAN RICE (8 - 10 SERVINGS)

Colourful and spicy rice.

INGREDIENTS

5 tablespoons ghee

3 onions, cut into long strips

Few peppercorns

2 cups rice

1/4 cup kidney beans (rajma)

2 tablespoons chilli sauce

3 tablespoons vinegar

Salt to taste

1 big carrot, cut into long strips

2 capsicums, cut into long strips

Pinch of soda bicarb

2 tomatoes, cut into 8 pieces

1/4 cup peanuts, fried

1 potato, cut into fine chips, fried

METHOD

(1) Heat three tablespoons of ghee in a flat pan. Add half of the chopped onions and peppercorns. Fry till light brown. Mix in washed rice, fry for five minutes. Pour hot water, cover and cook.

(2) When half done, add cooked kidney beans, two tablespoons chilli sauce, three tablespoons vinegar and salt to taste.

(3) Heat two tablespoons ghee in another pan. When it melts, add remaining half of the onions, carrot and capsicum strips. Mix a pinch of soda and salt to taste. Saute for few minutes. Mix these vegetables in the half cooked rice.

(4) Arrange tomato pieces, peanuts and potato chips on the rice when almost cooked. Cover and cook further for five minutes. Serve hot with curry.

(5) For parties, when rice is ready take out in a greased baking dish. Decorate with tomato pieces, peanuts and potato chips. Cover with aluminium foil and bake at 200°C for 20 minutes before serving.

BURITTO (MAKES 15 PIECES)

Burittos are round open mouth packets made of maize flour. They are stuffed, deep fried and served with crisp vegetables and easy red salsa.

INGREDIENTS

FOR THE RED PUMPKIN STUFFING

2 tablespoons oil

1 teaspoon cummin seeds

4 - 5 green chillies, chopped

3 - 4 cloves garlic, chopped

1/4 cup onions, chopped

1 cup red pumpkin, diced

1 cup potatoes, boiled, chopped

1/2 cup green peas, boiled

Salt to taste

2 tablespoons vinegar

FOR THE BURITTO COVERING

1 cup maize flour

1/2 cup flour

2 tablespoons oil

1/2 teaspoon salt

1/3 cup flour for the paste

FOR THE TOPPING

Cabbage, chopped

Spring onions, chopped

Easy red salsa as required

METHOD

FOR THE RED PUMPKIN STUFFING

(1)   Heat oil, add cummin seeds, green chillies, garlic and onion. Fry till soft. Add pumpkin pieces and salt to taste. Cover and cook on slow heat. Stir often.

(2)   Mix in chopped potatoes, green peas, salt and vinegar. Remove from gas and cool.

FOR THE BURITTO COVERING

(1)   Prepare dough like puri (slightly tight) out of maize flour, flour, oil, salt and water. Knead well and divide into 15 even sized balls. Roll them to five inches diametre rounds. Put stuffing in the centre and fold them keeping its mouth open. Stuffing should be below the mouth of the buritto and each one should have a base to stand.

(2)   Prepare a thick paste of one-third cup flour, quarter teaspoon salt and water. Apply about half teaspoon of the paste on the stuffing to seal it.

(3)   Deep fry in oil till outer layer is light brown in colour.

(4)   To serve : Top each buritto with chopped cabbage, spring onions and easy red salsa (see Pg. 146)

ENCHILADAS (6 - 8 SERVINGS)

A Mexican baked dish of stuffed pancake packets, covered with spicy sauces.

INGREDIENTS

FOR THE ENCHILADAS

1/2 cup maize flour

1/2 cup flour

1 teaspoon melted butter

3/4 cup water

1/2 cup milk

Salt to taste

Oil for shallow frying

FOR THE STUFFING

1/2 cup French beans

1/2 cup carrots

1 cup capsicum

2 green chillies

6 cloves garlic

2 tablespoons butter

1 onion

1/2 cup kidney beans (rajma), boiled in salt water

Salt to taste

FOR THE SAUCE

1 onion, chopped

5 cloves garlic, chopped

2 tablespoons butter

1/2 kg. tomatoes, extract juice

2 tablespoons sugar

Salt to taste

1 tablespoon vinegar

2 teaspoons red chilli powder

FOR PREPARING ENCHILADAS

1 cup white sauce (see Pg. 70)

Few rings of capsicum

1/2 cup cheese, grated

METHOD

FOR ENCHILADAS

Mix together all the given ingredients and make an even batter. Make pancakes with little oil and keep aside to cool.

FOR THE STUFFING

(1) Chop French beans, carrots, capsicums, chillies, and garlic into small pieces. Cook French beans and carrot pieces in salt water and drain.

(2) Melt butter and saute the onion, garlic, green chilli and capsicum till soft. Now mix in cooked beans, French beans, carrots and salt. Warm mixture for a few minutes and remove from gas.

FOR THE SAUCE

Fry onions and garlic in butter till light brown. Add tomato juice and all the seasonings. Simmer till sauce is thick.

TO ASSEMBLE ENCHILADAS

Take a baking dish, and grease it with butter. Put stuffing in the centre of each enchiladas and make neat packets. Arrange all these packets in a baking dish. Pour sauce over them. Then cover with thick white sauce, sprinkle grated cheese and capsicum rings. Heat oven to 200°C and bake for half an hour.

TACO BAR (6 - 8 SERVINGS)

There is more fun to a special party when you prepare tacos with more than one type of stuffings, sauces and toppings. This will give ample choice to your guests, to assemble their own taco, with desired stuffings, sauces and toppings.

INGREDIENTS

FOR THE TACOS (Makes 30 pieces)

1 - 1/2 cups maize flour (makai)

1 cup flour

3/4 teaspoon salt

2 tablespoons oil

Oil for frying

FOR THE BAKED BEANS AND GREEN PEAS STUFFING

1 can baked beans in tomato sauce (450 grams)

1/2 cup green peas, boiled in salt water

2 teaspoons red chilli powder

1/2 teaspoon salt

FOR THE EGGPLANT & GREEN PEA STUFFING

3 tablespoons oil

1/2 cup onions, chopped

3 - 4 cloves garlic, chopped

2 cups eggplant, peeled, diced

1/4 cup tomatoes, peeled, chopped

1/4 teaspoon cardamom powder

1/4 teaspoon clove and cinnamon powder

2 - 3 teaspoons red chilli powder

1/2 cup green pea, boiled in salt water

Salt to taste

FOR THE CORN STUFFING

1 tablespoon oil

2 - 3 green chillies, chopped

1 capsicum, chopped

1/2 cup corn, boiled

1 can baked beans in tomato sauce (450 grams)

Salt to taste

METHOD

FOR THE TACOS

Mix together the two flours, salt and oil. Make a soft dough like puri with water. Keep dough for at least half an hour and knead well. Make small balls and roll like puri. Deep fry in oil on both sides and then bend into a 'U' shape. Remove onto a brown paper. Store them in a box when cold.

FOR THE BAKED BEANS AND GREEN PEAS STUFFING

Combine all the given ingredients in a vessel. Warm them and mix well. Serve either cold or warm.

FOR THE EGGPLANT AND GREEN PEA STUFFING

Heat oil, add onions and garlic. Saute till soft. Add eggplant and tomato pieces. Mix salt to taste and cook on medium gas till they are soft. Add cardamom powder, cinnamon and clove powder, red chilli powder and green peas. Mix well and simmer for a few more minutes till the flavour sets in and the mixture is dry.

FOR THE CORN STUFFING

Heat oil and saute green chillies and capsicum for a minute. Add corn and baked beans in tomato sauce and salt to taste. Mix well and remove from gas.

FOR THE GREEN SALSA (SAUCE)
(Makes 1 cup)

100 grams green tomatoes

1 onion

2 green chillies

2 teaspoons vinegar

Salt to taste

FOR THE EASY RED SALSA (make 1 cup)

1/2 cup tomato ketchup

2 teaspoons chilli sauce

1/2 cup water

1 - 1/2 teaspoons corn flour

Salt, sugar and pepper to taste

FOR THE SALSA FRESCA

(Makes 1-1/2 cups)

2 tablespoons oil

1/2 cup onions, chopped

2 - 3 cloves garlic, flaked

3 - 4 hot green chillies minced

1/2 teaspoon cummin seeds

1/2 cup tomato puree (canned)

3/4 cup water

1 tablespoon flour

Salt to taste

1 tablespoon sugar

1/2 teaspoon oregano

1/4 cup canned mushrooms, chopped (optional)

FOR THE SUGGESTED TOPPINGS

Spring onions, chopped with tender green leaves

Lettuce, chopped

Cabbage, shredded

Cheese, grated

Raw or canned mushrooms, sliced

Spinach, chopped

Olives, sliced

Stuffed olives, sliced

Radish, sliced

Carrots, grated

FOR THE GREEN SALSA (SAUCE)

Cut tomatoes, onion and green chillies into big pieces. Add quarter cup water and cook. Cool and blend in a mixer till pulpy. Strain it. Finally add vinegar and salt.

FOR THE EASY RED SALSA (SAUCE)

Mix all the given ingredients and warm mixture till corn flour is cooked. Remove from gas and cool.

FOR SALSA FRESCA

Heat oil, add onion, garlic, chillies and cummin seeds. Fry till soft. Add tomato puree and water mixed with flour. Add salt to taste, sugar and oregano. Stir till sauce consistency is reached. Mix in mushrooms. Remove from gas and cool.

TO ASSEMBLE TACOS

Prepare taco shells just before serving time. In each fold of taco shell, fill two tablespoons of stuffing, any two to three items of toppings and one or two types of sauces.

CHILLIES RELLENOS (MAKES 12 PIECES)

Stuffed and fried chillies served with salsa.

INGREDIENTS

FOR THE RELLENOS

12 green chillies (short and broad chillies which are good for stuffing and not very hot in taste.)

2 tablespoons oil.

3 - 4 cloves garlic, chopped

1/2 cup potatoes, boiled, mashed

1 tomato, peeled, chopped

Salt to taste

1/4 teaspoon pepper powder

1 teaspoon vinegar

1 tablespoon coriander or parsley, chopped

FOR THE SAUCE

1 big tomato, peel and extract juice

2 - 3 cloves garlic, chopped

1 tablespoon coriander leaves, chopped

1 tablespoon oil

Salt to taste

METHOD

FOR THE RELLENOS

(1)   Split the chillies, open and remove seeds and sticks.
(2)   Heat oil and add the chopped garlic. Fry for a minute and then add potatoes, tomato pieces, pepper powder, salt, vinegar and coriander leaves. Mix and warm the mixture till a little dry. Remove from the gas and cool. Stuff this mixture in all the chillies.
(3)   Prepare a thick batter out of flour, water and salt. Dip each stuffed chilli in the batter and deep fry in oil.

FOR THE SAUCE

Prepare sauce by frying garlic. Add tomato juice, coriander leaves and salt to taste. Give a boil and remove from the gas. Serve with spicy hot chillies rellenos.

1. Kidney bean rolls in hot tomato salsa   p. 153
2. Corn tostados   p. 150
3. Chimichangos   p. 152
4. Buritto   p. 144

CORN TOSTADOS (MAKES 20 PIECES)

Crisp round tostados are topped with tasty corn topping, farm house salsoa and grated cheese. They are lightly baked to melt cheese.

INGREDIENTS

FOR THE TOSTADOS

1 - 1/4 cup maize flour

3/4 cup flour

1/2 teaspoon oregano

Salt to taste

3 tablespoons oil

FOR THE CORN TOPPING

2 tablespoons butter

4 - 5 green chillies, chopped

1 capsicum, chopped

2 tablespoons flour

3/4 cup milk

1 can cream style corn

1/4 cup cheese

Salt to taste

FOR THE FARM HOUSE SALSA

1 tablespoon oil

3 - 4 cloves garlic, chopped

2 - 3 green chillies, chopped

1 onion, chopped

2 green tomatoes, peeled, finely chopped

2 red tomatoes, peeled, finely chopped

1 teaspoon oregano

Salt to taste

METHOD

FOR THE TOSTADOS

Make dough out of flour, maize flour, oregano, salt, oil and water. Knead well and divide into 20 portions. Roll each portion to thin rounds of four inches diametre. Deep fry in oil till light brown in colour. When still hot, press on a base of a metal cup to get a depression in the centre. Store in an airtight box.

FOR THE CORN TOPPING

(1)   Heat butter, and saute the green chillies and capsicum till soft. Add flour and after a minute add milk. Stir till thick like a sauce. Now mix in cream style corn, cheese and salt to taste. Simmer till mixture is thick.

(2)   Spread hot corn topping on each tostado. Pour two teaspoons of farm house salsa and sprinkle some grated cheese. Put this on a greased baking plate. Bake at 200°C on upper shelf till cheese melts. Remove and serve immediately, with or without shredded cabbage and chopped onions.

FOR THE FARM HOUSE SALSA

Heat oil and saute garlic, chillies and onions, till they are soft. Add tomatoes, oregano and salt to taste. Cook till soft and thick like a sauce.

MEXICAN CUTLETS WITH SALSA VERDE (MAKES 10 PIECES)

Excellent dish for a buffet party.

INGREDIENTS

FOR THE CUTLETS

2 cups potatoes, boiled, mashed

1 tablespoon corn flour

Salt to taste

1/2 teaspoon pepper powder for potatoes

1 cup kidney beans, boiled, mashed

1 teaspoon chilli sauce

1/4 teaspoon pepper for kidney beans

A pinch citric acid

Oil for shallow frying

10 teaspoons cheese, grated

Few capsicum pieces

FOR THE SALSA VERDE

2 medium sized green tomatoes

2 green chillies

2 tablespoons coriander leaves, chopped

1 small capsicum

1 tablespoon vinegar

1 tablespoon sugar

Salt to taste

1 tablespoon corn flour

METHOD

FOR THE CUTLETS

(1)   Mix together potatoes, corn flour, salt and pepper. Divide into 20 portions. Flatten each portion into two inches diametre circles (like a thick puri).

(2)   Mix together the mashed kidney beans, salt, pepper, chilli sauce and citric acid. Divide into 10 portions. Flatten them into 1 - 3/4 inches diametre circles.

(3)   Sandwich kidney bean puri between two potato puries. Seal edges and shallow fry in oil.

(4)   Arrange all cutlets on a barbecue plate. Apply salsa verde. Sprinkle cheese and diced capsicum. Before serving, cover lid and warm cutlets for 10 minutes till cheese melts. Serve hot immediately or bake in oven till cheese melts.

FOR THE SALSA VERDE

Blend all ingredients together in a mixer. Then put on the gas to warm. Stir often till thick like a sauce. Remove from gas and cool to room temperature.

CHIMICHANGOS (MAKES 15 PIECES)

Chimichangos have recently become popular. Wheat tortillas are filled with stuffing and folded like envelopes. They are secured with a toothpick and deep fried till golden.

INGREDIENTS

FOR THE WHEAT TORTILLAS

2 cups wheat flour

1 teaspoon baking powder

1/2 teaspoon salt

1/2 teaspoon sugar

2 tablespoons oil

Warm water as required

FOR THE CHICKPEA STUFFING

1 - 1/2 cups chickpeas (Kabuli channa), boiled

2 pinches soda bicarb

Salt to taste

2 tablespoons oil

1 teaspoon cummin seeds

1 onion, chopped

4 - 5 cloves garlic, chopped

4 - 5 Kashmiri chillies, soaked in 2 tablespoons vinegar, ground to a paste

1/2 inch ginger, ground

1/2 cup potatoes, boiled, chopped

To decorate

Lettuce leaves, chopped

Tomato wedges

Cucumber flowers

METHOD

FOR THE WHEAT TORTILLAS

(1) Mix all the above ingredients and make a soft dough with hot water. Cover and keep for half an hour. Knead well. Divide into 15 portions. Form into balls.

(2) Roll each ball with little dry flour to six inches round and roast on tawa (iron griddle) on both sides till tiny red dots appear on its surface.

FOR THE CHICKPEA STUFFING

(1) Soak chickpeas overnight with two big pinches of soda bicarb. Next day, pressure cook them without changing water along with one teaspoon of salt. Drain off water. Roughly crush them.

(2) Heat oil, add cummin seeds, onion and garlic. Fry till they are soft. Add paste of ginger and chillies. Fry for a minute.

(3) Add the crushed chickpeas, potatoes and salt to taste. Mix well and allow to dry. Remove from gas and cool. Divide into 15 portions.

(4) Take a tortilla on a board. Put stuffing in the centre. Fold like an envelope. First fold one side over the filling. Then fold the two adjacent sides over. Finally fold the forth side over all and insert a toothpick to secure it firmly or stick ends with a thick paste of flour and water.

(5) Deep fry in oil till golden brown on both sides.

(6) Serve with salsa fresca (see Pg. 146) and garnish with chopped lettuce, tomato wedges and cucumber flower.

FOR THE CUCUMBER FLOWER

(1) Take about 2 inches piece of a cucumber. Peel it. Trim edges and round off both the ends.

(2) Make sharp, narrow zigzag cuts in the centre of the cucumber in such a way that the knife reaches its centre. Cucumber will open in two flowers.

(3) Scoop a tiny round portion from the centre and put a piece of glazed cherry or any other bright coloured vegetable, like beetroot, red radish or capsicum.

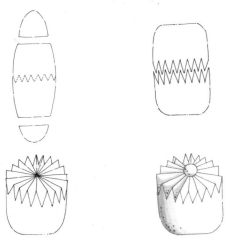

KIDNEY BEAN ROLLS IN HOT TOMATO SALSA (10 - 12 SERVINGS)

Tiny bean rolls floating in red hot tomato sauce.

INGREDIENTS

FOR THE BEAN ROLLS

2 cups kidney beans (rajma)

3 - 4 tablespoons oil

2 large onions, chopped (1 cup)

4 medium tomatoes

2 - 3 cloves garlic, chopped

2 teaspoons red chilli powder

Salt to taste

1/2 teaspoon black pepper powder

FOR THE RED HOT TOMATO SAUCE

1 kg. tomatoes

1 - 1/2 teaspoon ajwain

1 bay leaf

1 tablespoon oil

2 onions, finely chopped

3 cloves garlic, finely chopped

6 hot Kashmiri chillies, roast, powder

1 teaspoon maize flour

1/2 cup tomato ketchup

3 tablespoons sugar

1/2 cup cheese, grated

Salt to taste

1/4 teaspoon oregano

1/2 teaspoon chilli sauce

FOR THE COVERING

1 - 1/2 cups flour

1 - 1/2 cups maize flour

2 tablespoons oil

3/4 cup milk

Salt to taste

METHOD

FOR THE BEAN ROLLS

Soak kidney beans overnight. Heat oil in pressure cooker pan. Saute onions till transparent. Mix in tomatoes, garlic, red chilli powder, salt and pepper. Add beans and enough water. Cover and cook. Open lid and cook further till three-fourths of the water has evaporated. Cool and grind them in a mixer. Remove in the same pan and then warm kidney bean paste till dry and leaves the sides of the vessel. Remove from heat and cool. Shape into small oval rolls — 1" long and 1/2" thick.

FOR THE RED HOT TOMATO SAUCE

(1) Blend tomatoes in a liquidizer. Add bay leaf and ajwain. Put on the gas to boil for 15 minutes. Remove from heat.

(2) Heat oil in a vessel and saute finely chopped onion, garlic and Kashmiri chillies. Fry for a few minutes and add maize flour. Roast for half a minute. Add tomato ketchup, sugar, grated cheese, salt, oregano and chilli sauce. Boil everything together for a few minutes.

FOR THE COVERING

(1) Combine all the ingredients together. Make a thin batter using water. Keep aside for 10 minutes.

(2) Prepare rectangle pancakes on an iron griddle with oil. Take out on a wooden board. Cut strips long and broad enough to cover rolls. Secure each roll with a toothpick.

TO ASSEMBLE KIDNEY BEAN ROLLS

Take half of the hot tomato sauce in a serving plate. Arrange all kidney bean rolls with toothpick in rows. Pour remaining sauce over them.

ITALIAN DISHES

Italian cuisine is remarkably well suited to the needs, tempo and tastes of present day city life. It has great simplicity, considerable originality and is flexible enough to adapt to various tastes. The staple food of the Italians is rich with numerous varieties of pastas. Their housewives use a lot of fresh vegetables and fruits along with herbs, cheese, olives and olive oil.

Pasta is a common man's food. It is cheap, filling and quick to cook. It can easily combine with more expensive ingredients to produce an exotic dish. Pastas are made out of refined wheat flour. They are named according to their different sizes and shapes. **Macaroni** - has tubular shape, available in short pieces called elbow and also in long lengths. **Spaghetti** has solid tubular form, available in varied degrees of thickness. **Egg noodles** are the ribbon like pieces in varied widths. Now eggless, vegetarian noodles are also marketed. There are many other shapes like, **corrugated, alphabets, shells, stars** etc. Some pastas are made with eggs and green pastas with spinach. Some of the commercial egg pastas cook almost instantly while others take time to cook. Normally, pastas are never made at home, they are bought readymade and cooked further into various dishes.

ITALIAN SOUP (6 SERVINGS)

It is a clear vegetable soup served with a special dressing.

INGREDIENTS

100 grams cauliflower

1 onion

1 carrot

1/2 cup green peas

2 potatoes

1/2 cup small alphabet shaped macaroni

1/3 cup tomato ketchup

Salt to taste

FOR THE ITALIAN DRESSING

2 teaspoons mustard powder

2 teaspoons olive oil or refined oil

2 teaspoons vinegar

2 teaspoons cream

1 teaspoon salt

1/4 teaspoon pepper

METHOD

(1) Cut all the vegetables into small cubes. Boil in four cups of water, with little salt. Cook the vegetables and drain. Keep the stock.

(2) Mash quarter cup of these vegetables and mix with the stock. Boil the stock. Add one-third cup of tomato ketchup and macaroni. Bring to a boil.

FOR THE ITALIAN DRESSING

Mix mustard powder and olive oil in a dish. Add vinegar. Beat well. Then add cream, salt and pepper. Serve with soup. Add quarter teaspoon of the above dressing in one cup of Italian Soup.

TOMATO VERMICELLI SOUP (6 SERVINGS)

Simple and delicious soup with tender vermicelli.

INGREDIENTS

2 tablespoons butter

1/2 cup vermicelli

1/4 cup onions, grated

1 tablespoon parsley or coriander leaves, chopped

1 cup tomato juice

5 cups hot water

6 tablespoons cheese, grated

Dash of oregano (optional)

Salt and pepper to taste

Tabasco sauce to taste

METHOD

(1) Heat one tablespoon of butter and saute the vermicelli till light pink in colour. Remove on a plate.

(2) Heat one tablespoon butter and saute grated onions for two minutes. Add chopped coriander leaves and saute for another one minute. Add tomato juice and give a boil. Add hot water, half of the cheese, vermicelli, oregano, salt and pepper to taste. Simmer for 10 -15 minutes.

(3) Serve hot with cheese sprinkled on top and Tabasco sauce as required.

MACARONI RISSOTO (6 SERVINGS)

A moist rice with white sauce. It is covered with macaroni and tasty tomato-cheese sauce before baking.

INGREDIENTS

3/4 cup uncooked rice

3/4 cup thin white sauce (1 - 1/2 table-spoons butter, 3/4 tablespoon flour, 3/4 cup milk)

2 tablespoons oil

1/4 cup onions, chopped

4 cloves garlic, chopped

1/2 cup tomato ketchup

1/2 teaspoon chilli sauce

1/2 cup water

Salt, pepper, sugar to taste

2 - 1/2 tablespoons cheese, grated

Few curry leaves

1/2 cup macaroni

METHOD

(1) Cook rice in little salt water and cool. Mix with white sauce.

(2) Take oil in a pan and heat. Add chopped onions and garlic. Saute till slightly brown. Add tomato ketchup, chilli sauce, water, salt, pepper, sugar, cheese and curry leaves. Mix well. Boil for five minutes and remove.

(3) Cook macaroni in salt water. When cooked, drain and let it cool.

(4) Arrange rice in a greased dish. Put macaroni over it. Spread sauce on the top and bake for 20 minutes at 200°C (moderate).

TOMATO GINOCCHI (6 - 8 SERVINGS)

An excellent baked dish for a party. Creamy paneer spinach balls, covered with tomato sauce.

INGREDIENTS

FOR THE BALLS

1 cup milk

2 tablespoons butter

1/2 cup flour

1 bunch spinach, finely chopped

Pinch of soda bicarb

Paneer out of 1/2 litre milk

salt and pepper to taste

FOR THE SAUCE

1 kg. tomato

1 small carrot

1 small beetroot

2 tablespoons butter

1 big onion, ground

6 cloves garlic, ground

METHOD

FOR THE BALLS

(1) Boil milk and butter together. Add flour and stir properly for two minutes. Remove in a shallow plate.

(2) Take spinach in a pan and cook till soft. Add a pinch of salt and soda while cooking. Cook till dry. Add to the flour mixture.

(3) Now add paneer, salt and pepper to taste. Mix everything very well and make lemon sized balls.

(4) Boil water in a deep vessel. Add few balls at a time and boil for two to three minutes. Drain in a colander.

FOR THE SAUCE

(1) Cut tomatoes, carrot and beetroot into pieces and pressure cook them. Make puree.

(2) Melt butter fry the onion and garlic paste. Add the vegetable puree and seasoning. Boil till saucy consistency.

Salt, pepper and sugar to taste

1 tablespoon oregano seeds

FOR THE WHITE SAUCE

2 tablespoons butter

1 -1/2 tablespoons flour

1 - 1/2 cups milk

Salt and pepper to taste

1/2 cup cheese, grated

(3) Prepare white sauce with butter, flour and milk. Add salt and pepper to taste.
(4) Arrange half of the tomato sauce in a greased baking dish. Arrange spinach-paneer balls. Cover with remaining sauce. Top with white sauce and grated cheese. Bake at 200°C for half an hour.

MACARONI AND CORN-ROMAN STYLE (6 - 8 SERVINGS)

A simple but tasty dish with a combination of macaroni, vegetables and corn.

INGREDIENTS

1/3 cup salad oil or refined oil

2 cups macaroni, uncooked

1/2 cup onions, minced

1/2 cup capsicums, minced

4 cloves garlic, minced

3 cups tomato juice

1 teaspoon salt

1/2 teaspoon pepper

1 tablespoon sugar

2 tablespoons Worcestershire sauce

1 cup corn, boiled

1/2 cup cheese, grated

METHOD

Heat oil in a skillet and saute the uncooked macaroni, minced onions, capsicums and garlic for 10 minutes or until macaroni turns yellow. Stir in tomato juice, salt, pepper, sugar and Worcestershire sauce. Bring to a boil over high heat. Turn heat to low and cook further for 20 minutes. Add corns and mix well. Sprinkle cheese all over. Cover with a lid and cook on slow heat till cheese melts. Serve hot.

VERMICELLI BOXES (MAKES 10 - 12 PIECES)

An excellent snack for a tea party.

INGREDIENTS

FOR THE BOXES

1 - 1/2 cups flour

1/2 cup soft margarine

Ice cold water to mix

1/2 teaspoon salt

FOR THE FILLING

4 tablespoons oil

1 cup vermicelli

METHOD

FOR THE BOXES

(1) Sift flour with salt.
(2) Divide margarine into four parts. Put one part into the flour and mix well with finger tips till it resembles breadcrumbs. Make a dough with ice cold water.
(3) On a floured board roll out this dough into an oblong. Cut quarter of margarine into small bits. Spread over two-thirds of the pastry, half inch away from the edges. Fold pastry into three, seal

Salt to taste

Juice of 1 small lemon

1/4 teaspoon turmeric

1 teaspoon green chilli ginger paste

Little sugar

1/2 cup coriander leaves, chopped

edges, pressing lightly. Repeat process till all the margarine portions are used. Roll well and chill for 40 - 45 minutes.

FOR THE FILLING

(1)   Heat oil in a vessel. Add crushed vermicelli. Saute for a few minutes.
(2)   Add all the spices. Sprinkle half cup of water.
(3)   Mix well. Cook till water gets absorbed. Transfer onto a plate and cool. Mix in the chopped coriander leaves.

TO MAKE THE BOXES

Roll out the chilled pastry dough into an oblong shape of 1/4 inch thick. Cut into 10 pieces big enough to cover shallow pastry tins. Keep them in fridge. Roll the remaining dough thinly and cut six pieces to fit the pastry tins. Put filling in the centre of each tin. Apply water on edges. Cover them with thick pieces. Press edges and remove extra dough from the side. Use this dough to make thin layers for remaining tins. Apply little milk on the top for glaze. Bake in a hot oven (250°C) for 20 minutes. Then reduce temperature to 150°C and bake further for 20 minutes or till they become crispy.

BAKED NOODLES TRIO (6 SERVINGS)

A very colourful baked dish with a perfect blend of three different types of sauces.

INGREDIENTS

2 packets noodles

1/2 cup cheese, grated

FOR THE GREEN LAYER

1 bunch spinach, boiled, ground to a paste

2 green chillies, finely chopped

1 teaspoon cummin seeds

Salt to taste

1 tablespoon margarine

FOR THE WHITE LAYER

1 tablespoon margarine

1 - 1/2 tablespoons flour

1 cup milk

Salt and pepper to taste

FOR THE RED LAYER

1 onion, chopped

3 cloves garlic, chopped

1 tablespoon margarine

1 - 1/2 cups tomato puree

Salt, pepper and sugar to taste

1/4 teaspoon garam masala (see Pg. 287)

METHOD

(1) Boil the noodles in a lot of water with one tablespoon of salt. When soft, drain and keep aside.

(2) Fry the spinach paste in one tablespoon of margarine. Add half cup water. boil for a few minutes.

(3) Make a white sauce with margarine, flour and milk. Season with salt and pepper.

(4) Fry onions and garlic in one tablespoon of margarine. When light brown, add tomato puree and masalas. Boil for five minutes.

(5) Now divide noodles into three different parts. Mix each part with three different hot sauces. Take a greased baking tray. First spread spinach sauce, then white sauce layer and on the top the red tomato layer. Sprinkle grated cheese evenly. Bake in a preheated oven 200ºC for 25 minutes. Serve hot.

BAKED MACARONI AND CHEESE (6 SERVINGS)

A most delectable dish enjoyed by all.

INGREDIENTS

2 cups cut macaroni

2 tablespoons margarine

1 onion, minced

1 tablespoon flour

2 cups milk

1/2 cup cheese, grated

1 cup green peas, boiled

Salt to taste

1/4 teaspoon dry mustard powder

3/4 teaspoon pepper

4 teaspoons butter

3/4 cup breadcrumbs

3 slices toasts

2 tomatoes, sliced

METHOD

(1) In a large vessel boil macaroni till tender with one tablespoon of salt. Preheat oven to 250°C. Grease a casserole.

(2) Meanwhile melt margarine. Add the minced onion, flour and slowly stir in milk. Cook until smooth and hot, stirring often.

(3) To it add the grated cheese, stir till it melts. Add one cup boiled green peas, salt to taste, mustard powder and pepper.

(4) When macaroni is tender, drain into a colander and transfer into the greased casserole. Pour cheese sauce over it, tossing lightly with fork so that the macaroni is coated with sauce.

(5) Toss in breadcrumbs with four teaspoons of melted butter. Sprinkle over cheese sauce. Cut triangles out of toasts and arrange all round the casserole. Cut slices of tomatoes and arrange on the top.

(6) Bake uncovered for 20 minutes.

Note :

If your oven gets too much heat from the top, then arrange toast triangles after the dish is half baked. Otherwise they will turn too dark.

SPAGHETTI CROQUETTES (MAKES 20 PIECES)

A very convenient recipe for a large party. Croquettes are crisp outside and soft inside with a mixture of spaghetti and vegetables.

INGREDIENTS

1/2 cup poha (beaten rice,) thick variety

1 cup vermicelli, crushed

1/2 cup spaghetti, boiled

1/2 cup French beans, chopped

1/2 cup carrots, chopped

1/2 cup capsicums, chopped

1/2 cup onions, chopped

5 - 6 green chillies, chopped

Salt and sugar to taste

1/4 teaspoon citric acid

3 - 1/2 tablespoons flour

4 tablespoons butter

2 cups milk

METHOD

(1) Wash the poha and allow water to drain out.

(2) Boil French beans and carrots in salt water. Drain off water.

(3) Melt butter and fry the onions, capsicums and green chillies. When they are soft, add flour. Stir for a minute and add milk. Stir continuously till sauce is thick. Remove from gas and transfer the sauce to a thali. Cool.

(4) Now mix the boiled spaghetti, French beans, carrots and the drained poha to the prepared sauce. Also add citric acid, salt and sugar.

(5) Make oval shaped croquettes. Roll them in crushed vermicelli. Deep fry till golden in colour. Serve hot.

RAVIOLI (6 - 8 SERVINGS)

It is one of the most popular Italian dishes. Tiny little spinach stuffed packets are covered with a sauce and baked before serving.

INGREDIENTS

FOR THE STUFFING

2 bunches spinach, chopped, boiled and drained (measure 3/4 cup)

2 tablespoons butter

3 tablespoons cheese, grated

Salt to taste

FOR THE RAVIOLI DOUGH

1 - 3/4 cups flour

2 tablespoons ghee

1/2 teaspoon salt

Water to make a soft dough

FOR THE TOMATO SAUCE

1 tablespoon ghee

1 small onion, chopped

5 cloves garlic, chopped

1 carrot, grated

1 apple, grated

Salt, sugar to taste

1/2 teaspoon nutmeg and mace powder

1 pint tomato puree

2 tablespoons corn flour

1 cup cheese, grated

2 - 3 capsicums, chopped

METHOD

FOR THE STUFFING

Combine all the given ingredients well and keep aside.

FOR THE RAVIOLI

(1) Combine all the given ingredients for the dough. Knead well and leave aside for half an hour. Divide into 12 equal sized balls.

(2) Roll them thin. Cut with a zigzag cutter into 2 inches x 2 inches square pieces. Put half teaspoon of stuffing in the centre of a square. On the sides, apply thick paste of flour and water. Cover with another square and bind the edges properly. Repeat with the rest of the square pieces. Collect them in a dish or thali and cover. When all are ready, boil water in a big vessel. Put these pieces in the water and cook for five to seven minutes till they are soft. Drain and cool.

FOR THE TOMATO SAUCE

Melt ghee in a vessel. Saute the onions, garlic and grated carrot for a few minutes. Add grated apple and saute. Add seasonings and tomato puree. Bring to a boil. Mix dissolved corn flour to make the sauce a little thick. Pour over ravioli. Sprinkle cheese and capsicum pieces. Bake at 200°C till done.

MILANESE BAKED SPAGHETTI (6 - 8 SERVINGS)

A simple baked dish with unique flavour of spices like mace, white pepper, etc.

INGREDIENTS

FOR THE SPAGHETTI

1 cup spaghetti, broken into pieces

1 pint Italian sauce

Salt and pepper to taste

90 grams (3 ozs.) cheese, grated

1 cup potato icing

FOR THE ITALIAN SAUCE

1 small carrot

1/4 cup celery, finely chopped

1 small onion

1 pint milk

2 blades mace

12 white peppercorns

2 cloves

60 grams (1/4 cup) margarine

30 grams (1 oz.) flour

FOR THE POTATO ICING

2 potatoes, boiled, finely mashed

Salt and very fine pepper powder

1/4 cup milk

1 - 1/2 tablespoons butter

METHOD

FOR THE SPAGHETTI

(1)   Wash spaghetti and boil in salt water till tender. Drain and mix with Italian sauce, salt and pepper.

(2)   Stir over low heat until well mixed and quite hot.

(3)   Pour into a greased heat-proof dish. Grate cheese and sprinkle all over.

(4)   Decorate with potato icing. Bake at 250°C for 20 minutes or till light brown in colour.

FOR THE SAUCE

(1)   Clean the vegetables and chop them. In a pan, put the milk, mace, peppercorns, cloves and vegetables.

(2)   Keep on a low flame for atleast 15 minutes.

(3)   Melt margarine in a pan. Add flour, stir till it bubbles, then add scalded milk with vegetables. Stir till thick. Season to taste.

FOR THE POTATO ICING

Melt butter, add the mashed potatoes. Mix in the milk, salt and pepper. Stir till milk evaporates. Remove from the heat and cool. Fill in the piping bag. Decorate with a star nozzle.

1.   Spaghetti croquettes   p. 160
2.   Stuffed braided bun   p. 164
3.   Tomato vermicelli soup   p. 155
4.   Baked noodle trio   p. 159
5.   Pineapple and cheese tower   p. 165

STUFFED BRAIDED BUN (6 - 8 SERVINGS)

A bread with a difference. Bread dough is shaped like a braided bun and stuffed with a sweet mixture of apple and currants.

INGREDIENTS

FOR THE FILLING

1 large apple

2 tablespoons raisins

1 tablespoon currants, seeded

1/2 teaspoon cinnamon

1 tablespoon butter

4 tablespoons brown sugar

FOR THE BREAD

2 cups flour

1 - 1/2 teaspoons fresh yeast

1 teaspoon sugar

1/2 teaspoon salt

1 tablespoon margarine or butter

1/2 cup lukewarm water

METHOD

(1) Peel and core apples. Chop into tiny pieces. Melt the butter and put in the apple pieces, raisins, black currants and brown sugar. Cook on slow heat till apples are soft and the water has evaporated. Remove from the fire and cool. Leave aside.

(2) Melt sugar and salt in lukewarm water. Mix yeast directly in the flour and make a soft dough with the prepared water. Knead the dough for five minutes with margarine or butter. Keep this dough in an oiled vessel, covered with a wet cloth for 1 - 1/2 hours till it rises to double its volume.

(3) Reknead dough and make a ball. Put it on a floured surface and roll out into 12 inches by 9 inches rectangle. Arrange sweet apple filling in the centre lengthwise. Now put slant cuts on the two opposite longer sides with a knife at a distance of one inch.

(4) Pick up each strip and cover over the filling in such a way that they cross each other in the centre making a braided pattern. Refer to the given diagram.

(5) Preheat oven to 250°C. Keep this prepared bun on a greased baking tray, covered with a wet cloth. Leave aside to rise. Bake the bun for 25 minutes till golden brown on top. Remove from the oven and cool on a rack. Brush with melted ghee on top.

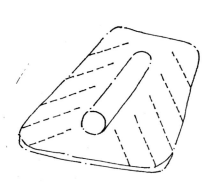 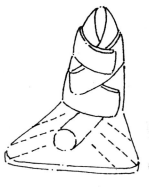 

MUSSACCA (6 SERVINGS)

A baked dish made with layers of eggplants, tomato sauce and cheese.

INGREDIENTS

12 thick slices big brinjals or eggplants (A thick seedless variety available in cold season)

12 slices potatoes

1 cup flour

Oil for deep frying

2 tablespoons butter

1 big onion, chopped

6 - 8 cloves garlic, chopped

1 kg. tomatoes, extract juice

Salt, sugar and pepper to taste

1 tablespoon oregano

1 - 1/2 tablespoons corn flour

1 cup white sauce (made out of 1-1/2 tablespoons butter, 1-1/2 tablespoons flour, 1 cup milk)

Cheese, grated as desired

1 - 2 capsicums, cut into rings

METHOD

(1) Prepare a thin paste of flour, salt and water. Dip slices of brinjals and potatoes in it and deep fry in oil. Keep aside.

(2) Heat butter, saute onions and garlic till transparent and soft. And tomato juice, sugar, oregano and pepper to taste. Allow it to boil for 10 minutes. Dissolve corn flour in little cold water and add to the boiling mixture. Stir for a few minutes. Remove from the gas.

(3) Grease a baking dish. Pour in one-third of the tomato sauce. Arrange half of the fried brinjal and potato pieces. Again pour one-third of the tomato sauce and sprinkle cheese. Arrange the second layer of brinjals and potatoes. Cover with remaining of tomato sauce. Again cover with white sauce, sprinkle grated cheese and arrange capsicum rings on top.

(4) Heat oven to 250°C and bake for 25 to 30 minutes. Serve hot.

PINEAPPLE AND CHEESE TOWER (6 - 8 SERVINGS)

This is an excellent combination - the sweetness of pineapple with a tangy taste of cheese. It is shaped into a decorative tower to be served at the end of a dinner party or as salad on a buffet table.

INGREDIENTS

3 tablespoons gelatine

1/2 cup sugar

1 big can pineapple tidbits or slices (850 grams)

1 cup syrup from pineapple can

3 tablespoons lemon juice

200 grams fresh cream

1/2 cup walnuts, chopped

1 cup cheese, grated

Lettuce leaves to decorate and glazed cherries

METHOD

(1) Soak gelatine and sugar in pineapple syrup.

(2) Cut slices into small pieces, keeping two slices aside for decoration.

(3) Warm gelatine mixture and melt it. Add lemon juice and pineapple pieces. Keep this mixture in fridge. When semi-set, remove and mix in whipped fresh cream, walnuts and cheese.

(4) Pour this mixture in a tall jelly tin and set in fridge.

(5) Unmould on a serving plate and decorate with lettuce, walnuts, pineapple and cherry pieces.

BURMESE DISHES

Burmese vegetarian dishes have a unique way of preparation. There is extensive use of coconut in many dishes. Rice is their staple food, offering many interesting and tasty dishes. Their food is simple, less oily and very sumptuous.

KWESHWE (6 - 8 SERVINGS)

A typical Burmese 'bhel', where specially prepared curry, spaghetti, sauces, crisp wheat strips, wafers are served separately. This gives ample scope to guests to prepare their own concoctions.

INGREDIENTS

FOR THE KWESHWE

500 grams cauliflower, cut into small pieces

100 grams carrots, cut into small pieces

100 grams French beans, cut into small pieces

3 potatoes, cut into small pieces

3 onions, cut into small pieces

250 grams green peas

1/2 cup ghee

Salt to taste

A pinch soda bicarb

1 tablespoon chilli ginger paste

7 - 8 cloves garlic, crushed

3 - 4 tomatoes, chopped into small pieces

1/2 coconut, grated, extract milk (1 - 1/2 cups)

1 tablespoon corn flour, dissolved in 1/4 cup cold water

200 grams spaghetti

Wheat strips

Mint liquid

100 grams potato straws

Chilli sauce to taste

Soya sauce to taste

FOR THE MINT LIQUID

3 - 4 sprigs mint, remove leaves

1 - 2 green chillies

1/4 teaspoon salt

2 tablespoons water

FOR THE WHEAT STRIPS

1 - 1/2 cups wheat flour

2 tablespoons oil

1/2 teaspoon salt

Ghee for frying

METHOD

FOR THE MINT LIQUID

Combine mint leaves, chillies and salt in a blender and grind to a smooth paste. Add water to the paste to form a liquid consistency.

FOR THE WHEAT STRIPS

Combine all the given ingredients and make a dough with water (like puri). Divide into three to four pieces. Roll very thin and then cut into long strips. Deep fry in ghee on medium heat till crisp. Fry them light brown and drain on an absorbent paper. Crush into smaller pieces while serving.

FOR THE CURRY

(1) Heat ghee in a big vessel. When hot, add cauliflower, carrots, onions, potatoes, French beans and green peas. Add salt to taste and a pinch of soda bicarb. Saute till vegetables become soft. Add little water and cook. Stir occasionally. After five minutes, add green chilli ginger paste, garlic and tomatoes. Cook further. When almost cooked, add coconut milk. Boil, add dissolved corn flour. Stir till thick. Remove from heat. Serve hot.

(2) Cut spaghetti into small pieces. boil in salt water till cooked. Drain and serve slightly hot.

TO SERVE

First take spaghetti in a plate. Pour curry over it. Sprinkle wheat strips and potato straws. On top add soya sauce, chilli sauce and mint liquid to taste.

RICE IN COCONUT SHELL (6 SERVINGS)

A unique way of cooking rice in coconut shells, which imparts unusual flavour to the rice.

INGREDIENTS

2 small fresh coconuts, with thin cream (malai)

1 - 1/2 cups rice

1 cup sweet lime juice

3 green chillies, chopped

1/4 cup coriander leaves

1/4 cup Worcestershire sauce

Salt to taste

12 small potatoes, boiled, fried

METHOD

(1) Cut off the tops of the coconuts and pour out the water. Do not scrape the creamy coconut from inside. Cut a slice from the bottom of the coconuts to enable them to stand upright.

(2) Wash rice and soak for 10 minutes. Cook in sweet lime juice and sufficient water. When almost cooked, remove from heat and mix in chillies, coriander leaves, Worcestershire sauce, salt and fried potatoes. Fill this lightly into coconut shells. **Do not pack coconuts too tightly.** Leave space for rice to expand. Cover with coconut tops and bake in a moderately heated oven (200ºC) till rice is properly done, in about half an hour. Serve hot in coconut shells. One can wrap coconuts in aluminium foil, to make them more presentable.

VEGETABLE DUMPLINGS (MAKES 18 PIECES)

Shallow fried vegetable dumplings are served with thin soya and vinegar sauce.

INGREDIENTS

FOR THE DUMPLINGS

1/2 cup potatoes, grated

1/4 cup onions, grated

1/2 cup carrots, grated

4 - 5 cloves garlic, minced

3 - 4 green chillies, finely chopped

3/4 cup flour

1/2 teaspoon baking powder

Salt to taste

Oil for shallow frying

Soya-vinegar sauce

FOR THE SOYA-VINEGAR SAUCE

5 tablespoons brown vinegar

5 tablespoons soya sauce

2 tablespoons sugar

METHOD

FOR THE DUMPLINGS

(1) Combine the grated potatoes, onions, carrots, garlic, chillies, flour, baking powder and salt in a bowl. Mix enough water to make a thick batter.

(2) Heat a non-stick or a heavy iron skillet. Shallow fry flat dumplings out of the above prepared batter about 1 - 1/2 inches diametre and 1/2 inch thick rounds. Fry till golden brown on both sides. Serve hot with soya-vinegar sauce.

FOR THE SOYA VINEGAR SAUCE

Combine all the above ingredients and stir well till sugar dissolves.

1.   Burmese banana curry   p. 170
2.   Sesame and turnip salad with tomato cucumber flower   p. 172
3.   Vegetable dumplings with soya vinegar sauce   p. 168
4.   Rice in coconut shell   p. 168

YELLOW RICE WITH SHREDDED PANCAKES (6 SERVINGS)

A coconut flavoured pullao accompanied with chickpea pancakes.

INGREDIENTS

1 - 1/2 cups rice

2 cups coconut milk

1/2 teaspoon turmeric powder

Salt to taste

3 - 4 cardamoms

FOR PANCAKES

1 cup chickpea flour

1/4 cup onions, grated

2 - 3 green chillies, finely chopped

2 tablespoons coriander leaves

2 tablespoons coconut, grated

Salt to taste

A pinch turmeric powder

METHOD

(1) Wash rice and soak for 10 minutes.

(2) Take coconut milk in a cooker pan and bring to a boil. To it, add the rice, turmeric powder, salt and cardamoms. Simmer till the milk evaporates. Now put in the pressure cooker with more water just enough to cook rice. Cook till done. Take out in a serving plate and decorate with shredded pancake pieces.

(3) To prepare pancakes: Combine all the ingredients in a vessel and add enough water to make a pancake batter. Shallow fry the pancakes on a heavy iron skillet or a non-stick pan till light brown in colour. Remove onto a board and shred them into long thin strips.

BURMESE BANANA CURRY (6 SERVINGS)

A slightly sweet curry which can be served with yellow rice and shredded pancakes.

INGREDIENTS

12 pieces raw bananas - 2" long and split in 2 pieces

1/2 teaspoon turmeric powder

Salt to taste

Oil for shallow frying

1 tablespoon oil

1/4 teaspoon fenugreek

1 - 2 pieces cinnamon

2 - 3 cloves

1/2 cup onions, chopped

3 - 4 green chillies, chopped fine

1/2 inch ginger, finely chopped

3 - 4 curry leaves

2 cups coconut milk

1 medium sized potato, boiled, mashed

1/4 cup green peas, boiled

METHOD

(1) Rub salt and turmeric to banana pieces and shallow fry them till cooked.

(2) Heat one tablespoon of oil. Add fenugreek, cinnamon and cloves. When hot, add onions, chillies, ginger and curry leaves. Fry till light brown in colour. Add turmeric powder and coconut milk. Bring to a boil.

(3) Mix in mashed potatoes, green peas and fried banana pieces. Simmer for 10 minutes and serve hot.

PINEAPPLE COCONUT DELIGHT (6 SERVINGS)

A light and satisfying pudding after a heavy meal.

INGREDIENTS

1 - 2/3 cups canned pineapple, crushed
1 cup pineapple syrup from the can
2 tablespoons gelatine
1/4 teaspoon vanilla essence
1/2 cup milk powder
1/2 cup ice water
2 tablespoons lemon juice
1/4 cup sugar
1/2 cup coconut, shredded

METHOD

(1)   Drain syrup from pineapple and add water to make one cup liquid.
(2)   Sprinkle gelatine in syrup to soften.
(3)   Place over low heat and stir until gelatine dissolves.
(4)   Remove from heat and add pineapple and vanilla essence. Chill to unbeaten eggwhite consistency.
(5)   Mix (with a beater) the milk powder with ice water in a bowl.
(6)   Beat until it becomes thick. Add lemon juice.
(7)   Beat further and add sugar.
(8)   Fold gelatine mixture and coconut into the whipped milk.
(9)   Chill pineapple coconut delight till firm.
(10) Decorate with pineapple slices.

BEAN SPROUTS IN WHITE RICE (6 SERVINGS)

Rice with mildly spiced bean sprouts. Serve with pungent sesame and turnip salad.

INGREDIENTS

1 - 1/2 cups rice
Salt to taste
1 tablespoon oil
1 cup bean sprouts - Chinese style
3 - 4 spring onions, chopped with all tender green leaves
2 - 3 cloves garlic, chopped
2 tablespoons soya sauce
2 teaspoons sesame seeds

METHOD

(1)   Wash rice and soak for 10 minutes. Add salt to taste and cook till almost done.
(2)   Heat oil, add bean sprouts, spring onions and garlic, for a few minutes on high flame. Add soya sauce, sesame seeds and salt to taste. Mix well.
(3)   Mix roughly the bean sprout mixture. Cover and cook till water is totally absorbed. Serve hot.

Note :
You can also make mushrooms in white rice by replacing bean sprouts with the same quantity of chopped mushrooms.

SESAME AND TURNIP SALAD (6 SERVINGS)

Pungent but crisp salad goes well with all types of Burmese dishes.

INGREDIENTS

2 fresh young turnips

Salt to taste

1 medium onion, thinly sliced

1 tablespoon soya sauce

1 tablespoon vinegar

1 tablespoon sugar

2 tablespoons sesame oil

1 tablespoon sesame seeds

Salad leaves to decorate

METHOD

(1) Either thinly slice turnips or cut them into thin long pieces.

(2) Rub salt little more than the normal taste. Keep for 10 minutes.

(3) Wash turnips in cold water.

(4) Now mix together the onions, soya sauce, vinegar and sugar.

(5) Heat oil. Add sesame seeds. When they stop spluttering, pour over the salad.

(6) Garnish with salad leaves and tomato-cucumber flower.

FOR THE SIMPLE TOMATO CUCUMBER FLOWER

(1) Select a firm red tomato with a flat base. It should not wobble. Cut 6 equal petals with a sharp knife by cutting only thick skin of the tomato.

(2) Open each petal carefully by separating it from the centre pulp.

(3) Arrange cucumber slices between the petals and the pulp ball. Slices should be smaller than the height of the tomato petals. Cucumber slices will keep the flower open and will also add colour to the flower.

GREEK DISHES

Greek cuisine is simple and not unduly rich. Great care is taken in its preparation in order to make it distinctive and delicious. Greek markets are well stocked with fruits, vegetables and nuts. Olive oil is extensively used in many dishes. There is a good balance of rice dishes and breads in daily menu and their sweets are often sticky and syrupy. They are generally fond of sweets and serve them at almost every meal.

MIXED VEGETABLES AND BARELY SOUP (8 - 10 SERVINGS)

Nutritious and satisfying soup unusually flavoured with nutmeg powder.

INGREDIENTS

1/4 cup barley, uncooked

2 tablespoons butter

2 cups turnip, cut into pieces

1/4 cup celery, chopped

1 cup carrots, cut into pieces

1/2 cup onions, cut into pieces

1/2 cup tomatoes, cut into pieces

Salt, pepper to taste

A pinch nutmeg powder

1 tablespoon corn flour

1 cup milk

METHOD

(1) Wash and soak barley for 15 minutes. Pressure cook it.

(2) Heat butter and add all the vegetables. Saute them for a few minutes. Add hot water enough to cover them. Cover and simmer till cooked, or pressure cook them with little less water. Put the mixture in a blender and blend to a puree.

(3) Mix together the vegetable puree and cooked barley with its water, salt, pepper to taste and nutmeg powder. heat and bring to a boil. Then mix in corn flour dissolved in milk. Stir for a few minutes. Put enough water to get the right consistency of the soup. Give a boil and serve hot with 'Greek rolls'.

LAYERED CHEESE AND SPINACH BAKE (6 SERVINGS)

A sumptuous baked dish with noodles and creamy spinach sauce. Can be served as a main dish.

INGREDIENTS

200 grams noodles, boiled

2 cups spinach, chopped

3 tablespoons butter

2 tablespoons flour

2 cups milk

1/4 teaspoon cinnamon, cloves, powdered

1/2 cup cheese, grated

Salt and pepper to taste.

METHOD

(1) Take spinach in a vessel with little water and cook it. Cool and blend to a fine paste.

(2) Heat butter, add flour, salt and pepper to taste. Stir for a minute. Add milk and stir till the sauce thickens. Mix in spinach puree, cinnamon and clove powder. Remove from gas.

(3) Take a baking dish and grease it with butter. Arrange half of the noodles, sauce and cheese.

(4) Bake at 250°C for 20 - 25 minutes until cheese is bubbly. Serve hot.

1. Greek rolls   p. 176
2. Bakhlava   p. 178
3. Ntomates me rizi   p. 176
4. Dolmas   p. 177

NTOMATES ME RIZI (TOMATO STUFFED WITH RICE) (6 SERVINGS)

Attractive baked tomatoes stuffed with rice. Can be served as a complete one dish meal.

INGREDIENTS

12 medium sized firm tomatoes

Salt, pepper and sugar to taste

2 tablespoons olive oil

1 medium onion, chopped

1/4 cup rice, uncooked

1/2 cup haricot beans, cooked

1/2 cup cheese, grated

1 tablespoon currants or chopped olives

METHOD

(1) Cut off the tops of tomatoes. Check whether they all can stand up right. Scoop them with a spoon and remove all pulp. Strain the juice to remove seeds and chop the remaining pulp. Sprinkle the inside with salt, pepper and sugar.

(2) Heat oil, add onions. Add washed and soaked rice, saute for a few more minutes. Add chopped tomatoes, salt to taste and enough hot water to cook rice. Cook till almost done. Mix in cooked haricot beans, pepper and half of the cheese. Also add currants or olives. Cook further till water is totally absorbed. Remove from gas and stuff this rice mixture in each prepared tomato. Top with the remaining cheese.

(3) Arrange the tomatoes in an ovenproof dish and bake at 200°C for half an hour. Serve hot or cold.

GREEK ROLLS (MAKES 8 ROLLS)

Stuffed Greek rolls give enough scope for variations. One can stuff them with any dry mixture.

INGREDIENTS

FOR THE DOUGH

2 cups flour

1 - 1/2 teaspoons fresh yeast

1/2 teaspoon salt

1/2 teaspoon sugar

1/2 tablespoon margarine or butter

FOR THE STUFFING

1/2 cup coriander leaves, chopped

1/4 cup coconut, grated

Salt to taste

1/4 teaspoon sugar

1/2 teaspoon chilli ginger paste

METHOD

(1) Sieve flour and mix in yeast.

(2) Melt salt and sugar in quarter cup of lukewarm water. Add to the flour.

(3) Make a soft dough. Knead with margarine. Put in a greased vessel. Cover with a wet cloth. Leave aside till double in size.

(4) Mix all the ingredients of stuffing and divide into eight parts.

(5) Knead the dough again for five minutes. Divide into eight balls. Flatten each ball. Put one portion of the stuffing in the centre of each ball. Cover up and make a round ball.

(6) Arrange in a greased baking tray. Cover with a wet cloth and allow them to rise for fifteen minutes.

(7) Bake at 250°C till slightly brown on top.

(8) Remove and cool on wire rack.

(9) Brush ghee on the top as glaze.

DOLMAS (6 SERVINGS)

Very unusual and attractive vegetable packets topped with cheese sauce.

INGREDIENTS

FOR THE DOLMAS

12 - 14 cabbage leaves (remove veins. If the leaf is very big, cut into 2)

4 big potatoes, grated

1 medium onion, chopped

1 tablespoon dill, (suwa bhaji) chopped

1/2 cup rice, washed

1/2 cup green peas

2 cloves garlic, chopped

Juice of 1/2 lemon

1/4 cup ghee

Salt and pepper to taste

FOR THE SAUCE

1 tablespoon margarine

1 tablespoon flour

1 - 1/2 cups milk

1/3 cup cheese

Salt and pepper to taste

2 tablespoons tomato ketchup

METHOD

FOR THE DOLMAS

(1) Boil water with one tablespoon of salt in a big vessel. Put prepared cabbage leaves. Let them boil till tender (for five minutes). Remove, drain, cool.

(2) Mix together the grated potatoes, onions, dill, washed rice, green peas, garlic, salt, pepper and lemon juice. Take this mixture (about 2 tablespoons) and put onto each cabbage leaf. Make a packet. Put them inverted in a deep pan. Pour leftover liquid on them.

(3) Pour melted ghee all round. Cover all the dolmas with water. Put a plate on the dolmas. Then cover the pan. Cook on medium fire till the entire liquid is absorbed (about 35 minutes).

FOR THE SAUCE

Melt margarine. Stir in flour. Gradually, pour in milk. Stir till it starts to thicken. Add grated cheese. Stir for five more minutes. Add salt and pepper. Remove hot dolmas on a serving plate. Pour sauce all over. Sprinkle tomato ketchup. Serve hot.

GREEN PEAS KEFTEPES (CROQUETTES) (MAKES 20 PIECES)

A quick and delectable snack for a tea party.

INGREDIENTS

2 cups small pieces bread without crusts

1 tablespoon oil

1/2 cup onions, chopped

5 - 6 cloves garlic, chopped

1 cup green peas, boiled, crushed

Salt and pepper to taste

1/4 cup coriander leaves or parsley, chopped

2 tablespoons vinegar

Oil for frying

METHOD

(1) Soak bread pieces in little water for five minutes. Squeeze out extra water and make into a pulp.

(2) Take one tablespoon of oil in a vessel and heat it. Add onions and garlic. Saute them till soft. Now mix in crushed peas, bread pulp, salt, pepper, parsley and vinegar. Mix well and then remove from gas. Cool it.

(3) Divide the mixture into 20 equal portions. Shape each portion into a croquette and deep fry in oil till golden brown or flatten them and shallow fry on a heavy iron skillet. Serve with tomato ketchup.

BAKHLAVA (6 - 8 SERVINGS)

Walnut stuffed crisp pastry pieces in sugar syrup.

INGREDIENTS

FOR THE PHYLLO PASTRY

2 cups flour

3/4 teaspoon baking powder

Water to make dough

FOR THE BAKHLAVA

12 phyllo pastry

1 - 1/4 cups walnuts, chopped

1/4 cup powdered sugar

1/2 teaspoon cinnamon powder

1/2 cup margarine, melted

FOR THE SYRUP

1/2 cup water

1 cup sugar

Few drops lemon juice

METHOD

FOR THE PHYLLO PASTRY

Mix the flour and baking powder together. Add enough water to make a firm dough. Knead as long as possible and put the dough aside for two hours. Knead and break off into 12 pieces. Roll these out into very thin pastry (use a thin rolling pin).

FOR THE BAKHALAVA

(1) Mix all the given ingredients well. Divide into six parts.

(2) Place two sheets of phyllo together. Heap walnut mixture on lengthwise edge and fold like a Swiss roll into a long roll. Gently push in this roll at each end to make it crinkle. Slice into two inches pieces. Repeat the process. Make six such rolls. Place the bakhlava pieces side by side in a greased baking tray. Pour melted shortening on top and bake till golden brown. (250°C little higher then moderate). Remove from the oven and cool.

FOR THE SYRUP

Heat sugar and water till sugar dissolves. Bring to boil, squeeze few drops of lemon juice. Remove from heat and pour over bakhlava. Cool and serve.

APPLE BASKETS (MAKES 10 PIECES)

Crisp baskets filled with juicy apple filling.

INGREDIENTS

FOR THE BASKETS

1/4 cup cheese, finely grated

3 tablespoons butter

2 tablespoons powdered sugar

1 cup flour

FOR THE APPLE FILLING

1 cup apple, cut into very small pieces

1/4 cup fresh breadcrumbs

1/4 cup walnuts, chopped

METHOD

FOR THE BASKETS

Blend together the butter, cheese and sugar. Beat till the mixture is light and fluffy. Mix in flour and make a soft dough. Take 10 patty pans. Divide dough into equal portions and press on sides of each pan. Fill with apple mixture and bake at 200°C for 35 to 40 minutes till apple pieces are done and the pastry is light pink in colour.

2 tablespoons seeded black currants or raisins

1/2 cup powdered sugar

1/4 teaspoon nutmeg powder

1 teaspoon lemon juice

1 tablespoon butter, melted

FOR THE APPLE FILLING

Mix all the ingredients given for the filling together and divide equally to fill in the prepared baskets.

BEETROOT PEONY FLOWER

(1)   Select a firm, big beetroot. Peel and trim it to 2 - 1/2 inches long and 1 - 1/2 inches round cylindrical shape. Cut off two side slices to make the two opposite sides flat.

(2)   Shape the upper curve edge throughout its length into small scallops or pointed lotus petals or rounded like rose petals as shown in the diagrams.

(3)   Now carve out petals, starting from top of one side of the petal, curving on the lower side and than cutting up on the opposite side. Each petal will come out like a cup with two petal shapes on both ends. Take out as many petals as possible. As you cut smaller petals, trim central portion from sides, so that it is thinner than the side end petals. Take out atleast 12 petals.

(4)   Take 1/2 inch broad and 1/ 2 inch thick slice from the beetroot. Cut wedges on the top surface to create a centre for the flower.

(5)   Take another small round piece of beetroot as a stopper. Insert in into a long thin stick.

(6)   Now starting with the largest petal, insert petals in the stick upto the stopper. Arrange petals in alternate positions to create peony flower. Complete flower by putting centre piece on top.

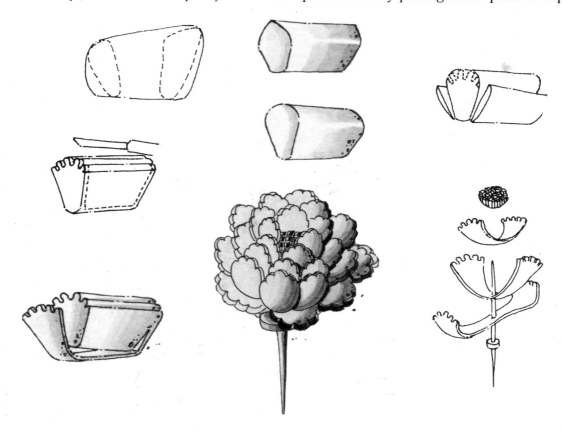

SRI LANKAN DISHES

Sri Lankan cuisine is full of surprises. Not only does it offer the fiery hot curries but gives you interesting combinations derived with Dutch and British influences, more so in non-vegetarian dishes.

In Sri Lanka, like in south India, rice is a staple food. Many varieties of curries are made with vegetables and fruits, which are served with plain or mildly spiced rise. Sri Lankans use a lot of coconut, hot chillies and spices in their food.

1. Papaya lamp   p. 187
2. Pineapple curry   p. 185
3. Idde appung   p. 182
4. Kalu dodol   p. 183
5. Yam and tomato salad with double petal tomato-cucumber flower   p. 182

IDDE APPUNG (STRING HOPPERS) (4 SERVINGS)

Many times string hoppers are served instead of bread or rice with spicy curries.

INGREDIENTS	METHOD
1 cup rice flour or flour	(1) If using flour, then wrap in a cloth and steam over boiling water. Open out flour, add salt and make a soft dough with hot water. In case of rice flour, add salt and hot water. Mix with a wooden ladle to make a soft dough.
1/2 cup hot water	(2) Put some of the mixture into a string hopper mould or sev press with fine holes.
Salt to taste	(3) Press in heaps into a wet cloth. Steam in an idli steamer for about five to seven minutes.
	(4) Serve them with hot curries.

YAM AND TOMATO SALAD (6 SERVINGS)

A salad with fresh curd, balances the hot food and climate of the island.

INGREDIENTS

1 cup yam pieces, cooked

1 tablespoon oil

1 teaspoon mustard seeds

2 green chillies, finely chopped

1/2 cup tomatoes, peeled, chopped

1 teaspoon sugar

Salt to taste

1 cup fresh curd, beaten

1 tablespoon coriander leaves, chopped

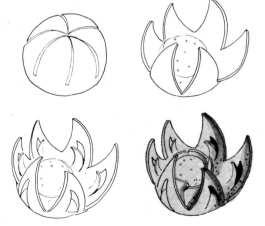

METHOD

FOR THE SALAD

(1) Steam a big piece of yam with its skin in a pressure cooker. Peel and cut into tiny pieces or roughly mash it.

(2) Heat oil, add mustard seeds. When they stop spluttering, add green chillies. Saute for half a minute, add tomato pieces, sugar, salt, yam pieces and beaten curd. Mix well and remove from the gas. Garnish with chopped coriander leaves and double petal tomato-cucumber flower.

FOR THE DOUBLE PETAL TOMATO-CUCUMBER FLOWER

(1) Select a firm red tomato with a flat base. It should not wobble. Cut six equal petals with a sharp knife by cutting only thick skin of the tomato.

(2) Open each petal carefully by separating it from the centre pulp. Cut out inner petals from each of the six petals. Push smaller petals inside and pull out the outer ones.

(3) Arrange cucumber slices between the petals and the pulp ball. Slices should be smaller than the height of the tomato petals. Cucumber slices will keep the flower open and will also add colour to the flower.

COCONUT RICE (6 - 8 SERVINGS)

Mildly flavoured coconut rice tastes good with many spicy curries.

INGREDIENTS	METHOD
1 - 1/2 cups good rice	Heat ghee. Saute onions and garlic till golden brown. Add cardamoms. Mix in washed rice and saute for five minutes. Add salt, turmeric and enough water to cook. When the rice is almost cooked, add lemon juice and sprinkle coconut. Cover and cook till done. Serve with dry curry.
1/4 cup ghee	
1 medium onion, chopped	
4 - 5 cloves garlic, chopped	
2 - 3 cardamoms	
Salt to taste	
1/2 teaspoon turmeric powder	
Few drops lemon juice	
1/2 cup fresh coconut, grated	

MINT CHUTNEY (MAKES 1/2 CUP)

This chutney can be served with snacks as well as with meals.

INGREDIENTS	METHOD
1 cup mint leaves	Combine all the given ingredients and grind to a paste in a wet grinder.
1/4 cup onions, chopped	**Note :**
2 - 3 green chillies	Omit lemon juice and replace it with half cup beaten fresh curd to make a loose consistency chutney.
2 tablespoons coconut, grated	
Salt to taste	
2 tablespoons lemon juice	

KALU DODOL (MAKES 15 - 20 PIECES)

A popular sweet dish - very nutritious and tasty

INGREDIENTS	METHOD
1 cup rice flour	(1) Take rice flour in a vessel. Add coconut milk gradually mixing all the time to avoid formation of lumps. Add the mashed jaggery, cardamom powder and a pinch of salt.
2 cups coconut milk	
1/2 cup jaggery	
1/2 teaspoon cardamom powder	(2) Stir continuously on medium gas, till mixture thickens and leaves the sides of the vessel. Mix a few drops of colour, mix well. Mix in cashewnut pieces. Remove in a greased shallow plate, cool and cut into diamond shaped pieces or mould into a shape and garnish with cashewnuts and glazed cherries.
Pinch of salt	
Few drops of cochineal colour	
1/2 cup cashewnuts, chopped	
Few glazed cherries	

CAULIFLOWER FRIKADELS (MAKES 15 - 20 PIECES)

A snacky dish which can be served with tea as well as at meal time.

INGREDIENTS

1/2 kg. cauliflower

1 onion, minced

5 cloves garlic, minced

Juice of 1 lemon

1/2 teaspoon chilli ginger paste

Few drops red colour

Curd, just enough to coat flower pieces or 1/2 cup (approx.)

1/2 cup coconut, grated

Salt to taste

1 - 1/2 cups gram flour

1/2 cup wheat flour

1/4 teaspoon soda bicarb

1/2 teaspoon chilli ginger paste for the flour

Oil for frying

METHOD

(1) Separate cauliflower into big pieces and boil for a few minutes till semi cooked. Drain. Now marinate these pieces in a mixture of minced onion, garlic, lemon juice, chilli ginger paste, red colour, curd, salt and grated coconut. Keep aside for two hours, turning often.

(2) Combine gram flour, wheat flour, salt, soda and chilli-ginger paste in a vessel and make a thick batter with water.

(3) Heat oil. Dip each cauliflower piece in the above batter. Deep fry till light brown. Serve hot.

DRY POTATO CURRY (6 - 8 SERVINGS)

Tiny ball like potatoes are nicely coated with a thick layer of spiced gravy. Serve with coconut rice.

INGREDIENTS

FOR THE GRINDING MASALA

2 tablespoons coriander seeds

2 tablespoons poppy seeds

2 small onions

1 inch ginger piece

1/2 dry coconut, grated

6 cashew nuts

6 almonds

2 green chillies

2 teaspoons red chilli powder

5 cloves garlic, flaked

1/2 teaspoon cummin seeds

1/4 teaspoon mustard seeds

METHOD

Heat ghee in a vessel. Fry the ground masala paste and curry leaves. When it emanates a good aroma squeeze in lemon juice and mix in the boiled potatoes. Fry for a few more minutes. Add three-fourths cup water. Simmer for 10 minutes. Serve with coconut rice.

1 teaspoon turmeric powder

1 tablespoon curry powder (see Pg. 287)

1/2 teaspoon powdered cinnamon and cloves

FOR THE CURRY

1/2 cup ghee

Few curry leaves

Juice of 1 big lemon

1/2 kg. small potatoes, boiled

Salt to taste

PINEAPPLE CURRY (6 - 8 SERVINGS)

A sweet and sour curry, tastes goods with mildly spiced pullao.

INGREDIENTS

2 cups canned pineapple or fresh pineapple, chopped

2 tablespoons oil

1 teaspoon cummin seeds

2 - 3 pieces cinnamon

3 - 4 cloves

Salt to taste

5 - 6 curry leaves

1/2 cup onions, thinly sliced

1/4 teaspoon turmeric powder

1 tablespoon lemon juice

FOR THE GRINDING MASALA

8 - 10 cashewnuts

2 tablespoons poppy seeds

3 - 4 green chillies

1/2 inch ginger

METHOD

(1)   If using fresh pineapple, then pressure cook the pineapple pieces with three tablespoons of sugar and one cup of water.

(2)   Heat oil, add cummin seeds, cinnamon, cloves, salt and curry leaves. Fry for a minute. Add the sliced onions and fry till golden brown. Add turmeric powder and the ground cashewnut paste. Fry till ghee separates. Add pineapple pieces, lemon juice and one and a half cups of water. Simmer curry for 10 minutes.

JACKFRUIT SAMBOL (6 - 8 SERVINGS)

Very tasty curry. It resembles and tastes like a mutton curry.

INGREDIENTS

FOR THE SAMBOL

1/2 kg. tender raw jackfruit pieces

1/4 cup oil

1 cup onions, chopped

Salt to taste

1 big tomato, peeled, chopped

1 tablespoon tamarind pulp

Coriander leaves to garnish

FOR THE GRINDING MASALA

8 - 10 cloves garlic

2 - 3 pieces cinnamon

5 - 6 black pepper seeds

2 - 3 cloves

2 - 3 cardamoms with seeds

2 - 3 green chillies

1 teaspoon red chilli powder

1/2 teaspoon turmeric powder

1/2 inch ginger piece

1/2 cup coconut, grated

METHOD

FOR THE SAMBOL

(1)   Heat oil in a cooker pan and fry the onions till golden brown. Add prepared masala paste, fry till oil separates. Add jackfruit pieces and salt to taste. Fry for a few minutes mixing everything well. Add about one and a half cups of water. Pressure cook the jackfruits.

(2)   Add the chopped tomato and tamarind pulp. Bring to a boil. Garnish with chopped coriander leaves with a chilli flower tucked in the centre. Serve with plain rice, chappati or bread.

FOR THE CHILLI FLOWER

(1)   Select a fresh green chilli with a stick which is straight and broad in shape.

(2)   Divide chilli into four to five petals by inserting a sharp pointed knife only skin deep. Do not disturb the seeds.

(3)   Carefully open each petal from the seeds. Immerse the chilli in ice cold water atleast for an hour. Each petal will open out making a pretty flower.

BANANA COCONUT PUDDING (6 SERVINGS)

Combination of bananas and coconut, topped with fresh cream, makes an excellent pudding.

INGREDIENTS

6 firm bananas

Good squeeze of lemon juice

1/2 cup powdered sugar

1 - 1/2 tablespoons butter

3 - 4 tablespoons desiccated coconut

200 grams fresh cream

METHOD

(1) Peel bananas and lay them in a fire proof dish. Squeeze lemon juice all over and sprinkle lavishly with sugar.

(2) Dot with little butter and scatter lightly with coconut.

(3) Bake in a fairly hot oven for about 20 minutes or till the bananas are soft but not squashy. Cool. Put in fridge. Just before serving, whip the cream with the remaining powdered sugar and pour on top of the bananas. Sprinkle yellow coloured desiccated coconut on top.

PAPAYA LAMP

METHOD

(1) Select a half ripe papaya with a good shape. Cut a slice from the bottom to make a base. Make a hole in the base to remove seeds.

(2) Mark papaya approximately in five equal portions with toothpicks.

(3) In each section, cut out geometrical shapes, like diamond, triangular, square etc. and other shapes to create a design. Remove toothpicks.

(4) Insert a candle from the bottom and light it at dinner table.

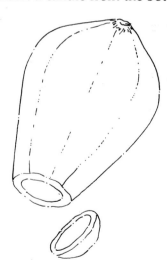
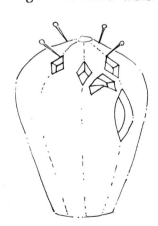

CHINESE DISHES

In recent years Chinese food has become extremely popular. It is one of the most sophisticated cuisines of the world. Basically, it is the Cantonese dishes that have become known as Chinese food, as the people of Canton province have travelled abroad and have introduced their culinary art. Szechuan food which is hot and spicy, has gained popularity in India.

The secret of its popularity is due to its delicious taste and is easy to digest. The food is economical, practical and high in nutritional value.

There are many vegetarian Chinese dishes which can be easily made at home. A typical Chinese menu consists of rice or noodle, with a bowl of soup and an assortment of different dishes, carefully chosen to complement each other.

HOT AND SOUR GREEN VEGETABLE SOUP (6 SERVINGS)

A soup specially for people who favour pungent food.

INGREDIENTS

2 tablespoons coriander leaves and

2 green chillies, minced

2 tablespoons oil

1/2 cup cabbage, shredded

1/2 cup French beans, shredded

1/4 cup capsicums, shredded

1/4 teaspoon aji-no-moto

1 teaspoon black pepper powder

6 cups water

2 tablespoons soya sauce

2 tablespoons vinegar

Salt to taste

4 tablespoons corn flour

METHOD

(1) Heat oil, add minced coriander-chilli paste. Fry for half a minute. Add all the green vegetables, aji-no-moto and black pepper. Fry for two minutes.

(2) Add six cups of hot water, soya sauce, vinegar and salt to taste. Bring to a boil.

(3) Melt corn flour in little water and add to the boiling soup. Stir constantly for a few minutes. Serve piping hot.

(4) Garnish with carrot curls (for method see Pg. 44).

WONTON SOUP (6 SERVINGS)

Delicious flour dumplings stuffed with vegetables in a clear vegetable soup.

INGREDIENTS

FOR THE WONTONS

3/4 cup flour

1 tablespoon oil for the dough

Salt to taste

1/2 tablespoon oil for vegetables

1/4 cup carrots, finely chopped

1/4 cup French beans, finely chopped

1/2 teaspoon soya sauce

A big pinch aji-no-moto

FOR THE SOUP

1 tablespoon oil

3 spring onions, sliced with leaves

1 big carrot, sliced

1/2 cup cauliflower pieces

1/4 teaspoon aji-no-moto

1 - 1/2 tablespoons soya sauce

5 cups hot water

Salt to taste

METHOD

FOR THE WONTONS

(1) Make dough out of flour, oil and salt (slightly tight). Cover and keep aside.

(2) Heat oil and add vegetables. Add salt, soya sauce and a pinch of aji-no-moto. Fry for five minutes. Keep aside to cool.

(3) Make big ball of the dough and roll out very thin. Cut 2 inches x 2 inches squares. Put half teaspoon stuffing in each square and fold wonton. Stick them around the stuffing leaving all ends loose. Collect all wontons in a plate.

FOR THE SOUP

Heat oil. Add vegetables, aji-no-moto and salt. Fry for a few minutes. Add soya sauce and five cups of hot water. Bring to a boil. Put in the wontons one by one and simmer for 20 - 30 minutes. Serve hot.

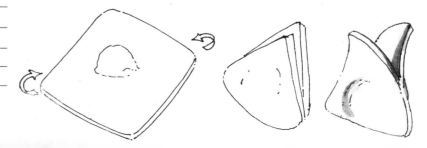

FRIED RICE (6 - 8 SERVINGS)

A rice dish is a must in every Chinese menu.

INGREDIENTS

2 cups rice

1 bunch spring onions, chopped

1 capsicum, chopped

1 carrot, chopped

3 tablespoons oil

Salt to taste

2 cloves garlic, chopped

1/4 teaspoon aji-no-moto

1 tablespoon soya sauce

METHOD

Cook rice in plenty of salt water. Drain and dry. Cut spring onions, capsicums and carrots into small sized pieces. Heat oil and saute all vegetables and garlic with little salt and aji-no-moto for three minutes. Add rice, soya sauce and required salt. Mix well and heat. Serve hot.

EIGHT JEWELS FRIED RICE (6 - 8 SERVINGS)

A fried rice with a difference.

INGREDIENTS

2 cups rice, uncooked

4 tablespoons oil

2 tablespoons almonds, sliced

2 tablespoons walnuts, sliced

1/4 cup each - peas, French beans, capsicums, cauliflower, carrots, spring onions with tender leaves and cabbage, finely chopped

1/2 teaspoon aji-no-moto

1/2 teaspoon ginger, minced

Salt to taste

4 tablespoons soya sauce

2 tablespoons vinegar

1 tablespoon chilli sauce

METHOD

(1) Cook rice in a rice cooker at least two hours before making fried rice. All grains should be separate.
(2) Heat oil and fry almonds and walnuts to light brown. Keep aside.
(3) Chop all the eight vegetables.
(4) Heat oil and when hot, add all the vegetables, aji-no-moto, minced ginger and salt to taste. Fry on high gas till vegetables are tender but crisp. Add soya sauce, vinegar and chilli sauce. Mix well. Add cooked rice and salt to taste. Mix well and take out in a serving plate. Decorate with toasted almonds, walnuts and simple carrot leaves.

FOR THE SIMPLE CARROT LEAVES

(1) Select a fresh carrot preferably orange coloured variety. Cut a piece of required length from its broad side. Peel it and trim to a thick leaf shape.
(2) Carve serrated edges on two opposite flat sides, by cutting straight and slant cuts.
(3) Cut out five to six slices of leaves out of each piece of carrot.

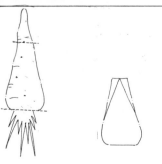

AMERICAN CHOPSUEY (6 - 8 SERVINGS)

Vegetables are mixed with sweet and sour sauce and topped with crisp fried noodles. It is one of the most popular Chinese dish.

INGREDIENTS

FOR THE SAUCE

1/2 cup vinegar

3/4 cup water

3/4 tablespoon soya sauce

1/2 cup sugar

1 - 1/2 tablespoons flour

4 tablespoons tomato ketchup

FOR THE FRIED NOODLES

3/4 cup flour

1 tablespoon oil

1/4 teaspoon salt

Oil for deep frying

FOR THE CHOPSUEY

100 grams French beans, cut into long strips

2 carrots, cut into long strips

Pinch of soda bicarb

Salt to taste

3/4 cup bean sprouts

4 tablespoons oil

2 big onions, sliced

400 grams cabbage, shredded

1 cup noodles, boiled

1 teaspoon aji-no-moto

1 teaspoon chilli sauce

METHOD

FOR THE SAUCE

Mix together all the ingredients given for the sauce and put on the gas. Stir constantly until thick. Keep aside.

FOR THE NOODLES

Mix the given ingredients together and make a slightly tight dough with water. Divide dough into four balls and roll each one very thin. Cut into long strips and deep fry in oil.

FOR THE CHOPSUEY

(1) Boil two cups water with little salt and a pinch of soda. Add French beans and carrot pieces. Boil for a few minutes. Strain and reserve the stock. Pour cold water over these vegetables and keep aside. Put the same stock on the gas and add bean sprouts. Boil for a few minutes and strain.

(2) Heat oil in a thick vessel. Add sliced onions. Saute till little soft. Now add cabbage, little salt and half teaspoon of aji-no-moto. Fry for a few minutes. Mix in boiled French beans, carrots, bean sprouts, noodles, remaining aji-no-moto, salt, chilli sauce and prepared sauce. Heat everything on a fast flame. Mix half of the fried noodles and remove from the gas. Top chopsuey with remaining fried noodles and serve hot.

STUFFED DUMPLINGS IN SWEET AND SOUR SAUCE (6 - 8 SERVINGS)

Steamed, stuffed dumplings, in various types of sauces - a speciality of Chinese cuisine.

INGREDIENTS

FOR THE STUFFING

1/4 cup carrot pieces, boiled

1/4 cup French beans, finely chopped, boiled

1/4 cup noodles, boiled

1/2 teaspoon soya sauce

Salt to taste

FOR THE DUMPLINGS

1 cup flour

2 tablespoons corn flour

1 teaspoon baking powder

1/4 teaspoon salt

4 - 5 tablespoons water

2 teaspoons oil

FOR THE SAUCE

3 tablespoons oil

2 tablespoons corn flour

1 teaspoon soya sauce

4 tablespoons vinegar

3 tablespoons tomato ketchup

1 bunch spring onions, chopped

4 tablespoons brown sugar

1 - 1/2 cups water

3 tablespoons oil

4 cloves garlic

1/4 teaspoon salt

METHOD

FOR THE STUFFING

Combine all the ingredients in a bowl and mix well.

FOR THE DUMPLINGS

Sieve flour, corn flour, baking powder and salt. Add oil, water and make a soft dough. Make small balls. Stuff little of stuffing in each ball. Arrange dumplings in a metal strainer, cover with a lid and steam in a cooker, without pressure on medium gas for 30 minutes.

FOR THE SAUCE

Saute onions in hot oil. Add all the other ingredients. Bring to a boil. Add dumplings and give one boil. Serve hot.

1. Eight jewels fried rice with simple carrot leaves   p. 190
2. Apple and nut fritters   p. 197
3. Chinese white cabbage with three petals red radish flower, spring onion curls   p. 195
4. Vegetable noodles with walnuts   p. 196
5. Hot and sour green vegetable soup   p. 189

VEGETARIAN MANCHURIAN (6 SERVINGS)

A recently popular dish similar to vegetable pakodas, mixed with hot and spicy soya sauce.

INGREDIENTS

FOR THE MANCHURIANS

1/2 cup cauliflower, chopped

1/2 cup carrot, chopped

1 cup flour

1/4 teaspoon soda bicarb

Salt to taste

FOR THE SAUCE

1 big onion, chopped

6 cloves garlic, chopped

3 green chillies, chopped

3 tablespoons oil

1 tablespoon soya sauce

1/4 teaspoon chilly sauce

1/3 cup water

Salt to taste

1/4 teaspoon aji-no-moto

METHOD

(1) Mix all the given ingredients for the manchurian and make batter like pakodas. Deep fry small balls in oil till light brown

(2) To prepare the sauce : Fry onions, garlic and chillies in three tablespoons of oil till brown. Add soya sauce, chilli sauce, water, salt and aji-no-moto. Give one boil. Mix in fried manchurians. Simmer and stir occasionally till sauce is absorbed and all the manchurians are evenly coated with it. Serve hot.

SESAME VEGETABLE FRITTERS (6 - 8 SERVINGS)

A Chinese snack, can be served at tea time or at meal time.

INGREDIENTS

FOR THE FRITTERS

6 - 8 carrots, sliced long

6 - 8 capsicums, sliced long

6 - 8 potatoes, sliced long

6 - 8 cauliflowerettes

4 teaspoons baking powder

1 tablespoon soya sauce

1 tablespoon vinegar

1/2 teaspoon red chilli powder

1/2 teaspoon black pepper

1 teaspoon sugar

Salt to taste

1/4 teaspoon aji-no-moto

METHOD

(1) Prepare a mixture of all the ingredients except the vegetables. Marinate the sliced vegetables in this sauce for half an hour. Stir and shake two to three times. Drain off excess liquid.

(2) Prepare a smooth batter with water.

(3) Dip each piece in the batter and deep fry in oil till light brown in colour.

(4) Serve hot with tomato ketchup.

3 tablespoons sesame seeds

Oil for deep frying

FOR THE BATTER

1/2 cup flour

1/2 cup corn flour

A pinch baking powder

1 teaspoon ground ginger

Salt to taste

CHINESE WHITE CABBAGE (6 SERVINGS)

A vegetable dish which can accompany fried rice.

INGREDIENTS

300 grams cabbage, cut in 2 inch pieces

2 tablespoons oil

1/4 teaspoon aji-no-moto

Salt to taste

1 cup milk

1 tablespoon soya sauce

1 tablespoon sugar

1 tablespoon vinegar

Few drops Tabasco sauce

3/4 tablespoons corn flour

METHOD

FOR THE WHITE CABBAGE

(1) Heat oil, add cabbage pieces, aji-no-moto and salt to taste. Stir for a few minutes.
(2) Mix all the remaining ingredients in milk. Add to the cabbage. Stir till cabbage is saucy.
(3) Serve hot, garnished with black pepper and chopped coriander leaves or with three petals red radish flower and spring onion leaf curls.

FOR THE THREE PETALS RED RADISH FLOWER

(1) Take a medium sized red radish. Cut off a slice from the bottom to make a base.
(2) Carve out three petals, each one attached at the base. Trim sides of each petal and shape them.
(3) Remove red top of the radish in such a way that only small round white centre remains, making it into an open type of dainty flower.
(4) Depending on the size of the radish, one can carve out four or five petals also.

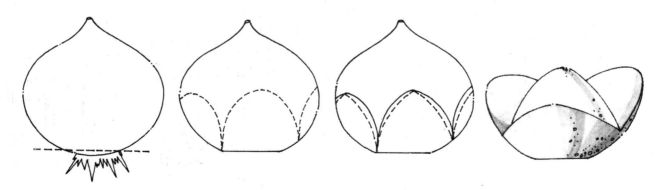

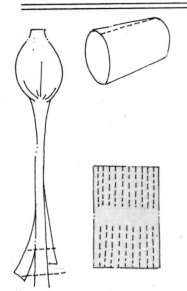

FOR THE SPRING ONION LEAF CURLS

(1)   Take about 3/4 inch tubular piece of a spring onion leaf. Cut it open in a flat strip.
(2)   Put this strip on a chopping board and cut small shreds with a pointed knife on both ends but attached in the centre.
(3)   Put in ice cold water. It will curl within half an hour.
(4)   Since these are very tiny leaf curls, similarly make several leaf curls.

VEGETABLE NOODLES WITH WALNUTS (6 - 8 SERVINGS)

A juicy dish with subtle taste of walnuts, served with rice.

INGREDIENTS

1/2 cup walnuts, broken into big pieces

3 tablespoons oil

1/2 teaspoon ginger, minced

1 tablespoon garlic, minced

1 cup small cauliflower, separate small flowerettes

1/4 teaspoon aji-no-moto

1 big capsicum, chopped into big pieces

1 cup noodles, boiled

1/2 teaspoon white or black pepper

Salt to taste

1 teaspoon soya sauce

1 teaspoon sugar

1 cup water

1 tablespoon corn flour

METHOD

FOR THE NOODLES

(1)   Heat oil. Saute walnut pieces until light brown and keep aside.
(2)   In the same oil, saute the minced ginger and garlic for half a minute. Add cauliflowerettes and a pinch of aji-no-moto. Saute for a few minutes. Add capsicums, noodles and remaining aji-no-moto, pepper and salt to taste. Stir for two minutes. Add soya sauce, sugar, water and walnut pieces. Bring to a boil. Add corn flour dissolved in little water. Simmer for two minutes. Serve hot.

EGGPLANT IN HOT GARLIC SAUCE (6 SERVINGS)

A delicious preparation for people who enjoy spicy flavours. French beans may be substituted for eggplant.

INGREDIENTS

| **METHOD** |

20 pieces eggplant (2" x 1")

5 Kashmiri chillies, soaked in 2 tablespoons vinegar

1 tablespoon garlic, minced

2 tablespoons oil

3 tablespoons tomato ketchup

1 tablespoon soya sauce

Salt to taste

Oil for frying

METHOD

(1) Deep fry the eggplant pieces. Drain on absorbent paper.

(2) Grind to a paste, the soaked chillies and garlic together.

(3) Heat two tablespoons oil. Add chilli garlic paste. Saute for two minutes. Add tomato ketchup and soya sauce. Stir for a minute. Add fried eggplant pieces and salt to taste.

APPLE AND NUT FRITTERS (MAKES 12 PIECES)

A delicious Chinese sweet dish.

INGREDIENTS

12 pieces apple (1/4 inch thick)

3/4 cup flour

1/4 teaspoon baking powder

2 tablespoons powdered sugar

Pinch of salt

3 tablespoons mixed nuts - walnuts, almonds and cashewnuts, chopped

Ghee for deep frying

Some more powdered sugar to sprinkle on top

METHOD

(1) Prepare apple pieces and keep them in water with a pinch of salt.

(2) Make a thick batter with flour, baking powder, salt and powdered sugar.

(3) Dip each piece of apple in the batter, roll in chopped nuts and deep fry in ghee till light brown in colour. Remove in a serving dish and sprinkle powdered sugar.

JAPANESE DISHES

It is the Japanese food that has gifted highest longevity in the world to its people. A lot of traditional food eaten in Japan today is from the sea. They consume great many varieties of seafood. Soyabean and its products like soya sauce, tofu, miso, etc. play an important role in Japanese cuisine. With the influence of Zen Buddhism from China, some of the good vegetarian food was introduced to them. but it is still difficult to find pure vegetarian varieties in Japanese food.

Japanese people take great pains in presentation of food. Each dish is served separately in individual bowls or plates per person. Care is taken to decorate delicately each serving. Rice is served throughout the meal.

1. Sesame fried tofu   p. 200
2. Tempura   p. 202
3. Cucumber flower cups with ginger   p. 203
4. Daikon soup   p. 200
5. Sushi-Rice cakes   p. 205

DAIKON SOUP (RADISH SOUP) (6 SERVINGS)

A thin soup with floating vegetable pieces.

INGREDIENTS

1/2 cup radish, diced

1/2 cup potatoes, diced

1/2 cup carrots, diced

1/2 cup spring onions, chop green leaves into small pieces and keep separate

1 tablespoon oil

1 inch ginger, minced

5 cups water

Salt to taste

5 - 6 teaspoon miso

Black pepper to sprinkle (optional)

METHOD

(1)   Cut all the vegetables into half inch pieces.

(2)   Heat oil, add ginger and all the vegetables except spring onion leaves. Saute for a few minutes stirring all the time. Add five cups of hot water and salt to taste. Simmer till vegetables are almost cooked. Add miso and green leaves of spring onions. Simmer for a few minutes. Serve hot with a dash of black pepper.

Miso (Bean paste)
It is the basic flavouring used in Japanese cuisine. It is made by mixing steamed soya bean with salt and a fermenting agent (Koji) made of rice. It is also mixed with soya sauce. Formerly, it was made in individual household but is now produced commercially. The colour, aroma and taste of miso differ according to the combination of ingredients which vary from place to place.

SESAME FRIED TOFU (MAKES 12 PIECES)

Delicious fried tofu served with soup or as an appetizer.

INGREDIENTS

12 - 2" x 1" pieces of well drained tofu

1/2 cup flour

1/4 teaspoon baking powder

Salt to taste

1 tablespoon black sesame seeds

2 tablespoons corn flakes, crushed

Oil for shallow frying

To decorate

Chopped green leaves of spring onions

Ginger, minced

METHOD

(1)   Combine flour, baking powder and salt together. Add water to make a thick batter. Dip each piece of tofu in the batter and then roll in corn flakes and black sesame seeds.

(2)   Shallow fry in hot oil till golden in colour.

(3)   Serve garnished with spring onion leaves and minced ginger.

Tofu (Bean curd)
It is made of soya bean. It is rich in proteins, vitamins and minerals. It is low in calories and saturated fats and is free of cholestrol. Tofu contains large amount of water. For some recipes where dry tofu is required, drain off water by the following method: Wrap tofu in a muslin cloth. Put it between two wooden blocks and allow the water to drain out.

YASAI SALAD (6 SERVINGS)

A vegetable salad with a pleasant aroma of sesame seeds.

INGREDIENTS

FOR THE SALAD

1 cup, 2" long pieces French beans

1 cup, 2" long pieces carrots

FOR THE SESAME SAUCE

4 tablespoons black sesame seeds

2 teaspoons sugar

2 tablespoons soya sauce

Salt to taste

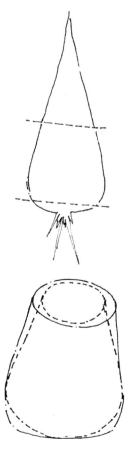

METHOD

FOR THE SALAD

(1) Boil French beans and carrots in salt water. When cooked, drain off water and pour cold water to retain the colour.

(2) Roast sesame seeds on low gas. Grind them coarsely in mortar and pestle or in a coffee grinder. Grinding gives out good aroma. Add soya sauce, salt and sugar. Mix well.

(3) Mix sauce evenly with the vegetables.

(4) Transfer salad in a serving plate. Decorate with a white radish flower in the centre.

FOR THE WHITE RADISH FLOWER

(1) Select a straight white radish. Cut out about 3 inches long piece from the stem end. Peel it.

(2) Taper this piece from the upper side. Keep top and the bottom flat to make it stand.

(3) On the top surface, carve out wedges, about 1/8 inch apart, like a checked pattern.

(4) Using a thin pointed knife and starting from the base end, cut out five half rounds around the radish. Cut second round of cuts alternating the first one. Make four to five layers of cuts upto the top. These half round cuts should be as close as possible and evenly spaced, so as not to show the bare stem, when petals are arranged.

(5) Cut out thin petals in graded sizes of uniform thickness from the leftover piece of radish.

(6) Insert the radish slices in each cut by opening carefully the half round cuts.

(7) After all the layers of petals are arranged, immerse the flower in ice cold water for at least 15 minutes, during which time, the petals will take natural curves, making a beautiful flower.

POTATO CROQUETTES (MAKES 20 PIECES)

A typical Japanese dish, served as a snack.

INGREDIENTS

2 tablespoons oil

1 tablespoon ginger, minced

1/4 cup spring onions with tender leaves, chopped

2 cups potatoes, boiled, mashed

1 cup green peas, crushed, boiled

1/4 cup carrots, boiled, chopped into small pieces

2 tablespoons soya sauce

2 tablespoons corn flour

1/2 teaspoon black pepper

1 tablespoon vinegar

1 tablespoon sugar

Salt to taste

3 tablespoons flour

Breadcrumbs, as required

METHOD

(1)   Heat oil, add ginger and spring onions. Stir for half a minute. Add potatoes, green peas, carrot, soya sauce, corn flour, black pepper, vinegar, sugar and salt to taste. Mix everything well. Remove from gas and cool.

(2)   Make 20 croquettes out of this prepared mixture. Apply paste of flour and then roll in breadcrumbs. Deep fry in hot oil.

TEMPURA (3 SERVINGS)

These are Japanese pakodas. They are dipped in thin liquidy sauce and eaten sizzling hot.

INGREDIENTS

FOR THE TEMPURA

6 capsicums, cut into big pieces

6 eggplant slices, or thin long small egg-plants

6 French beans, specially cut

6 sweet potato slices

6 potato slices

6 lady fingers, remove stems

6 mild variety green chillies, slit and remove seeds

METHOD

FOR THE TEMPURA

(1)   Prepare all the vegetables and keep them ready.

(2)   Mix all the given ingredients for the batter and make a loose batter like pakodas which will coat the vegetables lightly. Do not make a very thick layer. Keep this batter aside for 15 minutes.

(3)   Combine soya sauce, water, vinegar, salt and sugar together. Put on the gas to dissolve sugar. Bring to a boil. Remove from gas and cool.

(4)   Heat oil. Dip each vegetable in the batter and deep fry. Drain on brown paper. Serve each guest with a bowl filled with half a cup of sauce and one teaspoon of grated radish and quarter teaspoon of ginger. The guests will have to the serve themselves.

FOR THE BATTER

2 cups flour

2 teaspoons baking powder

Salt to taste

FOR THE TEMPURA SAUCE

1/3 cup soya sauce

1 - 1/2 cups water

1 tablespoon vinegar

Salt to taste

1 tablespoon sugar

3 teaspoons radish, finely grated

3/4 teaspoon ginger, minced, mixed with little lemon juice to get nice pink colour. Ginger can be served in small cucumber flower cups

FOR THE EGGPLANT CUTTING

Select tiny eggplants. Remove stem. Put slits from broad end, keeping them attached at the top. Spread with fingers. Keep in water till frying time.

FOR THE FRENCH BEAN CUTTING

String French beans and cut out 2 - 3 inches long pieces. Put slits on both ends of the French beans pieces, keeping it attached in the centre.

FOR THE CUCUMBER FLOWER CUP

(1)   Take about 2 inches long pieces of a cucumber. Peel it. Using a thin pointed knife, cut out a circle from top, atleast one inch deep to give thickness to the petals.

(2)   Cut out five petals out of the outer circle. Scoop the centre with a scooper and make a hollow to fill in the minced ginger.

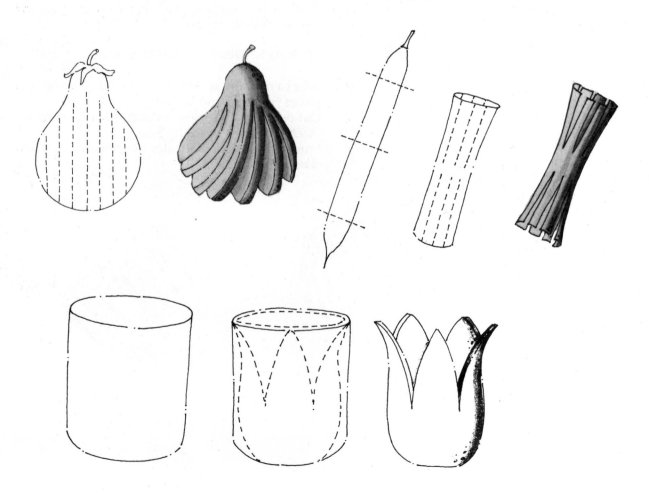

SHUMAI - STEAMED WONTONS (MAKES 12 PIECES)

A decorative main dish with a Chinese influence.

INGREDIENTS

FOR THE STUFFING

1/2 cup potatoes, grated raw
1/2 cup carrots, grated
Few green peas
3 tablespoons onions, grated
1 teaspoon minced ginger
1 tablespoon soya sauce
1 teaspoon sugar
Salt to taste

FOR THE SHUMAI

1 cup flour
1/4 teaspoon baking powder
Salt to taste
1 tablespoon oil

METHOD

FOR THE STUFFING

Mix all the ingredients together. Divide into 12 portions and use as filling. Put one pea on top of each shumai before steaming.

FOR THE SHUMAI

(1)   Make a soft dough like puri (slightly tight). Knead well and divide into twelve balls.

(2)   Roll each ball thin (like a puri) to 3 inches circle.

(3)   Put stuffing in the centre. Fold one side over the stuffing. Pinch and stick sides to form open mouth packet with a flat bottom to stand.

(4)   Arrange all the shumai on an oiled strainer and steam for 30 minutes or till done.

(5)   Transfer in a serving plate and decorate with red radish crysanthemum.

FOR THE RED RADISH CRYSANTHEMUM

(1)   Select a medium sized firm red radish. Slice off two pieces from top and bottom.

(2)   Cut out deep cuts, close to each other like checks, reaching almost upto the base.

(3)   Immerse it in ice cold water to open out. This will take atleast an hour.

SUSHI - RICE CAKES (MAKES 10 - 12 PIECES)

Most favourite dish of Japanese people. A rice cake stuffed with pickled or spicy vegetables and covered with seaweeds.

INGREDIENTS

FOR THE RICE

1 cup rice, cooked soft

2 teaspoons sugar

1 tablespoon vinegar

Salt to taste

FOR THE STUFFING

Pickled cucumber, carrot, cooked asparagus, fried mushrooms, etc. (see Pg. 284)

FOR THE COVERING

1 sheet of 'nori' seaweed or steamed coloccasia leaf - 10" x 8" strip

METHOD

(1)   Dissolve salt and sugar in vinegar and mix evenly with rice.

(2)   Put nori seaweed or a steamed coloccasia leaf on a bamboo mat. Spread rice evenly. Arrange one or two types of stuffing lengthwise. Make a tight roll with the help of a bamboo mat. Cut into 1 inch thick pieces.

Nori Seaweed

Nori seaweeds grow around bamboo stakes placed under water. When they are ready, they are taken out, washed, laid in thin sheets and dried. The best quality nori seaweed has glossy, black purple colour. They are used after roasting which brings out their flavour and texture. They contain lots of iodine.

PEACHES AND SWEET POTATO DESSERT (6 SERVINGS)

A light golden dessert with fruit pieces.

INGREDIENTS

1/2 kg. sweet potatoes

3/4 cup sugar

1/2 cup syrup from the peach can

2 tablespoons honey

6 pieces canned peaches

1 tablespoon toasted almond slivers

METHOD

(1)   Peel sweet potatoes. Cut into big pieces and pressure cook with little water. In an electric blender, put the sweet potatoes with water and blend to a smooth paste.

(2)   Add sugar, syrup from peach tin and honey. Put on the gas and stir continuously with a wooden spoon. First dissolve sugar, then continue cooking till the mixture leaves the sides of the vessel. Mix in peaches. Remove on a serving plate. Garnish with toasted almond slivers. Serve warm.

Note :

Same dessert can also be made with apricots and chestnut pieces.

EGGLESS BAKING

A beautifully decorated cake will certainly please everyone but it will be a complete success if it tastes as good as it looks. To achieve success in decorating and baking cakes, this chapter deals with a few good eggless cake recipes and useful hints for you to follow. Sponge cake, chocolate layer cake and checked cakes are good enough to decorate for special occasions as they have plain flat surfaces. While other cakes have nuts in them which make uneven surface for icing. They are good for coffee or tea parties. The cake you want to ice and decorate should be well proportioned and should have a levelled top. To bake a proper cake, it is important to understand the following points :

(1)   Choose a right size cake tin for the quantity of the cake mixture. Mixture should fill up 2/3 depth of the cake tin, leaving enough room for the cake to rise.
(2)   Prepare tin by lining inside base and sides properly with ghee (purified butter) and dust with flour. For extra precaution you may line the base of the tin with a greaseproof paper.
(3)   Level the cake mixture in the tin and make slight depression in the centre.
(4)   For the oven temperature, follow the instructions given in individual recipes. Do not open the oven door unnecessarily. Never bang the door while checking.
(5)   The cake is evenly baked when the top feels firm to the touch, or if a probing skewer or a thin narrow knife or a long toothpick, when inserted in the cake comes out clean. Then turn out cake on the wire rack to cool.
(6)   In case the top of the cake is slightly domed, turn out and stand it upside down to level it. If after some hours, it is still not levelled, then trim off the domed part and use the clean bottom side as the top surface for decorating.

COCONUT JAM CUPS (MAKES 15 PIECES)

Coconut biscuits packed in butterpaper cups and topped with jam.

INGREDIENTS	METHOD
3/4 cup powdered sugar	(1) Beat sugar and butter. Add vanilla essence.
6 tablespoons butter	(2) Sieve flour and mix in coconut.
1 teaspoon vanilla essence	(3) Add flour mixture to the creamed butter and mix well. Add little milk enough to make a piping consistency.
1 - 1/4 cups flour	
4 tablespoons desiccated coconut	(4) Fill this mixture in a piping bag with a big star nozzle.
Milk as required	(5) Pipe all round the inside of the cups, leaving little gap in the centre.
About 3 tablespoons mixed fruit jam	
15 paper cups	(6) Heat oven to 200°C. and then reduce to 150°C while placing cups for baking. Bake till light brown. It will take about 35 to 40 minutes. Remove and cool. Put jam in centre of each cup. Do not remove paper cups.

CHEESE BISCUITS (MAKES ABOUT 24 PIECES)

Animal shaped salty cheese biscuits, specially for tiny tots birthday party.

INGREDIENTS	METHOD
1 - 1/3 cups flour	(1) Sieve flour, salt, mustard powder and baking powder.
A pinch salt	
1/4 teaspoon mustard powder	(2) Rub in butter and grated cheese.
1/2 teaspoon baking powder	(3) Make dough with milk.
2 - 1/2 tablespoons butter	(4) Roll on a plastic sheet to about 1/4 inch thick. Cut out shapes with a biscuit cutter. Arrange them on a greased baking tray. Prick with a fork on top.
1/2 cup cheese, grated	
Milk to bind dough	(5) Bake at 200°C for about 15 to 20 minutes till light pink in colour. Remove and cool on wire rack.

MAWA BISCUITS (40 PIECES)

Simple crisp mawa biscuits topped with cashewnuts.

INGREDIENTS

6 tablespoons vanaspati ghee

2/3 cup powdered sugar

50 grams mawa (khoya)

30 ml. (1 fl. oz.) water

1/2 teaspoon vanilla essence

1 - 1/2 cups flour

1/4 teaspoon baking powder

Few cashewnuts, chopped

METHOD

(1) Using the palm of your hand, beat the ghee, sugar, mawa, water and essence in a thali (big shallow plate).

(2) Sieve flour and baking powder. Add to the above mixture and make a dough.

(3) Roll dough on a plastic sheet to 1/4 inch thickness. Cut with biscuit cutters. Arrange them on a greased baking tray. Apply milk on top and sprinkle chopped cashewnut pieces. Bake at 175°C. for 15 to 20 minutes till light pink in colour. Remove and cool on a wire rack.

Note :

Add about quarter cup of milk to mawa biscuit dough and make it soft. Press it through a cookie press to get biscuits in different shapes. Bake them at 175°C. for half an hour to get crisp biscuits.

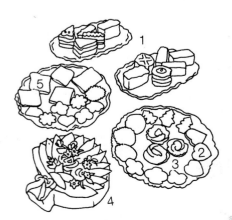

1. Pastries with butter frosting and chocolate frosting   p. 224 & 225
2. Mawa biscuits   p. 208
3. Coconut biscuits   p. 210
4. Fan cake   p. 226
5. Bee cookies   p. 215

COCONUT BISCUITS (MAKES 35 PIECES)

Crisp biscuits with an unusual taste of coconut.

INGREDIENTS

6 tablespoons vanaspati ghee

2/3 cup powdered sugar

1 teaspoon cardamom powder

1 - 1/2 cups flour

1 tablespoon custard powder

1/2 teaspoon baking powder

1/2 cup dry coconut, grated

Milk, as required

METHOD

(1) Using the palm of your hand, beat ghee, sugar and cardamom powder in a thali (big shallow plate).

(2) Sieve flour, custard powder and baking powder.

(3) Dry roast the coconut till crisp. Mix with flour.

(4) Now mix everything together and make a dough, adding milk as required.

(5) Roll dough on a plastic sheet. Cut with cutters. Arrange on a baking tray. Apply little milk on top.

(6) Bake at 175°C till light pink in colour. Remove and cool on wire rack.

NANKHATAI (MAKES 24 PIECES)

A very popular Indian style biscuit.

INGREDIENTS

1 cup cold vanaspati ghee

1 cup powdered sugar

1/2 teaspoon cardamom powder

1/4 teaspoon nutmeg powder

3/4 cup semolina

1 - 1/4 cups flour

A few pieces pistachios and almonds

METHOD

(1) Cut cold ghee in small pieces. Add sugar. Put in a thali (shallow plate) and beat very well with hand till light, white and fluffy. Add and mix cardamom and nutmeg powders.

(2) Then add flour and semolina Make a dough with very light hand. Make 24 balls and arrange them in a baking tray. Stick pieces of pistachios and almonds on top.

(3) Heat oven to 200°C then reduce to 175°C at the time of placing the tray in the oven. Bake till light brown in colour. Remove and cool.

WALNUT CAKE (6 - 8 SERVINGS)

A golden coloured cake with walnuts on top. A tasty cake for a tea party.

INGREDIENTS

2 cups self raising flour

1/2 teaspoon soda bicarb

1/2 teaspoon baking powder

1 cup walnuts, chopped

8 tablespoons brown sugar

3/4 cup water

6 tablespoons margarine

1 cup milk

1 cup ordinary sugar

1 teaspoon vanilla essence

METHOD

(1) Sieve together the self raising flour, soda bicarb and baking powder. Mix in nuts.

(2) Melt brown sugar in three fourths cup of water. Cool it. This is called treacle.

(3) Heat margarine with milk in a big vessel. Cool it. Mix in treacle, sugar and vanilla essence.

(4) Now mix in the dry ingredients. There should be no lumps in the mixture.

(5) Pour mixture in a greased tin.

(6) Bake at 200°C for about 40 minutes or till done. Remove from oven and keep for five minutes. Then invert on a wire rack and cool.

CHOCOLATE LAYER CAKE (6 - 8 SERVINGS)

A perfect cake for a birthday party. It can be decorated with frosting. A plain sponge cake can be made with the same recipe but deleting drinking chocolate and cocoa powder.

INGREDIENTS

FOR THE CAKE

270 grams (9 ozs.) self raising flour

2 teaspoons baking powder

1 teaspoon soda bicarb

2 tablespoons cocoa powder

2 tablespoons drinking chocolate

4-1/2 tablespoons margarine or butter, melted

1 can condensed milk (400 grams)

1 teaspoon vanilla essence

150 ml (5 fl. ozs.) lukewarm water

1/2 cup powdered sugar

FOR THE COFFEE CREAM

2 tablespoons margarine

90 grams (3 ozs.) icing sugar

1 tablespoon milk

1 teaspoon coffee essence

METHOD

(1) Sieve flour, baking powder, soda bicarb, cocoa powder and drinking chocolate.

(2) Melt butter in a big vessel.

(3) Add all the liquid ingredients and sugar.

(4) Then gradually mix in the flour mixture.

(5) Pour in two greased round sandwich tins. Preheat the oven.

(6) First bake for seven to eight minutes at 250°C and then for 20 to 25 minutes at 150°C. Remove from oven and keep aside for five minutes. Then invert on a wire rack or towel. When cool, apply coffee cream and sandwich the two cakes.

FOR THE COFFEE CREAM

Beat all the ingredients together in a vessel with a wooden spoon till light and fluffy.

BANANA NUT CAKE (6 - 8 SERVINGS)

A delicious cake, full of nutritious ingredients like wheat flour, banana, jaggery and curd.

INGREDIENTS

2 cups wheat flour or flour

2 teaspoons baking powder

1/2 teaspoon soda bicarb

6 tablespoons butter

1 cup jaggery

2 ripe bananas, mashed

2 tablespoons curd

1/2 cup milk

4 - 6 cashewnuts

3 - 4 walnuts

10 - 12 raisins

METHOD

(1) Sieve together flour, baking powder and soda bicarb.

(2) Take butter and jaggery in a big vessel. Put on the slow gas to melt. Remove from the gas and cool for a few minutes. Add mashed bananas and curd. Mix well.

(3) Add flour mixture and milk simultaneously. Mix lightly all the time, making an even batter. In the end, add nuts and raisins. Mix lightly. Pour in a greased baking dish of 8 inches diametre and 3 inches depth.

(4) Preheat the oven. Bake the cake at 200°C for 15 minutes. Then reduce to 150°C and bake for another 30 minutes, till done.

TUTTI FRUITI CUPS TOPPED WITH BUTTER-SCOTCH (MAKES 10 CUPS)

Delightful and easy-to-serve tiny cakes for birthday and tea parties.

INGREDIENTS

FOR THE CUPS

1 cup self raising flour

1/4 teaspoon soda bicarb

1/4 teaspoon baking powder

1/4 cup tutti fruiti, diced

1 cup granulated sugar

3 tablespoons margarine

100 ml. (3 fl. ozs.) water

1/2 cup milk

1/2 teaspoon vanilla essence

FOR THE BUTTER-SCOTCH TOPPING

3 tablespoons butter

105 grams (3 - 1/2 ozs.) brown sugar

3 tablespoons milk

90 grams (30 ozs.) icing sugar approximately

METHOD

FOR THE CUPS

(1) Sieve together the flour, soda bicarb and baking powder. Mix in tutti fruiti pieces.

(2) Take sugar, margarine, water and milk in a vessel. Heat till sugar and margarine dissolve. Remove from the gas and cool. Add vanilla essence.

(3) Gradually mix in flour mixture. Blend to avoid formation of lumps.

(4) Pour the mixture into 10 small greased cups to fill upto three-fourths only.

(5) Bake at 200°C for half an hour. Remove from oven and invert after five to seven minutes on a wire rack. On cooling, cover their tops with butter scotch topping.

FOR THE BUTTER-SCOTCH TOPPING

Melt butter and stir in brown sugar. Boil for a minute or two. Stir in milk and bring to a boil. Remove from heat and cool to lukewarm. Gradually stir in sufficient icing sugar to give a coating consistency. Spread over the cup cakes with a palette knife.

CHOCOLATE BUTTON RINGS (MAKES 8 PIECES)

Small cakes decorated with chocolate and white icing to form a ring pattern on top.

INGREDIENTS

FOR THE BUTTON RINGS

1/2 cup butter or margarine

1/2 cup powdered sugar

1/2 cup self raising flour

2 tablespoons custard powder

Milk as required

1/4 teaspoon vanilla essence

FOR THE SMOOTH CHOCOLATE ICING

2 tablespoons cocoa powder

2 tablespoons butter

2 tablespoons milk

90 grams (3 ozs.) icing sugar approximately

METHOD

FOR THE BUTTON RINGS

(1)   Cream butter and sugar till light and fluffy.
(2)   Sieve flour and custard powder together.
(3)   Gradually add flour and milk to the creamed butter. Mix lightly with a palette knife. Add milk till you get a dropping consistency. Mix in vanilla essence.
(4)   Fill butter paper cups to its three quarter capacity.
(5)   Bake at 200ºC from 25 minutes. Cool before decorating.

FOR THE CHOCOLATE ICING

(1)   Melt butter, cocoa powder and milk together in a small vessel placed over hot water. Beat in icing sugar. Remove for heat.
(2)   When the mixture begins to cool and is thick, spoon a little over each cake. Leave to set.
(3)   Now make a big flat star in the centre and a ring of small starlets all round the edges with white butter frosting. (refer recipe on Pg. 224)

PINEAPPLE UPSIDE DOWN CAKE (6 - 8 SERVINGS)

A decorative tea party cake. Can be served warm, fresh from the oven.

INGREDIENTS

FOR THE TOPPING

2 tablespoons butter

2 tablespoons brown sugar

1 small tin pineapple slices (450 grams)

Few glazed cherries

FOR THE CAKE

2 cups flour

1/4 teaspoon salt

3 teaspoons baking powder

1 cup powdered sugar

6 tablespoons margarine

1 cup milk

1 tablespoon vinegar or lemon juice

METHOD

(1)   Cream the brown sugar and butter and apply on the base and sides of a round cake tin of 9 inches diametre and three inches in depth. Arrange well drained slices of pineapple and cherries and keep the tin ready.
(2)   Sieve flour, salt and baking powder.
(3)   Cream powdered sugar and margarine with a wooden spoon till light and fluffy.
(4)   Add flour and milk gradually and mix with a palette knife to a dropping consistency. Mix vinegar or lemon juice.
(5)   Pour this mixture in the prepared tin. Bake at 250ºC higher than moderate for about 15 minutes. Then reduce to 150ºC till done.
(6)   Remove from the oven and cool for 10 minutes. Then turn it upside down on a wire rack. Now pineapple will come on top. Cut and serve triangular pieces.

CHECKED CAKE (6 - 8 SERVINGS)

A cake, which can be decorated for special occasions. When cut, it shows, a lovely pattern of white and brown checks.

INGREDIENTS

2 cups flour

1/4 teaspoon salt

3 teaspoons baking powder

1 cup powdered sugar

6 tablespoons margarine

1 cup milk

1 teaspoon vanilla essence

1-1/2 tabelspoons cocoa powder

2 tablespoons drinking chocolate

2 tablespoons mixed fruit jam

METHOD

(1)   Sieve flour, salt and baking powder.

(2)   Cream powdered sugar and 5-1/2 tablespoons of margarine with a wooden spoon till light and fluffy.

(3)   Add flour and milk gradually and mix with a palette knife to a dropping consistency. Mix in essence.

(4)   Divide this mixture in two parts.

(5)   Blend cocoa powder and drinking chocolate in half tablespoon of margarine.

(6)   Prepare three cake tins. Grease and flour them.

(7)   To half of the cake mixture, mix melted chocolate.

(8)   Now prepare three tins with alternate layers of both mixtures as shown in the diagram.

(9)   Preheat the oven. Bake at 200°C at moderate temperature for about 25 minutes.

(10) Remove from oven and cool for a few minutes. Then invert on a wire rack and cool.

(11) Stick all three layers alternately with mixed fruit jam, in such a way that on cutting the cake, we see brown and white checked pattern.

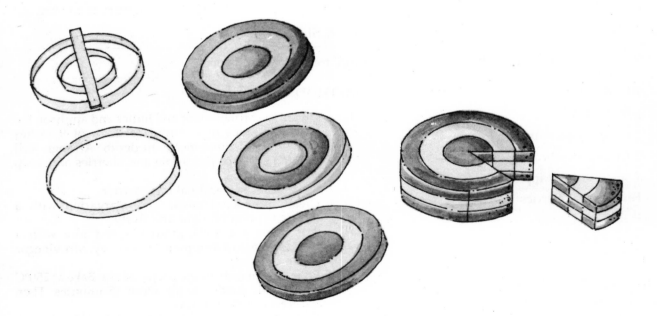

SHORT CRUST PASTRY OR SWEET PASTE

A basic dough recipe for biscuits, pies, flans etc.

INGREDIENTS

1/2 cup icing sugar

4 tablespoons margarine

1 - 1/3 cups flour

1 tablespoons custard powder

1/2 teaspoon lemon rind, grated

Milk as required

METHOD

(1) Mix and beat icing sugar and margarine with a wooden spoon till light and white.

(2) Add flour, custard powder and lemon rind. Mix with hand and make a dough. Use little milk, if required.

(3) Put this dough in a plate and keep in fridge till it becomes hard.

(4) Remove this hard dough from fridge and knead again. Make a ball and roll out on a floured plastic sheet. Cut to required size pieces. Arrange them on a greased baking tray. Prick with a fork.

(5) Heat oven to 300°C first, then reduce temperature to 200°C while placing the tray for baking. Bake till light brown. Remove and cool.

BEE COOKIES (MAKES 12 PIECES)

Colourful sweet cookies.

INGREDIENTS

1 recipe sweet paste

3 - 1/2 tablespoons sugar

2 tablespoons margarine

1 tablespoon fresh cream (from top of milk)

1 tablespoon honey

15 cashewnuts, chopped

8 glazed cherries, chopped

METHOD

(1) Roll out the cooled sweet paste to 1/4 inch thick square piece. Put it on a greased baking tray. Prick holes with a fork and bake. When sweet paste is half done, remove from the oven. Cool a little.

(2) Meanwhile combine sugar, margarine, fresh cream and honey in a vessel. Put on gas, keep stirring till mixture is thick. Mix in chopped nuts and cherry pieces.

(3) Immediately spread the topping on semicooked sweet paste. Put it back in the oven and bake for five to seven minutes. Cut rectangular pieces when slightly hot.

TARTS (10 PIECES)

Tiny tarts are easy to serve at a large party.

INGREDIENTS

1 recipe sweet paste

Jam as required

METHOD

(1) Roll out the cooled sweet paste to quarter inch thickness. Cut out rounds with a cutter, big enough to fit a tart mould. Arrange these circles in greased tart moulds. Prick holes with a fork.

(2) Bake blind at 200°C till almost done. Remove the tarts and fill with jam and bake further for a few more minutes. Remove and cool.

Note :

You can prepare empty tarts and fill with the same mixture as in Almond and Peach Flan.

CHEESE AND CORN PIE (6 SERVINGS)

A delicious savoury pie.

INGREDIENTS

FOR THE FILLING

2 tablespoons butter

1 onion, chopped

1 - 1/2 cups corn, boiled

1/2 cup cheese, grated

1 teaspoon mustard powder

Salt and pepper to taste

1 tomato, skinned and sliced

FOR THE SHORT CRUST PASTRY

1 - 1/3 cups flour

1/4 teaspoon baking powder

1/2 teaspoon salt

1 teaspoon powder sugar

4 tablespoons butter or margarine (cold)

Ice cold water to make dough

METHOD

FOR THE FILLING

Melt butter and saute onions till light brown. Add corn and half of the cheese. Season with mustard, salt and pepper.

FOR THE PIE

(1) Sieve flour and baking powder. Add salt and sugar.

(2) Cut butter into small pieces.

(3) Rub in flour gently till it looks like breadcrumbs.

(4) Now add cold water and make dough. Make two balls. Roll them out on a plastic sheet big enough to fit eight inches pie dish.

(5) Place one rolled out pastry in the greased pie dish. Prick few holes with a fork. Fill with filling. Cover with tomato slices and rest of the cheese. Apply water on edges.

(6) Now cover the filling with the other rolled out pastry. Stick properly. Trim edges. Decorate the edges or flute them. Roll trimmings and cut out some shapes like leaves. Stick them in position. Apply milk all over the pie. Prick some holes with a fork. Then bake.

(7) Heat oven to 200°C. Bake for at least half an hour till the top is light brown in colour.

(8) Remove. Serve hot or at room temperature.

PUFF PASTRY

A basic dough recipe which can be used for various preparations.

INGREDIENTS	METHOD
2 - 1/2 cups flour	(1) Divide flour into 2/3 and 1/3 parts. To 1/3 part mix butter. Put it on a small plastic sheet and then in fridge to harden. To the remaining 2/3 flour, mix in salt and make a soft dough with water. Knead well.
200 grams butter	(2) Roll dough oblong. Remove the cooled butter mixture from the fridge and put it in the centre of the rolled out dough and fold. Again put in fridge to harden for about 15 minutes.
1/2 teaspoon salt	(3) Remove dough on floured surface and roll as long as possible. Fold two ends in the centre and then place one side of the fold over the other. Sprinkle lavishly the dry flour whenever the dough tears and butter comes out in the initial stages of rolling. Put in fridge for 15 minutes to harden. Repeat this process four times.
	(4) Try the following three varieties of biscuits out of cooled puff pastry

PUFF PASTRY BISCUITS (30 PIECES)

(1) Remove the ready cooled puff pastry from the fridge. Roll to half inch thickness. Cut oblong pieces. Arrange them on a greased baking tray. Apply melted ghee on top of each biscuit as glaze.

(2) Heat oven to 250°C. Bake till they rise or for about 20 minutes. Remove tray. Arrange biscuits sideways in the tray, then bake at 100°C for 1-1/2 hours till very crisp.

CHEESE PUFF BISCUITS (MAKES 30 PIECES)

INGREDIENTS	METHOD
1 recipe puff pastry	(1) Roll out the dough twice. Then for the third time, sprinkle little cheese before folding. Repeat this process twice more.
1/3 cup cheese, grated, divide into 3 parts	(2) Roll out the cooled dough to half inch thickness and cut biscuit shapes as desired with a knife.
	(3) Baking process is the same as plain puff pastry biscuits.

PUFF PASTRY PIN WHEELS (MAKES 4 PIN WHEELS)

INGREDIENTS

1 recipe puff pastry

Mixed fruit jam as required

1/4 cup black currants, seeded and chopped

1/4 cup cherries, chopped

Milk and icing sugar as required

METHOD

(1) Cut the ready puff pastry into four parts. Roll each part thinly to an oblong, approximately 7" x 5".

(2) Thinly spread the mixed fruit jam. Sprinkle a mixture of currants and cherries. Roll up lengthwise like a swiss roll, sealing edges with water and trimming ends.

(3) Brush with milk. Mark six cuts with a knife on the surface.

(4) Bake at 200°C till golden brown.

(5) Remove from oven and cool on rack. Dust with icing sugar.

(6) Cut out biscuits at the markings.

ALMOND AND PEACH FLAN (6 SERVINGS)

An exotic peach flan made extra rich with nuts.

INGREDIENTS

1 small can peaches (450 grams)

1/2 cup syrup from the can

4 tablespoons powdered sugar

2 teaspoons corn flour

1 tablespoon mixed fruit jam

1 recipe sweet paste (see Pg. 215)

3 tablespoons cashewnuts, ground

A few almonds, blanched

100 grams fresh cream

METHOD

(1) Take out peaches from the can and drain the syrup. Take half a cup of syrup and to it add two tablespoons sugar. Boil it. Blend corn flour in little cold syrup and add to the boiling mixture. Stir till thick. When slightly warm mix in jam. Use this sauce as a glaze.

(2) Prepare one recipe sweet paste. Mix in ground cashewnuts and cool it. Remove after about 15 minutes and knead. Form into a ball and roll it to the size of a flan tray (8 inches).

(3) Put sweet paste in the greased flan tray. Make few holes with a fork. Bake blind (i.e. without any filling) at 200°C till light brown in colour. Cool.

(4) Whip fresh cream with two tablespoons of powdered sugar. Spread it at the base of flan. Arrange drained peach pieces over it. Put blanched and split almonds in between. Glaze top with prepared peach glaze. Cool in fridge. When properly set, remove and cut into pieces while serving.

APPLE PIE (6 SERVINGS)

A juicy apple pie, delicately flavoured with cinnamon and cloves.

INGREDIENTS

FOR THE FILLING

2 apples, chopped (without skin)

1/2 to 3/4 cup powdered sugar, or according to the taste of apples

3/4 teaspoon cinnamon and clove powder

1 tablespoon butter, melted

METHOD

Method of preparing pie is same as cheese and corn pie. For filling, mix all the given ingredients and fill in the centre.

Note :

Apple pie can be baked open without covering. Make in nine inches diametre pie dish. Cut strips from the remaining dough and arrange them across on top forming a trellis.

CAKE DECORATION

DECORATING INSTRUCTIONS

To decorate a cake is certainly an interesting art. You can decorate it as simply by just sprinkling icing sugar onto a cake with a sieve or a strip of paper. Cover cake with simple frosting and neatly arrange nuts, coloured candies, sweet silver balls etc. The sides of a cake can be left plain but it can be made more attractive by applying a thin layer of jam or butter frosting and then rolled in toasted or coloured coconut, nuts, or tiny chocolate scrapings. At the same time, you can decorate cakes as elaborately as you wish. For decorating, a person should have a basic skill and patience to practice different forms and designs. Once you get the knack of handling it, cake decorating is enjoyable and rewarding. To make the task easier few basic equipments are necessary :

(1)   Several mixing bowls of various sizes are required for working with different coloured icings.
(2)   A fine sieve for sifting icing sugar.
(3)   A wooden spoon for mixing small quantity of icing.
(4)   A rubber spatula is needed to scrape every last bit of icing out of a bowl.
(5)   A palette knife - It is a flat, flexible blunt knife. If helps when spreading icing over the top of the cake and around the sides.
(6)   A cake board - It is a firm card board cut to the size of a cake and is covered with a foil or greaseproof paper or a paper doily.
(7)   Piping syringe with several piping nozzles - A piping syringe can be filled with a stiff butter icing to decorate cakes. It can be fitted with different types of nozzles (decorating tubes) to get designs. There are six basic nozzles which can produce most of the designs used for decorating cakes. Each nozzle is available in different size but the basic decoration they produce are the same. For example, small star or a big star.

Round nozzle used for dots, balls, writing, strings etc. To get uniform dots, hold bag at a 90° angle, straight up and down with tube almost touching the surface of the practice board. Squeeze out a dot of icing, lift the tube carefully and pull away. More or less pressure will give bigger or smaller dot.

For writing, use softer icing to get smooth flow. Hold decorating bag at 45° angle to the surface and write with even pressure. Remember to move your entire arm, bending it only at the elbow.

Star nozzle : Most useful nozzle to make stars, shells, rosettes, ropes, zigzags etc. To get **star**, hold bag at 90° angle, straight up and down, with the tube touching the surface. Squeeze out a **star** of icing, stop pressure and gently pull away. Stars can make borders and if arranged close together, can cover the entire cake.

To get **shell**, hold bag at 45° angle, with tube just touching the surface, squeeze bag with a heavy pressure, lifting tube slightly until icing spreads out into a full shell base. Now relax pressure and pull tube down bringing shell to a point. Lift the bag gently. Uniformly made shells can make beautiful borders.

To get **rosette**, hold bag at 90° angle, straight up and down, with the tube touching the surface. Start to squeeze a star of icing, move tube down, around and up over star forming a rosette. Gently pull away the tube.

To get **ropes**, hold bag at 45° angle to the surface. Touch the surface and squeeze with medium pressure, move tube up, around and down in a curve, then stop pressure and pull tube away. Now put tube under arc of first curve and repeat to get rope border.

To get **zigzag**, hold bag at 45° angle to the surface. Touch the surface, squeeze out icing with even pressure, move tube, left and right slightly to form zigzag pattern.

Drop flower nozzle used for star and twisted flowers. To get **star drop flower**, hold tube at 90° angle to the surface, squeeze out a star drop flower, then stop pressure and gently pull away. Put a dot in the centre with a dot nozzle to complete flower.

To get **twisted drop flower**, hold tube at 90° angle to the surface, and squeeze a star drop flower. Then keeping the tube in the icing, twist with gentle pressure, then release pressure and gently pull away. Put a dot in the centre with a dot nozzle to complete flower.

Leaf nozzle is used for making various leaves. To get a **leaf**, hold bag at 45° angle to the surface, slightly tilting on the side. Squeeze with a heavy pressure to build the base of the leaf, then pull tube away, relaxing the pressure and end leaf with a point. To get ruffled leaf, press with a jiggling motion. (slight vibrating motion).

Rose nozzle used for making roses, ribbons, bows etc. To get a rose, use slightly stiff icing. Attach a small square wax paper on a flowernail, with a dot of icing. Hold tube at 90° angle and squeeze with heavy pressure. Build a good sized dome base for rose.

Hold bag at 45° angle. Touch wide end of the tube to near top of the icing dome with narrow end of the tube straight up. Now squeeze and pull the tube up and away from dome, stretching icing into a ribbon band as shown. At the same time, turn nail in the opposite direction to get a band of icing around the dome.

Touch wide end of the tube to icing dome with narrow tube end, pointing straight up. Turn nail in opposite direction and move tube up, around and down towards you in a half circle, to form a petal.

Following the same method, start at base of first petal, overlapping it slightly and squeeze out icing. Move tube up, around and down towards you to form a second petal. Following the same method, make third petal completing first set of petals.

Make second set of petals by following the similar procedure, but with petals alternating the first set. Continue making petals until you get the required size of rose. Dry rose on a flat board with the paper. One can store flowers until required.

Basket weave nozzle is used for making plain and ribbed stripes, basket weaving pattern etc. It is a tube with a flat mouth having one side serrated and the other plain. To make **plain stripe**, hold tube at 45° angle to the surface, with plain side on top. Pull away with even steady pressure.

To make **ribbed stripes**, keep serrated side of the tube on top.

Basket-weaving is a beautiful design to cover the side of a cake. Use medium consistency of the icing. With a serrated side up, squeeze out a vertical stripe of icing to the required length. Cover this stripe with short horizontal bars of icing with distance apart (size of the tube). Now squeeze out the second vertical stripe, where horizontal bars end. Cover this stripe with horizontal bars, fitting them between the spaces of the first row as shown in the diagram. Repeat the entire procedure over and over for basket weave pattern.

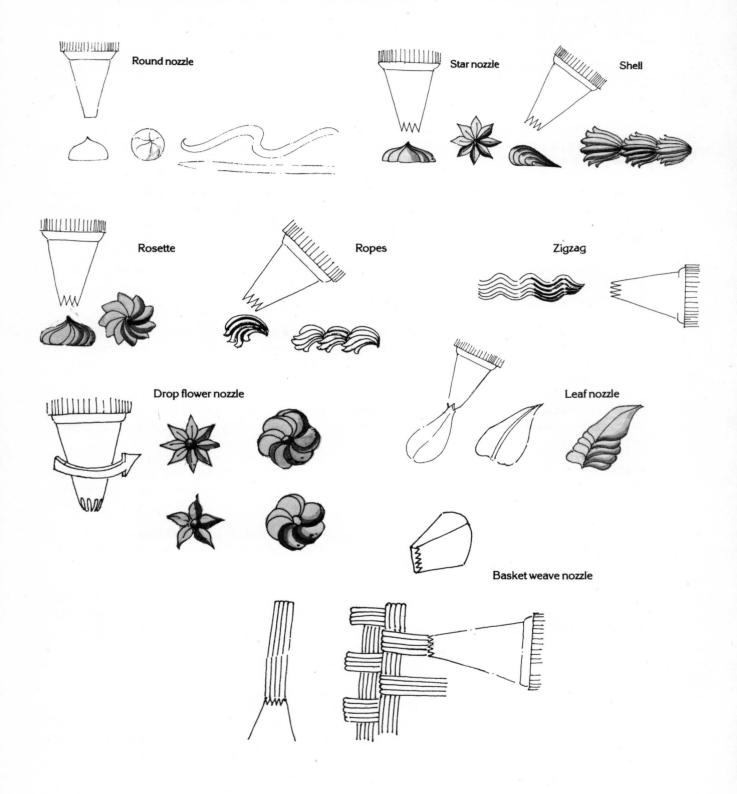

Round nozzle

Star nozzle

Shell

Rosette

Ropes

Zigzag

Drop flower nozzle

Leaf nozzle

Basket weave nozzle

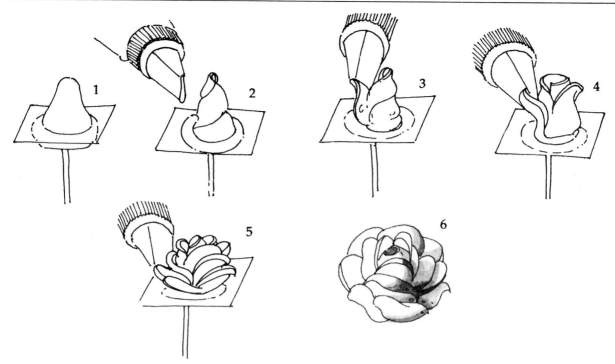

(8)   Paper cone - when you are planning cake decoration with several colours, it is not practical to wash syringe everytime you require to change a colour. So to solve this problem learn to make greaseproof paper cones. But remember paper cones are fragile and useful only for small icing jobs.

Take a 12 inches square greaseproof paper. Cut in half diagonally to form two triangles to make two cones. Now follow diagrams to get correct shape. Name three corners as A, B, C to give you a guideline. Fold corner B round inside corner A, and bring corner C round the outside of the cone, until it fits exactly behind A. All three corners must be together and the point of the cone neatly tight. Fold corner A over two to three times inward and then staple it to secure. You may snip off a tip of the cone to get tiny hole for writing or for dots etc. or cut off a large end, about 1/2 inch up from the tip and drop in a nozzle for fancy decoration.

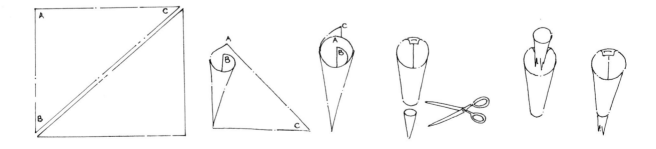

(9)   Nylon piping bag with a plastic coupler is readily available along with other tools for piping butter frosting. You can fill good quantity of icing in it. The plastic coupler is useful for changing nozzle without disturbing the icing in the bag.

(10)   Various food colours from reputed company which blend well with icing.

(11)   Paint brushes - one or two paint brushes are required to add colour to the icing and to tint dry icing decorations.

(12)   Flower nail - A flat, round (1 - 1/2 inches diametre) nailhead used as a turntable surface for making different icing flowers.

(13)   Big nozzles for nylon piping bag, used for getting big designs. Many a time used for decorating puddings and baked dishes.

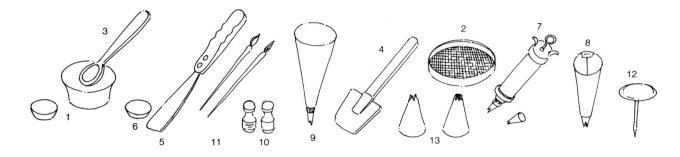

BUTTER FROSTING (MAKES 3/4 CUP)

Once you have the equipment to proceed with decoration, learn to make right type of butter frosting.

INGREDIENTS

6 tablespoons margarine

12 tablespoons icing sugar

Few drops lemon juice

Pinch of salt

1/2 teaspoon vanilla essence

Fresh cream as required

METHOD

(1)   Cream margarine with an electric beater or a wooden spoon till soft and fluffy.

(2)   Add icing sugar gradually and beat further. Also mix lemon juice and vanilla essence. For even mixing, scrape sides and bottom of the bowl often with a rubber spatula. Beat until light, white and fluffy.

(3)   Keep icing covered with a lid or a damp cloth and store in cool place or refrigerator when not in use.

(4)   While decorating, mix colour in small quantity of frosting as required.

(5)   To get right type of decoration, the consistency of the frosting should also be right. Add more icing sugar to make frosting stiff and add fresh cream to make it soft. Stiff frosting is needed for flowers and leaves. Medium consistency is good for boarders and softer flowing type of frosting for covering the entire cake, for writing and for string work.

CHOCOLATE FROSTING (MAKES 3/4 CUP)

INGREDIENTS	METHOD
1 recipe butter frosting (see Pg. 224)	Melt cocoa powder in melted butter and mix evenly in the butter frosting. For darker colour use more cocoa powder.
2 - 1/2 tablespoons cocoa powder	
1 tablespoon melted margarine or butter	

HOW TO MASTER THE ART OF CAKE DECORATION ?

To achieve a mastery over cake decoration, prepare one recipe of butter frosting, fill in the syringe and practice designs on the back of a flat oven tray. Try different nozzles and create new designs. When the tray is full, scrape your practice decoration off the tray and reuse the frosting in the syringe again. In case the frosting becomes loose due to handling, keep in fridge for a few minutes to harden. Remember right methods and patience will only make you perfect.

The angle at which you hold your decorating bag and nozzle is the key to produce correct designs. There are two main basic positions :
(a)   90° angle, the syringe or a bag is held perpendicular to the decorating surface to get stars, flowerets etc.
(b)   45° angle, the syringe or a bag is held at a slant to the decorating surface, mainly for borders. Some other nozzles have their own correct way of handling. You will learn these positions as you practice decorations.

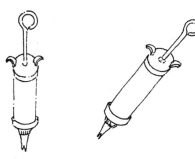

The pressure control over syringe is also important. The amount of pressure and steadiness with which it is applied to the syringe or a bag will determine the size and uniformity of any iced design. For example, if you give little pressure on a icing bag fitted with star nozzle, you will get a small star. But with more pressure it will become a big star. Some decoration require an even pressure, others a varying application of light, medium or heavy pressure.

FAN CAKE

Cakes are also decorated with marzipan, (almond paste). Marzipan recipe is on Pg. 272. **Make nice pliable paste. It should not crack** while bending but hold the given shape. **Following instructions will show you** how to decorate cake in a fan shape shown on colour Pg. 213 :

(1)   Prepare 8 inches diametre round cake.

(2)   Make 1 - 1/2 times recipe of marzipan.

(3)   Cut out two side pieces of the cake to get a handle of a fan. Apply soft jam or a thin layer of butter frosting all over on top and sides of the cake. Place the cake on the cake board.

(4)   Take two-third of the prepared marzipan and colour it pink. Knead it smooth. Roll this pink marzipan very thin - take corn flour if it sticks. Cut out a long strip to cover side of the cake. From the remaining, cut out a number of small and big petal shapes to cover top of the cake. Overlap each piece while placing on the cake.

(5)   Cut a circle big enough to cover handle and to hide uneven end of petals.

(6)   From the leftover pink paste, roll out and cut out three thin strips about 1/4 inch broad and 3 - 1/2 inches long. Take one strip and join two ends to make a circle. Press it in the centre. Attach two remaining strips making a bow. Place bow on the cake as shown in the diagram.

(7)   Make dainty flowers and leaves out of remaining marzipan and arrange like a flower bouquet on the cake. Finish with butter frosting (see Pg. 224) as shown.

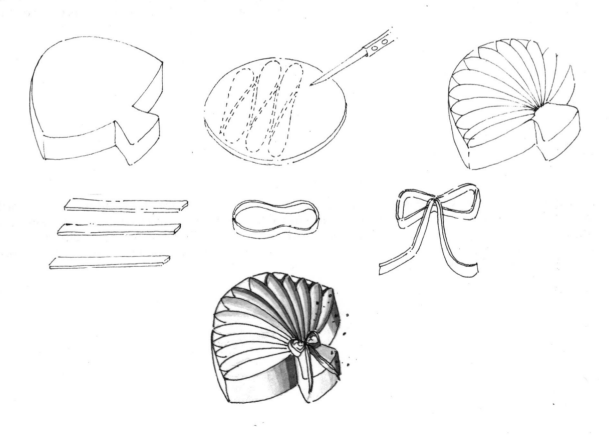

Rose

(1)   Add suitable colour to the required marzipan. Knead well and make it into very smooth and pliable dough. Use little corn flour in case it sticks to fingers.

(2)   Take a small lump of coloured marzipan and shape it into an oval petal. Make top margins thin and lower sides thick. Roll it from one end to form a centre bud of the rose. Flatten the lower base and make it stand.

(3)   Similarly make the second petal in an oval shape. Attach it to the centre bud in such a way that the end of the bud comes in the middle of the second petal. Fold petal from both ends to give shape. Flatten lower end and make it stand.

(4)   Attach three more similar petals, but slightly bigger oval shaped to get a complete rose flower.

(5)   Press middle of the lower side of the rose and separate the extra lump of the marzipan used as a stand. Arrange rose on the cake.

Rose bud

(1)   Make tiny rose buds with three petals as shown in the diagram. Take green lumps of marzipan, flatten it and cut it like calyx. Cover the lower side of the bud.

Leaves

Colour the marzipan green. Roll marzipan with a rolling pin. Cut with either a leaf cutter or with a pointed knife into assorted sizes of leaves. Mark veins with the knife.

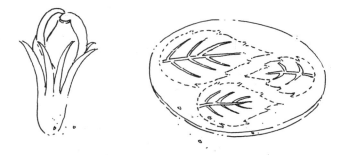

GELATINE SUGAR PASTE

A quicker and cheaper way of making a sugar paste for decoration than marzipan. Useful when small quantity is required.

INGREDIENTS

1 teaspoon gelatine

1 teaspoon margarine

1 - 1/2 tablespoons water

1 cup + 3 tablespoons (9 ozs.) icing sugar

METHOD

(1)   Take gelatine, margarine and water in a bowl and put it over a vessel with hot water. Heat until gelatine and margarine melts. Remove from heat.

(2)   Take half of the sifted icing sugar and mix in the gelatine mixture. Keep on beating and mixing. Add remaining icing sugar and mix into a smooth pliable dough. Knead well and add colour as desired for decoration. Store in a polyethelene bag.

WESTERN STYLE SNACKS AND SANDWICHES

CORN TOASTS (MAKES 10 PIECES)

Golden brown corny toasts made in a jiffy.

INGREDIENTS

1 - 1/2 cups flour

2 teaspoons baking powder

Corns from 4 corn cobs, boiled in salt water (1-1/4 cups)

1/2 cup cheese, grated

3 tablespoons butter

Salt to taste

1 teaspoon mustard powder

1 - 1/2 teaspoons red chilli powder

10 slices bread

2 - 3 tablespoons milk

Ghee to fry

METHOD

(1) Combine all the ingredients together except the bread slices and milk. Add little milk. Mix well. Apply about half an inch thick layer of this mixture on each slice of bread.

(2) Take two to three tablespoons of milk in a separate dish and with an teaspoon, pour the milk over the mixture on the bread slices. Apply milk evenly and make the surface smooth.

(3) Deep fry in hot ghee. When the crust side becomes brown, turn on the other side and fry till light brown. Remove on an absorbent paper. Serve hot with tomato ketchup.

Note :

For easy handling, you can cut each slice in two to make toasts.

PUFF PATTIES (MAKES 12 PIECES)

Crisp patties can be prepared in advance. Bake them just before serving time.

INGREDIENTS

1 recipe puff pastry (see Pg. 221)

FOR THE FILLING

1 tablespoon butter

1/4 cup onions, chopped

1 cup potatoes, boiled, cut into small pieces

1/2 cup green peas

1 tablespoon lemon juice

1/4 teaspoon cinnamon and cloves, powdered

Salt to taste

2 tablespoons parsley or coriander leaves, chopped

METHOD

(1) Heat butter, add the chopped onions. Saute till light pink in colour. Add potatoes, peas, lemon juice, powdered cinnamon and cloves and salt to taste. Mix well and remove from the gas. Cool Mix in parsley or coriander leaves. Divide into 12 portions.

(2) Take cooled ready puff pastry. Roll on floured surface to 1/4 inch thickness. Cut out 12 pieces big enough to cover pattie tins on top. Keep all these pieces in fridge. Take remaining pastry and roll out thinly. Cut 10 pieces big enough to line pattie tins. Keep them in greased tins.
Put filling in centre. Apply very little water on edges of pastry. Take out the cold pastry tops and stick them on top. Cut out trimmings. Make ball of the cut trimmings and make two remaining tins. Apply milk on each patty as glaze.

(3) Bake first for 20 minutes at 250ºC, then for 1 hour at 100ºC.

(4) When crisp, remove from tins and serve hot.

SAVOURY PICNIC BUNS (MAKES 8 PIECES)

Tasty buns with a sumptuous filling are good for picnics. They taste good even when cold.

INGREDIENTS

FOR THE FILLING

1/2 cup green grams or green peas, boiled

1/2 cup cabbage, chopped

1/2 cup carrot, grated

2 tablespoons coriander leaves or parsley, chopped

2 tablespoons capsicums, chopped

1 green chilli, chopped

1 tablespoon lemon juice

Salt to taste

1 tablespoon butter

FOR THE COVERING

1 teaspoon salt

1 teaspoon sugar

1 - 1/2 teaspoons yeast

2 cups flour

1 tablespoon butter

1/2 cup lukewarm water

METHOD

(1) Melt butter and add all the vegetables. Saute them on high flame till little soft. Add lemon juice and salt to taste. Remove from gas. Cool. Divide into eight portions.

(2) Melt salt and sugar in lukewarm water. Mix yeast in the flour. Make a soft dough with the above prepared water. Knead with butter for five minutes. Keep dough in an oiled vessel, covered with a wet cloth. Leave aside for 1 - 1/2 hours till the dough is double in size. Knead lightly again. Divide into eight balls. Spread out each ball and put stuffing in the centre, cover and arrange them on a greased baking tray. Cover with a wet cloth. Leave aside for about 25 minutes.

(3) Bake at 250°C for 15 to 20 minutes or till light brown on top. Remove buns from the oven, cool an wire rack. Apply ghee as a glaze.

CURRANT BUNS (MAKES 8 BUNS)

A milk bread with currants and cherries - a sure hit amongst children.

INGREDIENTS

1/4 cup milk

1/4 cup water

1 - 1/2 teaspoons fresh yeast

1 teaspoon sugar for the yeast

2 cups flour

1/2 teaspoon salt

1 tablespoon sugar for dough

1/4 cup mixture of black currants and glazed cherries, chopped

1 tablespoon butter or margarine

METHOD

(1) Warm milk and water together. Melt yeast, sugar and quarter cup of flour (out of 2 cups) in it. Keep this mixture for 10 minutes till it becomes frothy.

(2) Mix salt, ordinary sugar, chopped currants and cherries to the remaining flour. Make a soft dough with prepared mixture. Knead with butter or margarine for a few minutes.

(3) Keep dough in an oiled vessel till double in size or for 1 - 1/2 hours.

(4) Knead dough again and make about eight balls. Arrange them on a greased baking tray. Cover with an oiled plastic sheet till double in size.

(5) Brush milk on top of each ball. Sprinkle ordinary sugar on them.

(6) Heat oven to 250°C. Bake till buns are golden brown in colour about 15 to 20 minutes.

(7) Remove and cool on wire rack or cloth.

SPAGHETTI MUSHROOM TAKILA (MAKES 30 PIECES)

A tasty snack - ideal conversational pieces over cocktails.

INGREDIENTS

30 bread pieces, 1-1/2" x 1-1/2" cubes

FOR THE TOPPING

1 tablespoon butter

1 cup mushrooms, chopped (fresh or canned)

2 tablespoons oil

1/2 cup onions, finely chopped

8 cloves garlic, finely chopped

3 green chillies, finely chopped

1/2 inch ginger, finely chopped

4 tablespoons gram flour

1 cup spaghetti, boiled

1 tablespoon Worcestershire sauce

1/2 cup tomato ketchup

Salt to taste

FOR THE COATING

1/2 cup self raising flour

1/2 cup gram flour

1/4 teaspoon black pepper powder

Salt to taste

Oil for deep frying

METHOD

(1) Heat butter and saute the chopped mushrooms till cooked and dry. Keep aside.

(2) Heat oil, add onions and saute till light pink in colour. Add garlic, chillies and ginger. Saute for a few more minutes.

(3) Add gram flour. Saute for a few more minutes. Now add spaghetti, mushrooms, Worcestershire sauce, tomato ketchup and salt to taste. Mix well and stir mixture till dry. Remove from gas and cool.

(4) Over each bread cube evenly spread and press a little of the topping on one side. Keep aside.

(5) Make a batter of pouring consistency by mixing together the two flours, seasoning and water.

(6) With a teaspoon, pour a little of the batter on each cube. Coat them well on all sides with the batter.

(7) Heat oil. Deep fry the cubes placing the topping side in oil, first. Fry till light brown, turn on the other side. When done, remove on an absorbent paper and serve with 'hot and sweet sauce'.

PUFF STRAWS (MAKES 48 STRAWS)

Crisp straws with layered puffs can be stored like any snack and served with tea or soups.

INGREDIENTS

2 cups flour

1/2 cup ghee or butter

1/2 teaspoon salt

1/2 teaspoon caraway seeds

1/2 teaspoon black pepper, coarsely ground

3 tablespoons rice flour

Ghee for deep frying

METHOD

(1) Make a slightly tight dough out of flour, quarter of butter, salt, caraway seeds and black pepper. Knead well and leave aside covered for half an hour.

(2) Knead dough again and divide into six balls. Roll each ball as big as possible atleast eight inches in diametre like chappati.

(3) Prepare a paste by beating remaining quarter cup butter and rice flour.

(4)   Apply this paste evenly all over the surface of all the chappatis. Put one chappati over the other making a pair. You will get three pairs. Now fold each pair into a tight roll. Cut them into half an inch pieces. Roll each piece about 2 - 3 inches long by keeping its cut side up. Twist each piece. Deep fry in ghee on medium gas till crisp and light pink in colour. Remove on an absorbent paper.

WALNUT COFFEE BREAD (6 SERVINGS)

An unusual bread mildly flavoured with cinnamon and topped with walnut pieces.

INGREDIENTS

FOR THE DOUGH

1 medium sized ring mould

2 cups flour

1 - 1/2 teaspoons fresh yeast

1/2 cup lukewarm milk

1/2 teaspoon sugar

1/2 teaspoon salt

1 tablespoon butter or margarine

FOR THE TOPPING

2 tablespoons melted butter

3 tablespoons powdered sugar

1/2 teaspoon powdered cinnamon

3 tablespoons walnuts, finely chopped

METHOD

(1)   In a large bowl blend together quarter cup of flour (out of 2 cups) yeast, milk and sugar to make a batter. Keep aside till frothy for 10 minutes.

(2)   Mix salt in the remaining flour. Make a soft dough with frothy mixture of yeast. Use mixture of milk and water to make dough.

(3)   Knead dough with butter or margarine. Put in an oiled vessel. Keep it covered with a wet cloth till double in size.

(4)   Knead dough once again and divide it into 12 balls.

(5)   Roll each ball in melted butter and then in the mixture of powdered sugar, cinnamon and walnuts.

(6)   Arrange two layers of these balls in a greased ring mould, where each ball of the second row alternates with the balls of the first row.

(7)   Heat oven to 250ºC. Put the bread for baking in the middle of the oven. Bake till light brown on top, for about 20 minutes. Then put mould on the lower shelf and bake for another five minutes. Then remove from oven.

(8)   Unmould bread after few minutes and cool on wire rack.

GLAZED CINNAMON WHEEL (6 SERVINGS)

A decorative and tasty bread. Shows design of a wheel when sliced.

INGREDIENTS

A loaf tin

Recipe for the dough is same as Walnut Coffee Bread

FOR THE FILLING

2 tablespoons orange juice

3/4 teaspoon powdered cinnamon

2 tablespoons powdered sugar

A drop orange colour

3 drops orange essence

METHOD

(1) Make dough just like Walnut Coffee Bread upto double in size (method 3).
(2) Mix orange essence and colour in the orange juice.
(3) Knead dough with one tablespoon of orange juice. Make a ball and roll out 6" x 12" rectangular on a floured surface.
(4) Apply orange juice all over. Sprinkle mixture of sugar and cinnamon over it. Now roll up the dough from narrow side. Place in a greased 8 inches long loaf tin. Cover with an oiled plastic sheet and keep aside till double in size.
(5) Heat oven to 250°C and bake the cinnamon wheel for about 25 to 30 minutes or till crust becomes quite brown. Remove from oven, unmould and cool on wire rack. Apply sugar glaze on top when bread is still warm. Cut into slices and serve.
(6) For sugar glaze: Take equal amount of sugar and water in a small vessel. Melt sugar and boil till syrup is sticky. Use immediately.

WAFFLES

Waffles are one of the most favourite Western style dishes. There are many variations and combinations of preparing them.

HOW TO USE A WAFFLE IRON :

(1) Season waffle iron before using, to prevent it from sticking. To season, brush cold iron with oil. Heat to baking temperature, cool.
(2) When making waffles for the first time in a waffle iron, discard first waffle, since it will be very greasy. After that waffles made according to the recipe will come out well.
(3) Once waffle iron has been seasoned never wash it. If waffle particles stick to grids, before baking any more waffles, brush off particles.
(4) Always heat iron before making waffles, and put little ghee before pouring batter.
(5) Do not raise cover during baking.
(6) When a waffle is done, lift cover, loosen waffle with a fork, serve at once. Reheat iron before pouring in next waffle batter.
(7) (a) Waffles can be served for breakfast — with butter and honey, or golden syrup.
    (b) It can also be used as an accompaniment to curries, creamed vegetables etc.
    (c) As a dessert topped with fruit or icecream.

PLAIN WAFFLES (6 SERVINGS)

Enjoy plain waffles with many variations.

INGREDIENTS

2 cups flour

2 - 1/2 teaspoons baking powder

1/2 teaspoon salt

2 teaspoons sugar

4 tablespoons melted butter or margarine

1 - 1/2 cups milk

METHOD

(1) Sieve the flour with baking powder and salt and transfer into a pan.

(2) Mix in melted butter, sugar and milk to make a smooth batter. It should have a pouring consistency. Adjust it with water.

(3) Keep aside this batter for an hour before making waffles.

Variations -

(a) Add one cup of boiled corn in the batter before making waffles.

(b) Add one tablespoon of curry powder to the batter before making waffles. Serve with curry.

(c) Add one cup of grated fresh coconut to the batter before making waffles.

SWEET WAFFLES (6 SERVINGS)

Most commonly available in restaurants. They are delicious when served with butter and honey.

INGREDIENTS

2 cups flour

2 - 1/2 teaspoons baking powder

A pinch salt

2 tablespoons powdered sugar

4 tablespoons melted margarine or butter

1 - 1/2 cups milk

METHOD

(1) Sift flour with salt and baking powder and transfer into a pan.

(2) Add powdered sugar, melted margarine and milk. Make a smooth batter with a pouring consistency. Adjust with water. Keep this batter aside for an hour before making waffles.

Variation -

Sprinkle chopped walnuts or a mixture of walnuts and cashewnuts over batter as soon as it has been poured on to the iron.

RAISED WAFFLES (6 SERVINGS)

Golden brown crisp waffles are made spicy with chillies and coriander leaves.

INGREDIENTS	METHOD
2 cups flour	(1) Sieve flour.
1/4 cup water	(2) Melt sugar and salt in lukewarm water.
1 - 1/2 cups warm milk	(3) Mix in fresh yeast, melted butter and milk. Make a smooth batter.
1 teaspoon fresh yeast	(4) Cover this mixture and keep aside for 1 - 1/2 hours to rise.
2 teaspoons sugar	(5) Stir well before making waffles.
1 teaspoon salt	**Variation**
4 tablespoons melted butter	Add chopped coriander leaves and green chillies to the batter.

BUTTERMILK WAFFLES (6 SERVINGS)

Little sour taste of buttermilk in the waffles, balances with the sweetness of honey.

INGREDIENTS	METHOD
2 cups flour	(1) Sieve flour with salt, baking powder and soda bicarb.
1/2 teaspoon salt	(2) Add melted butter and buttermilk to make a smooth batter.
2 teaspoons baking powder	(3) Keep batter for an hour before making waffles.
1 - 1/4 teaspoons soda bicarb	(4) Serve hot with butter and honey or golden syrup.
1 - 1/4 cups thick buttermilk	
4 tablespoons melted butter	

SANDWICHES

Sandwiches are the most common and convenient for any occasion. It can be very casual or extremely fancy for celebrations.

Normally sandwiches are made of bread, butter and some kind of filling. White sandwich bread, brown bread, buns and rolls are normally used for making sandwiches. Ordinary butter and peanut butter are also required.

TYPES OF SANDWICHES

(1)   **Lunch pack or plain sandwiches**
      Two slices of plain or toasted bread are spread with butter and put together with a filing in between.
(2)   **Open Sandwiches**
      Bread is cut into different fancy shapes, spread with butter and topped with colourful filling.
(3)   **Toasted Sandwiches**
      Two slices of bread are spread with moist filling and the whole sandwich is grilled or toasted on gas in a special toaster. They are eaten hot.
(4)   **Fried Sandwiches**
      One slice of bread is spread with moist sticky topping and deep fried in oil or ghee.
(5)   **Double decker or club sandwiches**
      Three or more slices of bread or toasts are spread with butter and put together with different fillings in each layer. They are sometimes secured with a toothpick.

LUNCH PACK SANDWICHES

INGREDIENTS

(a)   Carrot and cheese filling (3 sandwiches)

3 tablespoons cheese, grated	**METHOD**
1 tablespoon butter	Mix together all the ingredients and use as filling for lunch pack, pinwheel or open sandwiches.
3 tablespoons carrot, grated	
Salt and pepper to taste	
Mayonnaise to bind (see Pg. 45)	

(b)   Apple and cheese filling (3 sandwiches)

3 tablespoons cheese, grated	Mix together all the ingredients and use as filling for lunch pack and open sandwiches.
1 tablespoon apple, chopped	
1 tablespoon walnuts, chopped	
Mayonnaise to bind (see Pg. 45)	

(c)   Garden Sandwich filling (8 sandwiches)

100 grams paneer, mashed
1 teaspoon green chillies, chopped
1 teaspoon capsicum, chopped
1 cup carrots, grated
1 tablespoon coriander leaves, chopped
Salt and pepper to taste
Mayonnaise to bind (see Pg. 45)

METHOD

Mix together all the ingredients and use as filling for lunch pack or open sandwiches.

(d)   Cucumber and cheese filling (3 sandwiches)

1 cucumber, grated, squeeze out water
2 tablespoons cheese, grated
A drop of green colour
Salt and pepper to taste

Mix together all the ingredients and use as filling for open or lunch pack sandwiches.

OPEN SANDWICHES

INGREDIENTS

(a)   Vegetable topping (12 - 15 sandwiches)

3/4 cup cabbage, shredded
1/2 cup cucumber, chopped
1/4 cup walnuts and cashewnuts, chopped
2 tablespoons capsicums, chopped
Salt and pepper to taste
Mayonnaise to bind (see Pg. 45)

METHOD

Mix together all the ingredients and spread on open sandwiches.

(b)   Coconut topping (3 sandwiches)

1 cup coconut, grated
1/4 cup onions, finely chopped
1 - 1/2 tablespoons butter
1/4 teaspoon turmeric powder
1/2 teaspoon red chilli powder
Salt to taste
1 tablespoon lemon juice
3 slices brown bread
3 slices white bread
Little tomato ketchup

Mix all the ingredients together and spread on square slices of bread. Cut out a ring from brown bread with a doughnut cutter. Apply butter on one side of this ring and place it on the spread. Dot centre with tomato ketchup or chilli sauce.

(c)   Green chilli topping (3 sandwiches)

1 tablespoon green chillies, finely chopped	Mix all the ingredients together and spread on open sandwiches.
1 - 1/2 tablespoons thick white sauce (see Pg. 70)	
Salt to taste	

(d)   Peanut topping (3 sandwiches)

1 tablespoon peanut butter	Spread peanut butter to an open sandwich. Apply lemon juice and then sprinkle ground peanuts.
Few drops lemon juice	
1 tablespoon peanuts, ground	

(e)   Apple and peanut topping (3 sandwiches)

1 tablespoon peanut butter	Spread peanut butter to an open sandwich. Put slices of apple and then apply lemon juice over it.
Few drops lemon juice	
Few slices apple	

(f)   Butterfly sandwich (1 sandwich)

Bread slice, cut in the shape of a butterfly	Apply butter to the shaped bread slice. Put mixture of tomato ketchup and peanut butter in the centre as body. Insert two small thin long pieces of carrot as whiskers. Arrange two round pieces of capsicum on two wings.
1 small carrot	
Little butter	
1/4 teaspoon tomato ketchup or chilli sauce	
A small piece capsicum	
1/4 teaspoon peanut butter	

TOASTED OR GRILLED SANDWICHES

To get nice golden toasted sandwiches, use butter on the outside of the bread slices, i.e. the sandwich filling is placed between the unbuttered sides of the bread slices. The filling can be made in advance, and slices can be buttered and kept ready in order to serve hot sandwiches in a jiffy. Serve with tomato ketchup, chutney or any spicy sauce.

(a)   Pizza filling (4 - 5 sandwiches)

2 tablespoons butter	(1) Melt butter and saute the capsicums, onions and garlic together till soft.
2 tablespoons capsicums, chopped	(2) Add breadcrumbs and saute for a minute longer. Add tomato juice, cheese and the seasonings.
2 tablespoons onions, chopped	
1 teaspoon garlic, chopped	(3) Mix well and cook for a few more minutes. Remove from gas and cool to room temperature before using in the toasts.
2 tablespoons breadcrumbs	
1 cup thick tomato juice	
1/4 cup cheese, grated	
1 teaspoon oregano	
1 teaspoon parsley flakes	
Salt, pepper and sugar to taste	

(b)   Russian salad filling (6 sandwiches)

1/4 cup potatoes, boiled, mashed	Mix well all the ingredients before using as filling for toasted sandwiches.
1/4 cup French beans, chopped, boiled	**Variations -**
1/4 cup carrots, chopped, boiled	(1) Add two tablespoons chopped pieces of canned pineapple and one tablespoon of chopped walnuts.
1/4 cup green peas, boiled	
Mayonnaise to bind (see Pg. 45)	(2) Add chopped and boiled pieces of capsicums.
Salt and pepper to taste	(3) Replace French beans and carrots with cucumber and salad leaves.

(c)   Mushroom and rice filling (6 - 8 sandwiches)

2 tablespoons butter	(1) Melt butter and saute onions till light pink in colour.
1/2 cup onions, chopped	(2) Add chopped mushrooms and saute till dry.
1/2 cup mushrooms (fresh or canned)	(3) Remove from gas and add rice, carrots cheese and seasoning. Mix well.
1 cup rice, soft cooked	
1/4 cup carrots, chopped, boiled	(4) Assemble the mixture on buttered slices of brown bread and toast.
Salt and pepper to taste	
1/4 cup cheese, grated	

(d) Savoury Banana filling (6 sandwiches)

2 special cooking bananas, (three faced raw bananas)	(1) Cook bananas in pressure cooker with their skin.
1/4 cup peanuts, roasted, pounded	(2) Peel and mash them. Add peanuts, chilli powder, salt, lemon juice, coconut and coriander leaves. Mix well.
2 teaspoons red chilli powder	(3) Use this mixture for toasted sandwiches.
Salt to taste	
2 tablespoons lemon juice	
1/4 cup fresh coconut, grated	
2 tablespoons coriander leaves, chopped	

(e) Cheese and sago filling (6 sandwiches)

1/4 cup sago	(1) Soak sago in water for five minutes. Drain off water and dry them on cloth for another 10 minutes.
2 tablespoons butter	(2) Melt butter and saute the chopped green chillies and sago. Stir and keep on the gas for two minutes.
1 teaspoon green chillies, chopped	(3) Add mashed potatoes, grated coconut, lemon juice, salt, sugar, peanuts and cheese. Mix well and remove from gas. Cool and use as filling for toasted sandwiches
1 cup potatoes, boiled, mashed	
2 tablespoons fresh coconut, grated	
1 tablespoon lemon juice	
Salt and sugar to taste	
2 tablespoons peanuts, ground	
1/4 cup cheese, grated	

(f) Vegetarian Chinese filling (6 sandwiches)

2 tablespoons oil	(1) Heat oil. Add potatoes, noodles, corn and carrots. Saute for a few minutes.
1/4 cup potatoes, boiled, chopped	(2) Add soya sauce, chilli sauce, vinegar and salt to taste. Mix well.
1/2 cup noodles, boiled	(3) Remove from gas, cool and use this as filling for toasted sandwiches.
1/4 cup corn, boiled	
1/4 cup carrots, chopped, boiled	
1 tablespoon soya sauce	
1 teaspoon chilli sauce	
1 teaspoon vinegar	
Salt to taste	

TRICOLOUR CLUB SANDWICH (MAKES 1 BIG SERVING)

A colourful club sandwich. One can toast the bread with the same filling.

INGREDIENTS

4 slices bread

1/4 cup paneer, mashed

1 tablespoon onion, grated

1 tablespoon fresh coconut, grated

Salt, pepper to taste

Green and orange colour

METHOD

Mix all the given ingredients except the colours. Divide mixture into three parts. To two parts put green and orange colours, and keep one part plain. Now spread filling on bread slices in such a way that it forms tricolour sandwich block.

CHECKED SANDWICH (MAKES 6 PIECES)

Unique and colourful sandwiches in checked pattern.

INGREDIENTS

4 tablespoons cheese, grated

4 tablespoons butter

Salt, pepper to taste

Mayonnaise to bind (see Pg. 45)

3 white slices bread

3 brown slices bread

METHOD

FOR THE CHECKED SANDWICHES

Mix all the given ingredients together and prepare a smooth paste. Apply this paste on slices and arrange them in alternate order. Now cut all these slices together into three blocks. Turn the centre block upside down. Apply remaining paste on both sides of centre block and then stick all three together. Cover this block in a wet thin cloth and keep in fridge to cool. Butter will harden and the bread pieces will stick properly with each other. Now cut slices in such a way that each one gets a checked pattern.

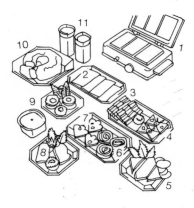

1. Plain waffle   p. 234
2. Raised waffle   p. 235
3. Checked sandwiches   p. 242
4. Butterfly sandwiches   p. 237
5. Carrot and cheese filling in lunch pack sandwiches   p. 236
6. Pinwheel sandwhiches   p. 245
7. Green chilli topping open sandwiches   p. 237
8. Corn toast   p. 229
9. Coconut tropping-open sandwiches   p. 237
10. Walnut coffee bread   p. 232
11. Grapes and apple cocktail   p. 34
12. Fancy carrot leaves   p. 246
13. Carrot rose   p. 246

SANDWICH CAKE (12 SERVINGS)

A sandwich made to appear just like a cake for special parties.

INGREDIENTS

1 small loaf bread, 8 inches long

FOR THE TOPPING

1 cup green peas, boiled, make a fine paste

1 - 1/2 tablespoons butter

1 tablespoon lemon juice

Salt and pepper to taste

A few drops green colour, if required

FOR THE FILLING

2 potatoes, boiled, cut into small pieces

1/4 cup carrots, chopped, boiled

1/4 cup French beans, chopped, boiled

Salt, pepper to taste

Thick white sauce to bind (see Pg. 70)

FOR THE POTATO ICING

1 potato, very finely mashed

Salt to taste

Little orange colour

1 tablespoon milk

1 teaspoon butter

METHOD

FOR THE CAKE

(1)   Remove crust from all sides of the bread loaf. Cut it horizontally into three thick slices. Apply butter to the lower slice. Spread half of the filling. Now butter the centre slice on both sides. Put over the filling. Spread second layer of filling. Butter the top slice on the lower side and place over the second filling.

(2)   Combine all the given ingredients for the topping. Now cover cake with this green pea topping. Level the surface smooth with the help of a palette knife dipped in water. Decorate with potato icing as normally done for cakes.

FOR THE FILLING

Combine all the given ingredients together and bind with the thick white sauce.

FOR THE POTATO ICING

Mix the given ingredients together and put on the slow gas. Stir till the mixture leaves the sides of the vessel. Use when cool.

PINWHEEL SANDWICHES (MAKES 12 PIECES)

Colour of the filling play an important role in these sandwiches. Any soft, colourful filling can be used to make these pinwheel sandwiches.

INGREDIENTS

3 slices bread, horizontally cut

1 cup purple yam, (ratalu) boiled, mashed

1 tablespoon lemon juice

Salt, pepper to taste

1 - 1/2 tablespoons butter

Few drops red cochineal colour, if required

METHOD

FOR THE PINWHEEL SANDWICHES

(1)   Mix all the given ingredients together except the butter and slices. Prepare a nice and smooth deep purplish red coloured mixture.

(2)   Apply butter to the slices. Then apply the mixture evenly over the slices. Roll each slice from the narrow end, into a tight roll.

(3)   Wrap these rolls in a wet cloth. Keep aside for 10 minutes. Cut into 3/4 inch thick slices. They will make colourful purple and white pinwheel sandwiches.

RIBBON SANDWICH (MAKES 12 PIECES)

A colourful combination of brown and white bread, green chutney and yellow chutney.

INGREDIENTS

FOR THE RIBBON SANDWICH

6 slices, brown bread

6 slices, white bread

4 tablespoons yellow chutney

6 tablespoons green chutney

3 tablespoons butter

FOR THE YELLOW CHUTNEY

1/2 cup coconut, grated

1 tablespoon peanuts, roasted

1 tablespoon grams, roasted (dalia)

1/2 teaspoon cummin seeds

1 Tablespoon lemon juice

2 green chillies

Salt to taste

Few drops yellow colour

METHOD

FOR THE RIBBON SANDWICH

(1)   Mix one tablespoon of butter in the yellow chutney and two tablespoons of butter in the green chutney.

(2)   Apply green chutney and yellow chutney evenly on three brown and three white bread slices and stick them alternately. Stick them firmly. Wrap in a wet cloth and leave in fridge for at least one or two hours. Remove before serving time and cut into slices. Each slice will have ribbon like colourful layers of bread and chutney. This recipe makes two blocks, resulting in 12 slices.

FOR THE GREEN CHUTNEY

See recipe on Pg. 126

FOR THE YELLOW CHUTNEY

Combine all the given ingredients in the wet grinder and grind to a fine paste.

CARROT ROSE

(1)   Cut out a 2 inches piece of a carrot from its broad end. Peel it and make it smooth rounded with a flat top. Carve out about five petals just below the flat top. Cut petals thin and rounded as possible.

(2)   Place the pointed knife at right angle from top and peel out a thin continuous ring from the inside of the carrot. It separates the petals and will give it fullness.

(3)   After completing the second step, it is just a matter of repeating these two steps, working towards the centre of the carrot. Cut these second set of petals in such a way that they alternate the first row. Similarly all layers of petals should alternate the previous ones. The more rows of thin petals you can carve out, the more striking and natural the rose will look.

(4)   One can carve similar rose out of beetroot, turnip, potato etc.

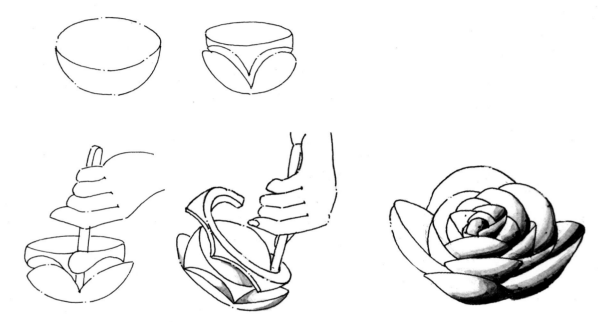

FANCY CARROT LEAF

(1)   Cut out a thin even slice from a carrot. Give it a curved leaf shape as shown in the diagram.

(2)   Cut out serrated edges by carving a straight cut and a curved slant cut.

(3)   Carve out small oval holes near each serrated edge and a curved vein in the centre.

(4)   Put this leaf in ice cold water so that it gets a natural curve and stiffness.

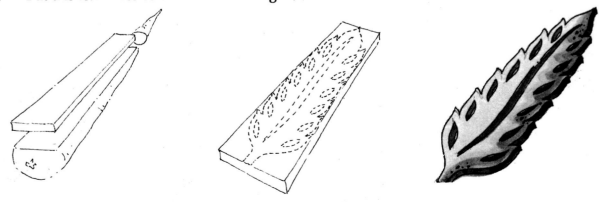

PUDDINGS AND DESSERTS

STRAWBERRY CHANTILLY (6 SERVINGS)

A souffle type of a soft, fluffy pudding which can be turned out in a jiffy.

INGREDIENTS

1 packet strawberry jelly crystals (85 grams) or follow recipe on Pg. 287

1/2 family pack vanilla icecream (200 grams)

1 cup strawberries mixed with 2 table-spoons powdered sugar

METHOD

(1) Set the dissolved strawberry jelly crystals partially. Divide into two parts. To one part, mix in vanilla icecream and whip on ice. Chill it. To the remaining half, mix in strawberries mixed with powdered sugar.

(2) Remove the chilled pudding in individual dessert bowls. Spoon strawberry jelly mixture on the top. Serve immediately.

PUDDING ON CLOUD (6 SERVINGS)

A quick chocolate pudding laced with cream.

INGREDIENTS

200 grams fresh cream

4 tablespoons powdered sugar, for fresh cream

2 cups milk

2 teaspoons cocoa powder

1/4 teaspoon salt

5 tablespoons sugar, for the custard

2 tablespoons custard powder

1 - 1/2 tablespoons corn flour

METHOD

(1) Whip fresh cream with powdered sugar on ice till stiff. Keep aside in the refrigerator.

(2) Heat milk with sugar. Dissolve cocoa powder, corn flour and custard powder in little cold milk. When the milk is hot, pour the above mixture and stir till thick. Remove from gas and cool. Chill till partially set.

(3) Divide the whipped cream into six individual glasses. Using the back of the spoon make a depression in the centre of each, and spread it up the sides of the glass. Spoon chocolate pudding in the centre. Chill thoroughly.

Note :
One can also serve this pudding on a bed of crushed biscuits. Mix about a cup of finely crushed biscuits, with melted butter. Press this mixture on the sides of the bowl and heap pudding in the centre. It can be laced with sweetened fresh cream.

CHOCOLATE SOUFFLE (6 SERVINGS)

Souffles are one of the finest desserts ever made. To get soft and spongy results, one has to have skill and alertness.

INGREDIENTS

FOR THE CUSTARD

2 cups milk

5 tablespoons sugar

6 teaspoons custard powder

1 - 1/2 tablespoons cocoa powder

1 tablespoon drinking chocolate

3/4 teaspoon vanilla essence

FOR THE GELATINE MIXTURE

2 - 1/2 tablespoons gelatine

3 tablespoons powdered sugar

1 cup water to melt gelatine

FOR THE CREAM

300 grams fresh cream

5 tablespoons powdered sugar

METHOD

(1) Combine milk and sugar in a pan and heat. Dissolve custard powder, cocoa powder and drinking chocolate in little cold milk. And add to the hot milk. Stir till thick. Remove from heat and cool. Mix vanilla essence.

(2) Mix gelatine and sugar in a pan. Add water and put on a double boiler to melt. Beat on ice till it looks like cream.

(3) Take out cream in a vessel. Add sugar and beat on ice till stiff but flowing. Keep aside little for decoration.

(4) Place a big vessel on ice. Add the cooled custard, cream and beaten gelatine. Stir often, scraping the sides till the souffle becomes almost thick.

(5) Pour in a prepared souffle bowl. Set in fridge. Take out foil and decorate with stiff cream.

To prepare a souffle bowl

Take a round bowl, much smaller than the quantity of the souffle mixture. Cut aluminium foil 3 inches wide and long enough to wrap around the bowl with half of its width above the rim. Fasten it with cellotape or tie with a thread.

PINEAPPLE SOUFFLE (6 SERVINGS)

INGREDIENTS

1 small can pineapple slices (450 grams)

FOR THE CUSTARD

2 cups milk

5 tablespoons powdered sugar

6 teaspoons custard powder

3/4 teaspoon pineapple essence

A few drops pineapple colour

FOR THE GELATINE

2-1/2 tablespoons gelatine

1 tablespoon sugar

1 cup syrup from pineapple can

2 tablespoons lemon juice

METHOD

(1) Combine milk and sugar in a vessel and heat. Dissolve custard powder in little cold milk and add to the hot milk. Stir till thick. Remove from heat and cool. Mix pineapple essence and colour.

(2) Mix together gelatine and sugar. Add pineapple syrup. Put on a double boiler to melt. Mix lemon juice. Beat on ice with an eggbeater till fluffy like cream.

(3) Combine fresh cream and powdered sugar. Beat on ice till cream is stiff but flowing. Keep little for decoration.

(4) Cut pineapple into tiny bits, reserving one or two rings for decoration.

FOR THE CREAM

300 grams fresh cream

5 tablespoons powdered sugar

(5) Place a big vessel on plenty of ice cubes. Mix in cooled custard, cream, beaten gelatine and pineapple pieces. Stir often, scrapping the sides till the souffle becomes almost thick.

(6) Pour in a prepared soffle bowl. Set in a fridge. Before serving, remove foil. Decorate with pineapple slices and stiffly beaten fresh cream.

ORANGE SOUFFLE (6 SERVINGS)

INGREDIENTS

Replace :

Pineapple syrup with orange juice
Pineapple pieces with orange segments
Pineapple essence with orange essence
Pineapple colour with orange colour

METHOD

Basic method remains same as pineapple souffle.

LEMON SOUFFLE (6 SERVINGS)

INGREDIENTS

Replace :

Pineapple syrup with water.
Pineapple essence with lemon essence
Pineapple colour with lemon colour

Omit pineapple pieces

METHOD

Basic method remains same as pineapple souffle.

CARAMEL CASHEWNUT SOUFFLE (6 SERVINGS)

INGREDIENTS

FOR THE SOUFFLE

Replace :
Pineapple syrup with water.
Pineapple essence with vanilla essence.

Omit
Pineapple colour.

FOR THE CARAMEL CASHEWNUT PIECES

90 grams (3 ozs.) sugar

30 ml (1 fl. oz.) water

90 grams (3 ozs.) cashewnut pieces

METHOD

(1) Basic method remains same as pineapple souffle.

(2) When the final souffle mixture is in the process of setting, add and mix half of the prepared caramel cashewnut pieces. To decorate souffle, sprinkle remaining cashewnut pieces on top.

(3) To prepare caramel cashewnuts, combine sugar and water in a thick pan. Melt sugar on low heat. Boil syrup till it turns light caramel looking like honey. Mix in cashewnut pieces and immediately spread over a greased plate. Cool under a fan. Remove from plate and crush into small pieces.

CHOCOLATE CHERRY PARFAIT (4 SERVINGS)

Highly decorative and tasty pudding.

INGREDIENTS	METHOD
1 packet red cherry jelly crystals-(85 grams) or follow recipe on Pg. 287	(1) Dissolve jelly in boiling water and cool. Chill until semi-set.
1-3/4 cups water to dissolve jelly crystals	(2) Blend icecream into half of the semiset jelly.
1 cup chocolate icecream	(3) Whip fresh cream with powdered sugar. Mix in cherry pieces.
1/4 cup glazed cherries, chopped	(4) Now spoon icecream jelly mixture into four individual dessert bowls. Add cherry- whipped cream topping, and top with the remaining half of the clear jelly. Chill till set.
200 grams fresh cream	
4 tablespoons powdered sugar	

IMPERIAL RICE PUDDING (6 SERVINGS)

A snow white pudding

INGREDIENTS	METHOD
2 tablespoons gelatine	(1) Soak gelatine in little water and then melt on low heat.
3 cups milk	(2) Boil milk and add prepared rice. Remove from heat and mix in sugar and almonds. Mix well and cool. Add vanilla essence.
3 tablespoons rice, boiled, mashed with little milk	
8 tablespoons sugar	(3) Leave this mixture in the refrigerator till semiset.
2 tablespoons almonds, blanched, powdered with little milk	(4) Meanwhile, whip fresh cream with four tablespoons of sugar, over ice cubes. Beat till stiff but flowing.
1 teaspoon vanilla essence	(5) Mix whipped cream with semiset milk mixture. Pour this pudding in a serving bowl. Set in fridge and decorate with blanched almonds and cherries.
200 grams fresh cream	
4 tablespoons powdered sugar	
TO DECORATE	
Few almonds, blanched	
Few glazed cherries	

1. Chocolate cherry parfait   p. 250
2. Sunshine pudding   p. 254
3. Lemon cream tarts   p. 255
4. Orange soufflé   p. 249

CHARLOTTE RUSSE (6-8 SERVINGS)

Very unusual and attractive pudding. It has an outer biscuit layer with soft cream inside and decorative jelly on top.

INGREDIENTS

FOR THE TOP LAYER

1 Packet lemon jelly crystals (85 grams) or follow recipe on Pg. 287

2-1/2 cups water to dissolve jelly crystals

A few glazed cherries

12 sponge fingers (readymade long crisp biscuits)

FOR THE BAVARIAN CREAM

1/2 litre milk

3 teaspoons custard powder

1 tablespoon sugar

2 tablespoons gelatine

1/2 teaspoon vanilla essence

1/4 cup walnuts, chopped

200 grams fresh cream

METHOD

(1)   Prepare jelly by dissolving it in two an a half cups of water. Cool. Pour jelly in a six inches round deep tin forming a 1/2 inch layer. Put in fridge to set. Arrange pattern of cherries on this jelly and set carefully. Cover with a little more jelly. Set remaining jelly and use for decoration.

(2)   Trim sponge fingers and fit closely round the side of the tin.

(3)   Melt gelatine in little water and cool.

(4)   Prepare custard with milk , custard powder and sugar. Cool. Add gelatine, vanilla essence and chopped walnuts.

(5)   Now whip cream with four tablespoons of powdered sugar. Mix with cooled custard and gelatine. Pour at once into the prepared charlotte tin. Leave in fridge to set.

(6)   Dip the bottom of the tin in warn water and then invert on a serving plate. Jelly and pattern of cherries will be seen on top. Sponge fingers will be all round enclosing soft pudding inside.

(7)   Chop remaining set jelly into small pieces and spoon around the pudding.

APRICOT DELIGHT (6 SERVINGS)

A simple pudding with a spicy apricot sauce.

INGREDIENTS

FOR THE CUSTARD

1/2 litre milk

6 teaspoons sugar

2 heaped tablespoons corn flour

1/2 teaspoon vanilla essence

FOR THE SAUCE

15 apricots

1 cup water

4 teaspoons sugar

1/4 teaspoon powdered cinnamon and cloves

METHOD

(1)   Heat milk and sugar. When it boils, add corn flour dissolved in cold milk. Stir till thick. Remove from heat and cool. Add vanilla essence. Pour in a rinsed mould. Put in a fridge to set.

(2)   Boil apricots with water. When soft, add sugar, cinnamon and clove powder. Cool. Remove seeds, crush with a spoon. Cool in fridge.

(3)   Unmould pudding in a serving dish and serve with cold apricot sauce.

FRUIT TRIFLE (6-8 SERVINGS)

A fruity pudding liked by all guests.

INGREDIENTS

2 cups milk

1-1/4 cups powdered sugar

2 tablespoons custard powder

300 grams fresh cream

1/2 teaspoon vanilla essence

1 small sponge cake

3-4 tablespoons mixed fruit jam

Cleaned and chopped fruit pieces :1 apple, 2 oranges, 1 sweetlime, 1 banana, 100 grams grapes

METHOD

(1) Boil milk with six tablespoons of powdered sugar. Dissolve custard in little cold milk and add to the hot milk. Stir constantly till thick. Cool.

(2) Take fresh cream in a vessel. Add three-fourth cup of powdered sugar and beat over ice cubes. Reserve one fourth of cream for decoration.

(3) To the cooled custard, add vanilla essence and the remaining fresh cream.

(4) Spread half of the cream custard in a pudding tray. Spread half of the fruits. Cut cake into slices. Apply jam on one side and arrange them over fruits. Spread remaining fruit. Pour remaining custard cream over the surface, spread till smooth. Decorate with stiffly beaten fresh cream and some fruit pieces.

Variation

One can make chocolate trifle by using chocolate cake instead of plain sponge cake and chocolate custard instead of plain vanilla custard.

CARAMEL CREAMS (4 to 6 SERVINGS)

A creamy pudding, tastes good when thoroughly chilled.

INGREDIENTS

1/2 cup sugar for caramel

1/2 cup+1 tablespoon (5 fl. ozs.) water for caramel

4 teaspoons custard powder

1/2 litre milk

30 grams (1 oz.) sugar for milk

1/4 teaspoon vanilla essence

2 tablespoons gelatine

100 grams fresh cream

2 tablespoons powdered sugar

A few walnuts

METHOD

(1) First make the caramel. Put sugar and water in a heavy pan. Melt sugar and strain if there is any dirt. Boil sugar syrup rapidly on a fast flame. Stir occasionally. Boil until it is caramelised. When caramel is ready remove from the flame and dip the base of the pan in cold water to check heat and prevent further browning.

(2) Blend custard powder in little cold milk. Heat remaining milk and sugar. Add dissolved custard and stir constantly till thick.

(3) Pour prepared custard over caramel. Heat pan again and stir till caramel melts and is mixed thoroughly with custard. Remove from gas, cool and mix in vanilla essence.

(4) Soak gelatine in little water for a few minutes and then melt on slow heat. Add to caramel custard mixture.

(5) Fill this pudding in a serving bowl or in six individual cups. Put in fridge to cool and set.

(6) Whip cream with two tablespoons powdered sugar till stiff. Decorate pudding with this cream and walnuts.

SUNSHINE PUDDING (6-8 SERVINGS)

Very delicious pudding for a special party.

INGREDIENTS

100 grams walnut macaroon biscuits

1 large can pineapple (850 grams)

2 tablespoons gelatine

18-1/2 tablespoons powdered sugar

2 cups milk

6 teaspoons corn flour

300 grams fresh cream

Juice of 1 lemon

2-3 drops lemon colour

METHOD

(1)   Break macaroons into small pieces.

(2)   Keep big rectangular mould in a fridge to cool.

(3)   Drain four pineapple slices and cut into small pieces. Keep aside remaining slices for decoration.

(4)   Take one and a half cups of pineapple syrup in a vessel. Mix in gelatine and six tablespoons of powdered sugar. Keep on double boiler to dissolve the sugar completely.

(5)   Make custard with milk, six and a half tablespoons of powdered sugar and corn flour. Cool.

(6)   Whip 200 grams of fresh cream with four tablespoons of powdered sugar.

(7)   Add lemon juice to the dissolved gelatine and whip on ice till it looks like cream.

(8)   Place a big vessel on ice. Mix in cooled custard, whipped cream and gelatine. Also add macaroon pieces and pineapple pieces. Scrape sides often till the pudding is semiset. Pour into a big mould and set in fridge.

(9)   Unmould on a serving plate.

(10) Whip 100 grams of fresh cream with two tablespoons of powdered sugar, till stiff. Add one or two drops of lemon yellow colour. Decorate pudding with pineapple slices and cream.

LEMON CREAM PIE OR TARTS (6 SERVINGS)

Pie is convenient for a small group of guests. Tarts can be prepared and served easily to a larger group of guests.

INGREDIENTS

1 recipe, sweet paste (see recipe on Pg. 215)

6 teaspoons custard powder

1-1/4 cups (10 fl. ozs.) water

Little lemon rind

Juice of 1-1/2 lemons

1/2 cup sugar

100 grams fresh cream

2 tablespoons powdered sugar

1/2 cup custard (use in case of pie only)

1 tablespoon gelatine (use gelatine in case of pie only)

1 banana or orange

METHOD

(1) Make pie shell or tarts out of sweet paste and bake them blind. Cool.

(2) Melt custard powder in little water.

(3) Boil water, lemon rind, lemon juice and sugar. Strain the mixture after sugar has dissolved.

(4) Put it again on gas. Add dissolved custard powder. Stir till cooked. Cool.

(5) Fill tarts with lemon cream and put a slice of orange or banana.

(6) Whip fresh cream till stiff with two tablespoons of powdered sugar.
OR

(5) Fill pie shell with a mixture of banana slices, custard and melted gelatine.

(6) Cover with lemon cream.

(7) Decorate with fresh cream whipped with two tablespoons of powdered sugar, green peels and glazed cherries.

PINEAPPLE CREAM TARTS (MAKES 12 TARTS)

A delightful recipe for serving at the end of a sumptuous dinner.

INGREDIENTS

1 recipe sweet paste (see Pg. 215)

2/3 cup milk

1-1/2 tablespoons sugar

1-1/2 tablespoons corn flour

1/3 cup pineapple syrup

2 slices pineapple from can

1 tablespoon butter

1/2 teaspoon pineapple essence

Few glazed cherries for decoration

METHOD

(1) Make tarts out of sweet paste and bake them blind. Cool.

(2) Heat milk with sugar. Dissolve corn flour in little cold milk. Add to the hot milk. Stir continuously till thick.

(3) Remove from gas and add pineapple syrup, pineapple pieces essence and butter. Stir and beat mixture till evenly mixed and becomes cold.

(4) Divide the mixture equally into all tarts. Top with glazed cherries and cool in fridge till serving time.

ICECREAMS

Icecreams have become very popular in this century, thanks to the modern developing technology which has made it possible to freeze icecream mixtures. It is also possible now to make icecreams in advance and store for a longer period. Homemade icecreams have that personal touch which make them pure and rich in their flavours.

Icecreams can be easily made at home by following two methods :
(1)   In the refrigerator
(2)   By hand or electric churner.

It is easy to achieve success if few of the following points are remembered while making icecreams :

(1)   Always turn the control in the refrigerator to highest point an hour before putting icecream in the ice compartment. Once the icecream sets, then put the control back to its normal temperature.
(2)   Keep box touching the base of the ice compartment for perfect and quick setting.
(3)   Keep icecream box covered with polythelene bag to prevent formation of crystals.
(4)   For perfect results, always taste the icecream mixture before freezing, because on cooling icecream tastes less sweet. So mixture should be sweeter than the normal taste.
(5)   Beat icecream atleast twice during the process of setting in the freezer to break formation of crystals.

As homemade icecreams do not contain any preservatives which are normally found in commercial products, they cannot be stored for the same length of time. Most of the icecreams should not be kept for more than a couple of weeks. They loose their flavour and change texture.

Before serving most of the homemade icecreams should be transferred to the main part of the refrigerator. It will soften the icecream evenly. Very cold icecream will be too hard and will not taste good. Time needed in the refrigerator depends on the richness of the mixture and the amount of the icecream. Rich icecreams need less time than the other. Allow about 30 minutes for a box of 1" x 6" x 4" to set.

CUSTARD APPLE ICECREAM (12 SERVINGS)

The natural sweetness and creamy texture of the custard apples, make the icecream more delectable.

INGREDIENTS

1-1/2 litres milk

3/4 to 1 cup sugar

1 tablespoon custard powder

1 teaspoon gelatine powder

1 cup custard apple pulp

1 teaspoon vanilla essence

200 grams fresh cream

METHOD

(1) Boil milk for 15 minutes. Add sugar and boil for another 10 minutes. Blend custard powder in little cold milk and add to the boiling milk. Stir for a few minutes. Remove from the gas and cool.

(2) Melt gelatine powder in little water, cool and mix in the cooled milk. Mix in custard apple pulp, vanilla essence and fresh cream.

(3) Make icecream in an icecream churner or leave in the freezer compartment till well set.

CHICKOO ICECREAM (12 SERVINGS)

This icecream is made the same way as custard apple icecream by using three fourth cup of chickoo pulp (made in mixer) instead of custard apple pulp. Serve icecream in a cup with chickoo leaves tucked on sides.

Method for chickoo leaves :
(1) Select ready to eat chickoo. Peel it and cut out a slice. Shape slice like a leaf.
(2) Cut serrated edges by carving alternately straight and slant cuts.

MANGO ICECREAM (12 SERVINGS)

Quick and easy to make when mangoes are in plentiful.

INGREDIENTS

1-1/2 litres milk

1 cup sugar or more, according to the taste of mangoes

2 teaspoons gelatine powder

6 medium sized mangoes

METHOD

(1) Boil milk for 15 minutes, add sugar. Boil for another 10 minutes and then cool.
(2) Melt gelatine in little water and cool.
(3) Cut small pieces of three mangoes and extract pulp from the remaining mangoes.
(4) Mix mango pulp, pieces and gelatine in the milk.
(5) Fill this mixture in a churner box and make icecream.
(6) If you want to make this icecream in the fridge, then mix in mango pieces after beating the milk mixture at mushy consistency.

PINEAPPLE ICECREAM (10 SERVINGS)

Rich and creamy icecream with a tangy taste of pineapple and lemon.

INGREDIENTS

1 small can pineapple slices (450 grams)

3/4 cup sugar

1 tablespoon gelatine powder

3 tablespoons lemon juice

1/2 litre milk, boil for 15 minutes, cool

400 grams fresh cream

METHOD

(1) Make pulp of pineapple pieces with its syrup in a mixer.

(2) Mix sugar and gelatine powder into pineapple pulp. Heat on gas till gelatine powder and sugar dissolves. Cool. Mix in lemon juice and milk.

(3) Pour this mixture in a box. Cover it with polythelene and put in freezer till mushy in consistency. Remove and beat with an egg beater. Add fresh cream and beat again till properly mixed. Put it back in freezer till set.

CHOCOLATE ICECREAM (12 SERVINGS)

Like chocolates, chocolate icecream is also a favourite amongst kids.

INGREDIENTS

1-1/2 litres milk

3 teaspoons cocoa powder

3 teaspoons drinking chocolate

3 teaspoons custard powder

1 to 1-1/4 cups sugar

200 grams fresh cream

1 teaspoon gelatine, dissolved in little water

1 teaspoon vanilla essence

METHOD

(1) Boil milk for 20 minutes.

(2) Dissolve cocoa powder, drinking chocolate and custard powder in little cold milk. Add to the boiling milk and stir for five minutes. Add sugar and boil for another five minutes. Remove from gas and cool.

(3) Add fresh cream, vanilla essence to the cooled milk and dissolved gelatine.

(4) Set icecream in fridge or in a icecream churner.

HONEYDEW ICECREAM (12 SERVINGS)

A nutty icecream with a rich taste of honey.

INGREDIENTS

1-1/2 litres milk

2 tablespoons corn flour

1-1/2 cups sugar

1 teaspoon gelatine, melted

200 grams fresh cream

1/4 cup walnut pieces

1/4 cup cashewnut pieces

1/2 cup fig pieces

1/4 cup honey

1/4 cup water

METHOD

(1) Boil milk for 20 minutes. Dissolve corn flour in little cold milk and add to the boiling milk. Add sugar and stir constantly till thick. Remove from the gas and cool. Add melted (in water) gelatine and fresh cream.

(2) Chop walnuts, cashewnuts and figs into small pieces. Combine with honey and water in a vessel. Heat on gas and stir often till liquid is absorbed. Remove from gas and cool. Add to the prepared milk. Now set icecream in fridge or make in a churner.

STRAWBERRY ICECREAM (12 SERVINGS)

A rich and creamy icecream of fresh strawberries and cream.

INGREDIENTS

1 cup fresh strawberries

1/2 cup powdered sugar

1-1/2 litres milk

1 tablespoon custard powder

3/4 cup sugar

1 teaspoon gelatine powder

200 grams fresh cream

METHOD

(1) Cut strawberries into half. Mix half cup of powdered sugar in it and keep for two hours.

(2) Boil milk for 20 minutes. Melt custard powder in little cold milk. Stir for a few minutes. Add sugar and boil for another five minutes. Remove from the gas and cool. Add half of the strawberries with the syrup.

(3) Dissolve gelatine powder in little water and cool. Mix with prepared milk.

(4) Pour this milk mixture in a box. Keep in the freezer, covering with a polythelene bag, till semiset.

(5) Take out from freezer. Beat with an egg-beater till fluffy, and mix in fresh cream. Beat again.

(6) Finally add remaining strawberries. Now cover with polythelene bag and keep back in fridge till set.

Note :
If making icecream in a churner, add all the strawberries with syrup in the cooled milk.

VANILLA ICECREAM (12 SERVINGS)

Most commonly prepared which also serves as a base to a number of dessert preparations.

INGREDIENTS

1-1/2 litres milk

1 can condensed milk (400 grams)

Vanilla essence

Sugar, if required

METHOD

(1) Boil milk for 20 minutes. Cool a little and add the condensed milk. Mix vanilla essence. Taste and adjust proportion of sugar.

(2) Set icecream in freezer or churner.

VANILLA ORANGE SURPRISE (12 SERVINGS)

Vanilla icecream balls with a generous topping of orange sauce.

INGREDIENTS

FOR THE VANILLA ICECREAM

1-1/2 litres milk

2 tablespoons corn flour

1-1/2 cups sugar

1 teaspoon gelatine

1 teaspoon vanilla essence

200 grams fresh cream

FOR THE ORANGE SAUCE

1-1/2 cups orange juice

3/4 cup sugar

1 tablespoon corn flour

1 tablespoon butter

1 tablespoon lemon juice (if orange juice is sour omit lemon juice)

A few drops orange colour

A few drops orange essence

FOR THE VANILLA ORANGE SURPRISE

1 recipe vanilla icecream

1 cup orange segments

1 recipe orange sauce

METHOD

FOR THE VANILLA ICECREAM

(1) Boil milk for 20 minutes. Dissolve corn flour in little cold milk and mix to the boiling milk. Add sugar, stir mixture till thick and the sugar dissolves. Remove from gas and cool.

(2) Melt gelatine in little water and add to the milk. Add vanilla essence and fresh cream. Make icecream in a churner or leave in the freezer till well set.

FOR THE ORANGE SAUCE

Combine all the above ingredients except orange colour and essence in a vessel. Heat on medium gas till sugar dissolves and sauce is thick. Cool to room temperature. Mix in orange colour and essence.

FOR THE VANILLA ORANGE SURPRISE

(1) Prepare vanilla icecream.

(2) Take one scoop of icecream. Put a few orange segments in the centre and make a ball. Similarly make other scoops.

(3) Arrange all these scooped balls in a box and freeze them. Serve each scooped ball with a tablespoon of orange sauce.

VANILLA PINEAPPLE SURPRISE (12 SERVINGS)

Two-in-one icecream balls topped with pineapple sauce.

INGREDIENTS

FOR THE PINEAPPLE SAUCE

1 small can pineapple slices (450 grams)

1/2 cup sugar

1 tablespoon corn flour

1 tablespoon butter

1 tablespoon lemon juice

A few drops yellow colour and pineapple essence

FOR THE VANILLA PINEAPPLE SURPRISE

1 recipe vanilla icecream (see Pg. 261)

1 cup pineapple sections, canned

1 recipe pineapple sauce

METHOD

FOR THE PINEAPPLE SAUCE

(1) Take out pineapple slices from the syrup. Drain them well, cut into small pieces and use for stuffing in vanilla icecream.

(2) Combine all the syrup from the pineapple can, sugar, corn flour, butter and lemon juice in a vessel.

(3) Heat on gas till sugar dissolves and the sauce is thick. Cool sauce and mix in pineapple essence and yellow colour. Keep to room temperature.

FOR THE VANILLA PINEAPPLE SURPRISE

(1) Make vanilla icecream.

(2) Take one scoop of icecream, stuff pineapple pieces in the centre and form into a ball. Arrange these balls in a box and freeze them.

(3) Serve each scooped ball with pineapple sauce.

LEMON SPONGE ICECREAM (6 SERVINGS)

A decorative mould lined with Swiss roll spirals.

INGREDIENTS

FOR THE LEMON SAUCE

1 cup water

1 cup sugar

1 tablespoon corn flour

1 tablespoon butter

1/4 cup lemon juice

Few drops lemon colour and essence

FOR THE ICECREAM

1 jam Swiss roll

1/2 recipe vanilla icecream (see Pg. 261)

1 recipe lemon sauce

METHOD

FOR THE LEMON SAUCE

(1) Combine water, sugar, corn flour, butter and lemon juice in a vessel. Heat on gas till sugar dissolves and the sauce is thick.

(2) Mix in lemon juice. Remove from gas and cool. Mix lemon essence and colour. Keep to room temperature.

FOR THE ICECREAM

(1) Cut the Swiss roll into quarter inch thick slices. Stick them all round a fancy shaped (hexagonal or boat or heart shape) mould.

(2) Fill vanilla icecream leaving a dent in the centre. Arrange remaining Swiss roll slices in the centre.

(3) Now put this mould in a plastic bag and then in the freezer till set.

(4) To unmould, pass knife all round the sides. Keep mould outside for a few minutes and then unmould on the serving dish. Serve with lemon sauce.

ORANGE ICECREAM (12 SERVINGS)

A sumptuous icecream with a sweet 'n' sour taste of fresh oranges.

INGREDIENTS

1-1/2 litres milk

1 tablespoon corn flour

1 tablespoon custard powder

1-1/2 cups sugar

1 teaspoon gelatine

200 grams fresh cream

1 cup orange juice

Few drops orange colour and essence

METHOD

(1) Boil milk for 20 minutes. Blend corn flour and custard powder in little cold milk and mix in the boiling milk.

(2) Add sugar, stir constantly till sugar dissolves and the milk is thick. Remove from gas and cool.

(3) Melt gelatine in little water and add to the milk. Mix in fresh cream, orange juice, colour and essence. Make icecream in a churner or leave in the freezer till set.

RIPPLED ICE-LOAF (12 - 15 SERVINGS)

A wonderful combination of vanilla icecream with chocolate or apple sauce.

INGREDIENTS

FOR THE CHOCOLATE SAUCE

1 tablespoon drinking chocolate

1/2 tablespoon cocoa powder

2 tablespoons sugar

1/4 tablespoon custard powder

1/3 cup water or milk

1 tablespoon butter

FOR THE APPLE SAUCE

1 big apple

1 tablespoon lemon juice

1/4 teaspoon powdered cinnamon and cloves

1/4 cup sugar

Few drops of red colour

FOR THE RIPPLED ICE-LOAF

1 recipe vanilla icecream (see Pg. 261)

Chocolate sauce or apple sauce

METHOD

FOR THE CHOCOLATE SAUCE

Combine all the ingredients together in a vessel and heat. Stir constantly till sauce is thick. Cool to room temperature.

FOR THE APPLE SAUCE

Peel and chop apple into tiny pieces. Add water, enough to cover the pieces. Cook on gas till soft. Mash apple pieces and pass through a sieve. Now mix in lemon juice, cinnamon and clove powder and sugar. Heat again on gas till sugar dissolves and has a saucy consistency. Add colour and mix well. Remove from gas and cool to room temperature.

FOR THE RIPPLED ICE-LOAF

Prepare one recipe vanilla icecream and one recipe of either chocolate sauce or apple sauce. After preparing vanilla icecream, when it is still soft mix sauce with a fork very roughly. Then fill in loaf tins (two) without much mixing. Put tins in plastic bags and set in freezer. For serving remove tins, pass knife all round edges and keep outside for a few minutes or hold sides under running tap water. Then put upside down in a serving plate. Sprinkle grated milk chocolate on top. Cut slices and serve. Each slice will show marble effect.

KULFI

It is an Indian style of icecream. Milk is boiled and is reduced to half its original volume. This gives typical pinkish brown colour and milky taste. It is never thickened with corn flour or custard powder, but it is made rich and thick by adding either of the following items :

(a)   Mashed mawa (khoya) 'pedas' (Indian sweet)
(b)   Khoya
(c)   Homemade fresh cream (top of the cold milk)
(d)   Fresh crustless bread slices soaked in milk and thoroughly mashed.

Artificial essences can be avoided in kulfis. Kulfi is normally set in special cone shaped aluminium moulds. Sometimes kulfi can be served with boiled 'falooda sev' which is available in packets. Sometimes small earthenware cups are used to set in the kulfis.

MALAI KULFI (12 KULFI MOULDS)

INGREDIENTS	METHOD
1-1/2 litres milk	(1) Boil milk on medium gas till it is reduced to half its original quantity. Add sugar and boil for another 10 minutes. Remove from gas and cool.
3/4 cup sugar	
2 khoya pedas or 50 grams khoya	(2) Mash peda or khoya and mix it thoroughly, first with little milk in a small bowl and then add to the lukewarm milk.
	(3) Fill milk mixture in special cone shaped kulfi, moulds or in a box. Leave in the freezer till well set.

PISTA KULFI (12 KULFI MOULDS)

INGREDIENTS	METHOD
1-1/2 litres milk	(1) Boil milk on medium gas till it is reduced to half its original quantity. Add sugar and boil for another 10 minutes. Remove from gas and cool.
1/2 to 3/4 cup sugar	
1/4 cup pistachios, finely chopped	(2) Add fresh cream, pistachios and green colour.
Few drops green colour	(3) Fill in the special kulfi moulds or in a box and leave in the freezer to set.
1/2 cup thick fresh cream (top of the cold milk)	

BADAM AND KESAR KULFI (12 KULFI MOULDS)

INGREDIENTS	METHOD
1-1/2 litres milk	(1) Boil milk on medium gas till it is reduced to half its original quantity. Add sugar and boil for another 10 minutes. Remove from gas and cool.
1/2 to 3/4 cup sugar	
1/4 cup almonds, blanched and finely chopped	(2) Add prepared almonds and saffron.
	(3) Remove crust from bread slices and soak in quarter cup of milk for 15 minutes. Make a fine pulp of this in a blender and add to the cooled milk.
Few strands saffron, dissolved in little milk	
3 big slices bread	(4) Pour in kulfi moulds or in a box and leave in a freezer to set.

MANGO KULFI (12 KULFI MOULDS)

INGREDIENTS	METHOD
1-1/2 litres milk	(1) Boil milk on medium gas till it is reduced to half its quantity. Add sugar and boil for another 10 minutes. Remove from gas and cool.
1/2 to 3/4 cup sugar	
1 cup mango pulp, fresh or frozen	(2) Mix in mango pulp and quarter cup of fresh cream.
1/4 cup fresh cream (top of the cold milk)	(3) Fill in the kulfi moulds or an aluminium box and leave to set in freezer compartment.

Note :
Same kulfi can be made by using, custard apple pulp and chickoo pulp.

WHITE PUMPKIN KULFI (12-15 KULFI MOULDS)

An unusual variation of kulfi.

INGREDIENTS	METHOD
3 slices bread	(1) Remove crust from bread slices and soak them in three-fourth cup of milk for 15 minutes.
1-1/2 litres milk	
1 cup white pumpkin, grated	(2) Grate white pumpkin and cook on slow gas covered with a lid. Add little water if required. Cool.
1 cup sugar	
1 teaspoon powdered cardamoms	(3) Make a fine pulp of the cooked pumpkin and bread in a blender.
	(4) Boil milk on slow gas till it is reduced to half its original quantity. Add sugar and boil for another 10 minutes. Remove from gas and cool.
	(5) Mix milk with pumpkin-bread pulp and cardamom powder. Fill in the special moulds or in an aluminium box and leave in the freezer to set.

CASSATA (12-15 SERVINGS)

A multi coloured mould, layered with different flavoured icecreams.

INGREDIENTS

FOR THE SIMPLE ORANGE ICECREAM

1 litre milk

1/2 cup sugar

2 teaspoons corn flour

100 grams fresh cream

1/2 teaspoon gelatine, melted

Few drops orange colour and essence

TO ASSEMBLE CASSATA

1 recipe simple orange icecream

1 recipe simple pista icecream

1/2 recipe vanilla icecream (see Pg. 261)

1/4 cup tutti fruiti pieces

1/2 cup peanuts, roasted and coarsely ground

A set of three aluminium bowls.

Largest bowl of 9" diametre and 6" deep

METHOD

FOR THE SIMPLE ORANGE ICECREAM

(1)   Boil milk for 20 minutes. Add sugar and boil for another five minutes. Add the dissolved corn flour and simmer for a few more minutes. Remove from the gas and cool.

(2)   Add fresh cream, dissolved gelatine and orange colour and essence.

(3)   Make icecream in a churner or leave in the freezer till well set.

FOR THE SIMPLE PISTA ICECREAM

Recipe is the same as simple orange icecream but replace colour and essence with pista or vanilla essence and green colour.

TO ASSEMBLE CASSATA

(1)   Put the biggest bowl in fridge to chill. Line its side and base with simple orange icecream. Press middle bowl over it. Cover and freeze until firm. Remove the bowl and spread simple pista icecream over simple orange icecream. Press the smallest bowl over it. Cover and freeze. Remove the bowl and fill the centre with the mixture of vanilla icecream and tutti fruiti pieces. Level icecreams and cover and freeze for atleast six hours.

(2)   To serve, hold sides of the bowl under running tap water. Unmould on a serving plate. Stick nuts all over the cassata icecream. Cut triangular slices in such a way that each serving gets all three layers. One can unmould cassata on a thin layer of sponge cake too.

SANDWICH SUPREME WITH VANILLA YOGHURT ICECREAM AND BUTTER-SCOTCH SAUCE (12 SERVINGS)

Sponge cake sandwiched with yoghurt icecream and topped with delicious butter-scotch sauce.

INGREDIENTS

FOR THE VANILLA YOGHURT ICECREAM

1 cup yoghurt (fresh curd)

1 cup fresh cream

1/4 cup golden syrup

1/3 cup powdered sugar

1 teaspoon gelatine, dissolved in little water

1/2 teaspoon vanilla essence

FOR THE BUTTER-SCOTCH SAUCE

60 grams sugar

1/2 cup boiling water

1-1/2 tablespoons butter

1 tablespoon flour

1/2 cup milk

FOR THE SANDWICH SUPREME

1 sandwich sponge cake (400 grams approx.)

Mixed fruit jam, as required

1 recipe vanilla yoghurt icecream

1/4 cup walnuts and almonds, chopped

Butterscotch sauce

METHOD

FOR THE VANILLA YOGHURT ICECREAM

Put all the ingredients in a vessel and blend them until smooth. Pour in an airtight box and freeze. Whisk at least twice during the process of setting. When it is 95 percent set, use as required.

FOR THE BUTTER-SCOTCH SAUCE

(1)   Take sugar in a vessel and heat it. Keep stirring till it dissolves and caramelises. (like dark honey). Remove from gas.
(2)   Gradually mix in boiling water, and stir till it mixes evenly. Cool it.
(3)   Heat butter, add flour and stir for a minute. Mix in milk and stir till it forms an even sauce. Remove from gas and cool. Mix with caramel syrup. Keep at room temperature.

TO ASSEMBLE

(1)   Split sandwich cake into three horizontal layers. Over the first layer spread half of the vanilla yoghurt icecream. Sprinkle nuts. Cover with second layer of cake. Spread half of the icecream and the nuts. Cover with the top layer of the cake to complete the sandwich. Keep covered in the ice compartment to set.
(2)   Remove from freezer and leave it on the lower shelf of the refrigerator for 30 minutes before serving time. Cut into slices and serve with butter-scotch sauce.

MARZIPANS, CHOCOLATES, FUDGES ETC.

COOKED MARZIPAN

A sweet paste of ground cashewnuts or almonds, moulded into different shapes to decorate a cake.

INGREDIENTS

1 cup (100 grams) cashewnut pieces

3/4 cup (170 grams) sugar

METHOD

(1) Grind cashewnuts. Make a paste with little water on a grinding stone like chutney, or make a fine powder and then grind in a wet grinder.

(2) Take sugar in a thick pan. Add water enough to soak sugar. Put on gas and stir with a wooden spoon till sugar dissolves. Add two to three drops of lemon juice to remove the scum. Strain through a muslin cloth. Put on the gas again.

(3) Add cashewnut paste and mix evenly. Stir continuously with a wooden spoon till it becomes thick. Switch off gas and continue stirring till mixture becomes dry. Remove from gas and transfer the mixture on a marble table.

(4) Make a very fine paste by grinding with the side of a glass bottle. If you feel the mixture is dry, then sprinkle few drops of water. It should become a very smooth, pliable dough. Marzipan should be stored in a plastic bag or an airtight box.

MARZIPAN MOSAICS

Colour small quantities of marzipan into delicate contrasting colours. Roll out each colour to an identical size. Brush the surface of one lightly with egg white or water and press a second colour in place, use a spatula to lift it. Continue until all colours are used. The finished slab should be more than 1" thick. Pat it gently and evenly with a rolling pin. Cut in strips and then in cubes or oblongs. Place in sweetcase so that the rainbow sides are uppermost.

NUT DELIGHTS

Roll out marzipan very thinly. Cut small circles with a fluted 1-1/4 inch biscuit cutter. Chop any kind of nuts, fairly coarsely, knead them into a very small quantity of thick mixed fruit jam. Put sufficient quantity of the mixture in the centre of each circle to allow the fluted edges to be pressed upwards to seal the nuts in. Decorate each with a piece of crystallized cherry. One can stuff seedless dates also.

COCONUT BALLS

Make marzipan into small balls and brush with either egg white or very little apricot or mixed fruit jam and roll in desiccated coconut.

MARZIPAN FRUITS

Take a little piece of natural marzipan and add required colour. Give a nice dainty fruit shape. Put green peel or cinnamon as a stick and clove for calyx. You can use toothpicks to give impressions on the surface. Small artificial leaves and sticks can be used. Leave these fruits to dry before packing in boxes.

(1)   **Marzipan Apple**
Colour the marzipan to a pleasant apple green. Form into the shape of tiny apples. Dip a very fine brush into pink colouring and shade on the outside, to look like a ripe apple. Press a clove into the base and tiny cinnamon as stalk into the top.

(2)   **Marzipan Carrot**
Colour the marzipan with orange colouring. Form into carrot shape, making one or two slight imperfection' marks with a fine needle or toothpicks. Cut three tiny stalks from green marzipan for artificial sticks. Put them on top.

(3)   **Marzipan Banana**
Colour the marzipan yellow like a banana. Form into tiny banana shapes. Dip a fine paint brush into either strong coffee or rather thin diluted chocolate and brush brown marks of banana.

(4)   **Marzipan Peach**
Take two small balls of marzipan. Colour one with pink or orange and the other with yellow. Mix both the balls and roll into peach shape. Put artificial stick and leaf on the top.

(5)   **Marzipan Pears**
Colour the marzipan into green and little brown. Roll to form pear shape. Put artificial leaf and stick on the top. Put small clove at the base.

(6)   **Marzipan Strawberries**
Colour the marzipan a very delicate pinkish red with cochineal red and two or three drops of saffron yellow so that it is not too mauvish red in colour. Form into strawberry shapes and top with tiny green marzipan stalk and leaf shapes. Roll this strawberry into coloured (powdered red colour) sugar.

(7)   **Marzipan Orange**
Colour marzipan into orange and shape like an orange. Roll over a coarse sieve to get impressions.

(8)   **Marzipan Chickoo**
Colour marzipan brown by mixing cocoa powder. Shape like a chickoo and put artificial stick and a leaf.

(9)   **Marzipan Watermelon slice**
Take two balls of marzipan. Colour one pink and the other green. Shape green ball for the outer skin and the pink as inner soft. Fix them together with little water. Put cardamom seeds in place of watermelon seeds.

(10) · **Marzipan Mango**
Mix yellow and green marzipan. Roll them to form mango shape. Put artificial leaf and stalk.

CHOCOLATE COATED MARZIPAN

Make marzipan. It is easier to handle if the chocolate marzipan is a little softer than usual. So either a few drops of liquor or sugar syrup, could be blended with marzipan. Dip into the melted chocolate. Then dry on butterpaper before wrapping in aluminium foil.

GOLDEN TOFFEE (50 PIECES)

Yummy toffees — too hard to resist !

INGREDIENTS

55 grams margarine

1/2 cup sugar

55 grams liquid glucose

45 grams golden syrup

4 tablespoons condensed milk

1/2 cup milk

2 tablespoons soyabean powder or arrowroot powder

METHOD

(1) Mix all the ingredients in a thick pan.
(2) Put over medium heat. Stir till sugar dissolves
(3) Boil mixture till it becomes fairly thick.
To test, put drop of the mixture over ice. It should turn hard.
(4) Make a frame with wooden planks. Grease the floor and sides of the wooden frame.
(5) Pour the mixture, allow to cool. When almost set, cut pieces with heated knife. Cool.
(6) Wrap cold pieces into aluminium foil.
Note :
Similarly coconut toffees can be made by mixing two tablespoons of dessicated coconut at stage 3.

VARIETIES OF PLAIN MILK CHOCOLATE

A basic chocolate dough which can be varied in shapes and sizes.

INGREDIENTS

2 tablespoons icing sugar

1 tablespoon milk powder

2-1/2 tablespoons drinking chocolate

1 tablespoon cocoa powder

A few drops lemon juice

METHOD

(1) Combine all the dry ingredients together and sieve them atleast thrice with a very fine sieve to remove tiny lumps.
(2) Add lemon juice and make a firm dough using water. Lemon juice gives shine to the mixture. There should not be any cracks in the dough while making a ball. Wrap in a polythene bag to avoid drying. This is a basic plain milk chocolate dough which can be used in various ways.

(1)   **Moulded fancy shapes**
Special rubber moulds for chocolates are available. They are flexible for easy removal of chocolates. They have various shapes like flowers, fruits and animals. For easy removal, it is better to grease moulds from inside with a thin coat of melted ghee. This can be done with a small paint brush. Wet fingers with melted ghee and make a smooth ball of chocolate big enough to fit in the mould. Press chocolate in the shape, lightly pat on top to push in every groove of the mould. Fill up all shapes of the mould. Allow mould to dry for an hour or two and then unmould. Allow to dry on a plate, before using.

(2)   **Nut chocolates**
Mix two tablespoons of finely chopped mixture of nuts, almonds, cashewnuts and walnuts, whilst making the plain milk chocolate dough. Give shapes like triangle, square, rectangle, round, oval, etc. with fingers greased with melted ghee. Allow these nut chocolates to dry on a plate before use.

(3)   **Fancy chocolate figures**
Prepare plain milk chocolate dough. Make a smooth big ball. Roll to about one eighth inch thickness between two sheets of polythene. Cut out figures of animals and other shapes with biscuit cutters. Allow them to dry on a plate. Decorate them with lemon-butter frosting.
To prepare lemon-butter frosting, take one tablespoon of butter or margarine. Mix with two tablespoons of icing sugar and few drops of lemon juice. Add colour if needed. Beat with a wooden spoon till light and fluffy. Use this frosting to decorated figures with a fine nozzle. Make outline of figures or eyes etc. Dry them before use.

(4)   **To coat centres**
Use milk chocolate mixture for coating chocolate dry centres.

CHOCOLATES WITH DIFFERENT CENTRES

For these types of chocolates we have to prepare different varieties of centres. First thoroughly dry the centres. Then coat them with specially prepared coating mixture. Again dry chocolates on butterpaper and then wrap with decorative foil. Dry centres can be stored in an airtight box for a few days. Chocolates can be preserved in an airtight container for about two weeks.

(1) Plain Centre (4-5 pieces)

INGREDIENTS	METHOD
1-3/4 tablespoons icing sugar, sieved	Mix all the above ingredients with water (use dropper to add water, and make a firm dough. Then divide into four to five parts and shape as desired. Let them dry for atleast five to six hours.
1-1/2 tablespoons milk powder	
3 drops any essence	
Few drops suitable colour	

LIST OF COMBINATIONS OF DIFFERENT COLOURS AND ESSENCES

Colour of the Centre	Colour	Essence
White	No colour	Almond, icecream, vanilla or cardamom
Yellow	Lemon or pineapple	Lemon or pineapple
Orange	Orange	Orange
Green	Green	Pista or peppermint
Pink	Strawberry or rose or raspberry	Cochineal or strawberry or rose or raspberry
Violet	Violet	Vimto or grape

(2) Marzipan Centre (4-5 pieces)

INGREDIENTS	METHOD
2 tablespoons icing sugar	(1) One can add any colour to marzipan. Make tricolour marzipan block as follows. Divide marzipan into three parts. To one part add the green colour, to the second add red or orange colour and keep the third part plain. Mix colours evenly and roll all to same thickness and size. Stick them in order of green, white and pink or orange. Cut smaller pieces for coating.
1 tablespoon milk powder	
3 tablespoons almonds or cashewnuts, blanched, ground. (Use almond essence if cashewnuts are used)	(2) Marble effect can be given in marzipan centre. Divide dough into two parts. To one part add any dark colour. Then roughly mix both and roll them, making marble balls ready for coating.

(3)   Coffee Centre (3-4 pieces)

INGREDIENTS	METHOD
1-1/2 tablespoons icing sugar	Make dough by combing all the ingredients with a little water. Give different shapes. Dry them.
1 tablespoon milk powder	
3/4 teaspoon instant coffee — If you want a strong flavour, add a little more coffee.	

(4)   Coconut Centre (6-8 pieces)

INGREDIENTS	METHOD
1-1/2 tablespoons icing sugar	Make a dough by mixing together all the ingredients with a little water. Make small centres and dry.
1-1/2 tablespoons milk powder	
4 tablespoons desiccated coconut	
Any colour (no essence)	

(5)   Chikki Centre (10-12 pieces)

INGREDIENTS	METHOD
3 tablespoons sugar	Melt sugar on a low heat. Add ground peanuts. Mix properly with a spoon. Drop small portions of the mixture on a greased plate. Coat them when dry.
2-1/2 tablespoons peanuts, ground	

(6)   Nut and Cherry Centre (4-6 pieces)

INGREDIENTS	METHOD
1 tablespoon tutti-fruity mix, chopped	Mix all the ingredients with water and make a dough. Divide and shape as desired.
2 tablespoons cashewnuts and walnuts, chopped	
1 tablespoon icing sugar	
1-1/2 tablespoons milk powder	

(7)   Date and Nut Centre (10-12 pieces)

INGREDIENTS	METHOD
6 pieces seedless dates	Melt butter, add dates and warm. Keep on smashing the dates, till they become pulpy. Mix in nuts and remove from the gas. Make balls for the centre when mixture is still warm.
2 tablespoons almonds and pistachios, chopped	
1 teaspoon butter	

(8)   Crystallised Ginger Centre

Cut crystallised ginger into appropriate size and coat with chocolate mixture.

(9)   Cream Biscuit Centre (12 pieces)

INGREDIENTS
3 tablespoons sugar
1 tablespoon water
1 tablespoon milk powder
1 tablespoon cocoa powder
24 tiny round biscuits (1/2 inch diametre)

METHOD

Take sugar and water in a vessel. Melt sugar and then boil it till syrup consistency is reached. Remove from gas and mix in milk powder. Add cocoa powder. Apply immediately on biscuits and make sandwiches.

Note:

For flavoured cream biscuits, use two tablespoons of milk powder and omit cocoa powder. Also add essence and colour in the combinations suggested on Pg. 274. Take small biscuits which can be directly used for coating or make sandwiches out of bigger biscuits, then cut them carefully to required sizes.

(10)   Assorted Centres

Aamras papad (dried mango pulp sheets), small biscuits, whole pieces of walnuts, cashewnuts, seedless dates and almonds can be coated with chocolate mixture.

CHOCOLATE COATING

A chocolate mixture enough for coating 15 to 20 dry centres.

INGREDIENTS
5 tablespoons icing sugar
2 tablespoons milk powder
2 tablespoons drinking chocolate
1/2 teaspoon cocoa powder
2 teaspoons ghee, melted
Few drops lemon juice
Few drops water

METHOD

(1)   Sieve all the dry ingredients twice to remove lumps. Put the mixture in a pan and add ghee and lemon juice. Hold the pan over another pan of boiling water, and beat the mixture, adding cold water gradually till it attains a coating consistency.

(2)   To coat the chocolate, dip dry centres, one by one and place them on butterpaper. Let them dry for about five to six hours. When chocolates are dry, wrap them in decorative foil.

OR

Follow the first method till the mixture is of coating consistency. Then remove vessel from heat and cool it. When the mixture is easy to handle, wet fingers with melted ghee and take a little lump of the coating mixture and cover the dry centre and make them nice and smooth. Arrange them on a plate or a butterpaper sheet. Dry thoroughly before wrapping in decorative foil.

KHOYA FUDGE (MAKES 30 PIECES)

Delicious fudge with milky flavour. A good sweet for children's party.

INGREDIENTS

100 grams sugar

Water just enough to soak sugar

200 grams khoya

METHOD

(1)   Combine water and sugar in a thick vessel. Dissolve sugar on medium gas. Boil till it is of two thread (chasani) sugar syrup consistency.

(2)   Crumble khoya into tiny crumbs. Add to the boiling syrup. Stir continuously till mixture becomes light brown and leaves the sides of the vessel. Take out on a greased plate. Allow it to cool. Make small balls when mixture is still warm. Allow to cool completely on the greased plate. Wrap pieces in thin decorative foil, which is normally used for wrapping chocolates.

Note :

One tablespoon of desiccated coconut can be added to the thick fudge mixture before removing it from the gas. To make 'coconut khoya fudge'.

PRESERVES

SQUASHES

Squashes are made out of fresh fruit juices and pulps mixed in proportion with sugar, water, citric acid, essence and colour. A preservative is also added to maintain its freshness for a few months. Homemade squashes are economical and convenient to serve, when made in appropriate fruit season. For serving, only 1/3 glass of squash is taken and mixed with cold water or sometimes with chilled soda. Most popular among squashes are orange, pineapple, lemon, raw mango and ripe mango. For quick reference the following table will be helpful.

	Orange	Pineapple	Lemon	Raw Mango	Mango
Fruit Juice (ML)	1000	1000	1000	1000	1000
Sugar (Grams)	1700	1700	1700	2500	1000
Water (ML)	1300	1300	1300	1000	1000
Citric Acid (Grams)	40	35	-	1/4Tsp	1Tsp
Essence (Teaspoon)	1/2	1/2	1/2	-	-
Colour	Orange	Pineapple Yellow	Lemon Yellow	Lemon Yellow	-
Preservative Potassium Meta-bisulphate i.e. K.M.S. (Grams)	2.8	2.8	2.8	2.8	2.8

Basic Method for Squash Preparation :

(1)   Select nice fresh fruits — Do not use over-ripe fruits. Extract juice.
(2)   Sieve juice.
(3)   Measure juice.
(4)   Measure water and sugar accordingly.
(5)   Boil water with sugar, give a boil or two. Add citric acid. Give one more boil. Strain to clear syrup. Cool completely.
(6)   Mix juice and syrup.
(7)   Use little syrup to dissolve preservative. Add to juice and syrup.
(8)   Add colour and essence.
(9)   Fill in sterilized bottle and wax them. Label and store in a cool dark place.

Hints: For Squashes

(1)   2.8 Gms. K.M.S. = 1/4 (Level) teaspoon.
(2)   Citric Acid = 1 teaspoon level = 6 grams.
(3)   If we take 1000 ml. juice and follow the recipe it usually gives 6 bottles — 24 ozs. each.
(4)   80-100 lemons usually give 1000 ml. lime juice.
(5)   Pineapple not being a juicy fruit, it is better to peel, chop and steam cook, then blend with little water and extract juice. Reduce that much of water in the recipe.
(6)   Fill squash bottles upto neck only. Leave space for chemical reaction of preservatives.
(7)   Squashes cannot be preserved without preservatives.
(8)   Always cool and fill squashes in a bottle.
(9)   Citric acid is added to clear syrup and to help avoid sugar from separating.
(10)   To preserve squashes, wax their mouth. Take paraffin wax in a vessel or empty food tin. Melt it. Remove from gas. Tighten the cap of the squash bottle and dip its mouth upto the neck into the hot melted wax. Give two to three coats of wax. This will make it airtight.

LEMON-GINGER SQUASH

A squash pleasantly flavoured with ginger.

INGREDIENTS	METHOD
1 recipe lemon squash (refer the table)	(1) Soak crushed ginger in lemon juice for an hour. Strain juice and measure it. Then follow the lemon squash recipe.
100 grams fresh ginger, peeled, crushed	(2) It makes an excellent pink coloured squash.

GRAPE SQUASH

A fantastic idea to enjoy grapes throughout the year.

INGREDIENTS	METHOD
2-1/2 kgs. black grapes, Black Princess, Bangalore variety is preferable	(1) Wash fruit and crush it with hand. Pour in a vessel and boil till very soft. Strain and cool juice.
5 kgs. sugar	(2) Add sugar to water. Heat, stir often till sugar dissolves. Add citric acid and boil for 10 minutes. Strain and cool.
100 grams citric acid	
2-1/2 litres water	(3) Mix in cooled juice and syrup. Also add essence and colour. Measure the quantity and remove the preservative accordingly. Dissolve in little squash before mixing into the large quantity.
1 tablespoon cola colour	
1 tablespoon grape essence	
1/2 teaspoon sodium benzoate preservate per litre	(4) Fill in sterilized bottles, wax and seal them.

COCUM SQUASH

It is an excellent red coloured squash with lots of medicinal value. It is good to drink cool cocum squash, especially in summer.

INGREDIENTS	METHOD
4 kgs. fresh cocum (red sour fruit, resembling plums)	(1) Cut cocum into pieces and mix with sugar. Keep for 1-1/2 hours. Then add water. Pressure cook till five whistles. Strain syrup and remove pulp.
8 kgs. sugar	(2) Put syrup on the gas and add citric acid. Dissolve and remove from gas. Measure the quantity.
1-1/2 litres water	
30 grams citric acid	(3) Take the preservative and measure it according to the quantity of squash. Dissolve first in little squash before mixing it in. Fill in glass bottles. Wax and seal them.
1/4 teaspoon preservative (potassium metabisulphate) per 1 litre of end product.	

Note :

Fresh cocums are available in April, May i.e. summer months only.

SYNTHETIC SYRUPS

Unlike squashes, in synthetic syrups, no fresh fruit juices are added, but made entirely out of sugar, water, citric acid, colour and essence. These syrups are easy to preserve than squashes. They can blend very well with milk preparations like milkshakes, falooda, icecreams etc. Following table will help in quick reference while making popular syrups like rose, raspberry, strawberry, khas, orange and pineapple.

Synthetic Syrups	Rose Syrup	Raspberry	Strawberry	Khas	Orange	Pineapple
Water (ML)	1000	1000	1000	1000	1000	1000
Sugar (Grams)	1800	1800	1800	1800	1800	1800
Essence (Teaspoon)	Rose	Raspberry	Strawberry	Khas	Orange	Pineapple
Colour	Red	Raspberry	Strawberry	Green	Orange	Pineapple
Citric Acid (Grams)	15	28	16	25	25	25

Basic Method for Syrup Preparation :
(1)   Dissolve sugar in water. Add citric acid.
(2)   Boil for 10 minutes.
(3)   Strain and cool.
(4)   Add colour and essence.
(5)   Pour in sterilized bottles, label, wax and store.

CARDAMOM AND SAFFRON SYRUP

A multipurpose syrup.

INGREDIENTS

1 kg. sugar

800 ml. water

2 teaspoons citric acid

30 cardamoms

30 black peppercorns

1/2 teaspoon saffron

METHOD

(1)   Grind together cardamoms with skin and peppercorns. Slightly warm saffron in a small vessel and crush the strands.

(2)   Combine sugar, water and citric acid in a vessel. Put on the medium gas. Dissolve sugar and let it boil for 10 minutes. Add cardamom, pepper and saffron powders. Boil for another five minutes. Remove from gas and close the vessel to retain flavours. Cool. Strain through a muslin cloth. Fill in sterilized bottles.

This syrup can be used in many ways.

(1)   For sherbet : Add one and a half tablespoons of syrup to one glass (6 ozs.) of chilled water with an ice cube.

(2)   For milkshake : Take two tablespoons of syrup to one glass (6 ozs.) of chilled unsweetened milk and blend in a mixie till frothy.

(3)   For icecreams with cardamom saffron flavour : Add enough syrup to less sweetened and thickened cold milk, before making icecream.

(4)   For cardamom-saffron lemonade : Add two tablespoons of syrup with one tablespoon of lemon juice and a bottle of chilled soda.

(5)   For cardamom-saffron sweet buttermilk (lassi) : To a glass of chilled unsweetened buttermilk, add two tablespoons of syrup.

FRUIT JAMS

Jams are always made from fruit pulp and they are not transparent.

INGREDIENTS

1 kg. fruit pulp (fruit in season)

1 kg. sugar

6 grams pectin powder

6 to 7 grams citric acid

1 teaspoon mixed fruit essence, if necessary

Colour according to the fruit combination

GRAPE JAM

1 litre grape juice from black grapes

1 kg. sugar

4 grams citric acid

PAPAYA JAM

1 kg. papaya

1 kg. sugar

8 grams citric acid

BANANA JAM

1 dozen yellow skin bananas

Sugar equivalent to the pulp of bananas

6 grams citric acid

MIXED FRUIT JAM

(a) 3 oranges

3-4 apples, cooked

2-3 bananas

1 small pineapple, cooked

Juice of 3 lemons

(b) 1 pineapple

3 oranges

3-4 apples

1/2 kg. grapes

1-2 guavas

(c) 3-4 apples

1/4 kg. grapes

1 pineapple

1/4 kg. strawberries

1 guava

Juice of 3 lemons

(d) Mango-Select ripe mangoes which have less fibres in it like Totapuri variety.

(e) 1/2 kg. strawberries

2 bananas

METHOD

(1) Peel and remove seeds from fruits. Soft fruits do not need cooking. But hard fruits such as pineapple, and guava need cooking. Always use one of the fruits having pectin in it, e.g. guava, papaya, apple etc. which will help to thicken the jam. Cook fruits with just enough water to cover. Cook in pressure cooker. Cook till soft. Mash fruits well or put them in a mixer. When the proper mixture of fruits is ready, measure it.

(2) Measure sugar in proportion to the amount of fruit pulp. Combine the two in a thick bottomed vessel or non stick vessel and cook. Stir often with a wooden spoon till sugar dissolves. Allow to boil. Boil till it starts to thicken. Add pectin powder mixed with little sugar (to avoid formation of lumps). Mix immediately. Check the consistency of jam by putting a drop in a plate. It should not move or spread.

(3) Add citric acid, colour and essence, if necessary. Mix well and remove from heat.

(4) Pour hot in sterilized jars till brim. Cool, seal, label and store.

FOR THE BANANA JAM

Cook the bananas in little water. Mash them. Add sugar as much as the pulp of bananas and citric acid.

FRUIT JELLY

Fruit jellies are made from clear fruit juices. They are transparent and used like jams. They can only be made out of fruits which have high pectin content such as, apples, papaya, guava, jackfruit, etc.

INGREDIENTS

1 litre pectin extract from a fruit (seasonal)

1 kg. sugar

6-7 grams citric acid

METHOD

(1) Wash and cut fruit into small pieces. Cook with 1-1/2 times water for half an hour. Strain pectin extract juice. Do not take pulp. Measure it.

(2) Take sugar in proportion to the juice. Dissolve sugar in pectin extract. Stir with a wooden spoon, boil and strain, if necessary.

(3) Cook till it starts to thicken. A drop of the mixture should not move or spread. Then add citric acid. Mix well, remove from gas and fill into a sterilized bottle upto the brim. Cool, seal, label and store.

Note for jams and jellies

(1) Always fill in bottles when hot before the jam or jelly starts to set.

(2) Always fill upto the brim.

(3) No preservative is needed if equal amount of sugar and juice or pulp are used.

(4) Avoid using too much of any dark fruit like chickoo as it does not give a pleasing colour to the jam.

(5) For sealing, allow jam or jelly to set and cool completely. It will create little space at the mouth. Pour hot wax on jam till top. Allow it to set and then close the cap.

MARMALADES

Marmalade is a jelly but with fruit peels. The peel of the fruit like orange, lemon, etc. is added to give bitter taste and natural flavour. Normally, marmalade is made from orange, lemon and grapefruit. To remove excessive bitterness from the skin, boil several times in water. Then cut fine strips before adding to marmalade. British marmalades are much more bitter than American ones.

ORANGE MARMALADE

INGREDIENTS

1 litre pectin extract

1 kg. sugar

6-7 grams citric acid

Peel from half orange

METHOD

(1) Wash oranges, remove skin.

(2) Separate segments and remove seeds.

(3) Cook in little water. Boil over medium fire for 15-20 minutes. Strain through a muslin cloth.

(4) Measure pectin extract, add equal amount of sugar. Cook as in jelly and follow the same method.

(5) Take peel of half an orange or even less. Cook in water. Change water and cook again. Repeat this process four to five times. Now cut the peel into very thin long strips. Add citric acid. Allow marmalade to cool for a few minutes before pouring in sterilized bottle.

STRAWBERRY CRUSH

It is used for milkshakes, icecream topping or certain desserts. Crush made from raspberries is equally good.

INGREDIENTS

1/2 kg. strawberries

2 kgs. sugar

2 cups water

35 grams citric acid

1/2 teaspoon preservative — sodium benzoate per 1/2 litre of end product

METHOD

(1) Wash, pick and clean strawberries.

(2) Mix strawberries with sugar and leave overnight to soak. Next day pick up strawberries from the liquid sugar and make a puree in a mixer. Add water in the liquid sugar and boil for 15 minutes to prepare sugar syrup. Cool and mix with strawberry puree. Measure it.

(3) Mix sodium benzoate in proportion to its measurement.

(4) Fill in sterilized bottles, seal, label and store.

TAMARIND PULP

Ready tamarind pulp is very convenient in cooking. It saves a lot of time and trouble whenever you need small quantity of tamarind for chutnies, curries and many other dishes for daily cooking.

INGREDIENTS

1 kg. tamarind

6 grams pectin powder

2 teaspoons acetic acid, glacial

Little sugar

METHOD

(1) Clean tamarind and soak in enough water to cover, keep overnight. Put through a mixer. Strain it. Put on the gas and boil it. Reduce to little less than half its quality.

(2) Add pectin powder mixed with little sugar.

(3) Boil for sometime and then mix acetic acid. Remove from gas and fill in sterilized jars. When cold, cover with plastic caps.

DRY ONIONS

Slice onions finely into very long pieces. Spread them on a cloth and dry under hot sun till very crisp without moisture.

Fry them in oil to make crisp golden brown onions for pullaos, biryanis, etc. This saves time and consumes less oil while frying.

MUSHROOMS — PRESERVED IN OIL

These mushrooms can be preserved for a year and are very tasty in salads, sandwiches and soups.

INGREDIENTS

1 kg. mushrooms

3 tablespoons salt

1/2 litre vinegar

4 bay leaves

6 cloves

1 tablespoon white peppercorns, partly crushed

3/4 litre olive or salad oil

METHOD

Clean and wash mushrooms well. Slice them. Cover them with salt and vinegar. Leave for an hour. Boil them for 10 minutes until soft. Drain. Arrange mushrooms in a jar. Add spices between layers of mushrooms. Cover with salad oil.

HOT MANGO PICKLE

INGREDIENTS

1 dozen medium sized raw mangoes

Wash and cut into small pieces

1 cup salt

1 tablespoon turmeric

FOR THE MASALA (mixture of spices)

1 cup split mustard seeds without skin

2 cups split fenugreek seeds without skin

2 tablespoons asafoetida

1 tablespoon turmeric powder

4 cups red chilli powder

6 cups salt (dried in sun)

5 cups sesame oil

METHOD

(1) Apply one cup of salt and one tablespoon of turmeric to the mango pieces. Cover and keep aside for 24 hours. Remove the pieces from the water that have oozed out from the mango pieces. Dry mango pieces on cloth under sunlight for 1-2 hours.

(2) To prepare masala, take a big deep plate. Put asafoetida in the centre. Then arrange a circle of mustard followed by a circle of fenugreek. Heat two cups of oil and pour over the asafoetida and around it. Cover and set aside to cool. Add to it chilli powder, turmeric powder and salt. Mix well.

(3) Take a big glass jar. Spread a thick layer of masala at the bottom. Take half of the remaining masala and mix with mango pieces. Make alternate layer of masala and mango pieces. Press everything well in the bottle. Cover and keep aside for three days.

(4) On the fourth day, press layers of pickle, again. Heat remaining oil. Cool and then pour over the pickle. Allow it to get soaked right till the bottom. Finally, a thick layer of oil should remain at the top.

(5) The pickle is ready to use after a fortnight. If kept properly clean, pickle can be preserved for more than a year.

Note :

Some pickles can be made with a mixture of "gunda" and mango pieces. Gunda is a fruit with thick green skin, sticky juice and a stone inside. They are available in summer only. To prepare gundas for stuffing, split on one side. Remove sticky stone from inside with the help of a stick dipped in salt. Stuff the prepared masala in the hollow of the gundas. Arrange alternate layer of mango pieces and stuffed gundas in the bottle.

CHHUNDA

Sweet and sour mango pickle.

INGREDIENTS	METHOD

INGREDIENTS

6 raw mangoes — Rajapuri variety if possible, peeled, grated to measure 10 cups

3/4 cup salt

15 cups sugar

1/2 cup cummin seeds -

roasted, coarsely powdered

1 cup red chilli powder

METHOD

(1) Mix grated raw mango and salt. Rub and mix well till good amount of water oozes out.

(2) Add sugar and mix well till sugar almost melts. Cover and keep aside for 12 to 24 hours.

(3) Tie a thin cloth at the mouth of the chhunda vessel. Keep this vessel under scorching Sun. Stir chhunda everyday in the evening. Keep vessel over a plate containing a little water, to avoid collection of ants. Continue this process every day till sugar syrup gets fairly thick, or when you put a drop of syrup in a plate it should not run but remain steady like a dot. The process will take about eight to ten days.

(4) Now mix in the roasted cummin powder and red chilli powder. Keep in Sun for one more day.

(5) Next day fill in the glass jar. Chhunda can be preserved for more than a year.

CHAAT MASALA

Pungent masala used for seasoning, specially prepared the chaats.

INGREDIENTS

1/4 teaspoon asafoetida

1 teaspoon black pepper

1 teaspoon black salt

2 teaspoons roasted cummin seeds, ground

1 teaspoon ginger powder

3 teaspoons dry mango powder (amchur)

1-1/2 teaspoons salt

2 teaspoons red chilli powder

METHOD

Mix everything well and make a fine powder in a dry grinder. Preserve in an airtight bottle.

CHILLI SAUCE (WITH OR WITHOUT GARLIC) (MAKES 1/2 CUP)

A spicy sauce served with variety of hot snacks.

INGREDIENTS

50 grams dry red chillies, preferably Kashmiri variety

5 cloves garlic, flaked (optional)

8-10 black peppercorns

2 teaspoons cummin seeds

4 cloves

1 inch stick cinnamon

2 teaspoons salad oil

1 tablespoon sugar

Salt to taste

3 tablespoons vinegar

1/2 teaspoon sodium benzoate

METHOD

(1) Break chillies into pieces and soak in 100 ml. water for two hours. Make paste of chillies and garlic.
(2) Grind together, peppercorns, cummin seeds, cloves and cinnamon.
(3) Take salad oil in a vessel and fry chilli-garlic paste till oil separates. Add the ground spices, sugar, salt and vinegar. Mix well, add preservatives. Remove from gas. Cool and grind to a fine paste in a mixer.

JELLY CRYSTALS

Jelly can be easily prepared with various combinations of colour and essences.

INGREDIENTS	METHOD
6-1/2 teaspoons gelatine	(1) Mix gelatine, citric acid and sugar in a vessel.
1-1/4 teaspoons citric acid	(2) Add water and soak for ten minutes. Heat on gas to melt gelatine and sugar. Remove from gas and mix appropriate colour and essence, e.g. lemon colour and lemon essence. (Refer combination chart on Pg. 274)
6-1/2 tablespoons sugar	
2-1/2 cups water	
1/2 teaspoon any colour	
1/2 teaspoon any essence	

GARAM MASALA (MAKES 1/3 CUP - 3 OZS.)

It is used in many savoury dishes and curries.

INGREDIENTS	METHOD
2 tablespoons black pepper	Pick and clean all the ingredients. Grind them in the dry grinder till very fine. Store in an airtight bottle.
25 large pieces cinnamon	
100 cloves (approx.)	
25 cardamoms	

CURRY POWDER (MAKES 1/2 KG.)

Frequently used in many curries and vegetable dishes.

INGREDIENTS	METHOD
3/4 cup (50 grams) coriander seeds	Fry all spices in little oil except mace and dry ginger powder. Cool and grind to a very fine powder. Store in an airtight bottle.
1/2 cup (50 grams) aniseeds	
3 tablespoons (25 grams) mustard seeds	
1/2 cup (50 grams) cummin seeds	
1/2 cup (50 grams) fenugreek seeds	
1/3 cup (50 grams) peppercorns	
1/2 cup (50 grams) cloves	
2/3 cup (50 grams) big cardamoms	
1/4 cup (25 grams) caraway seeds	
1/2 cup (50 grams) dry ginger powder	
1-1/3 cup (50 grams) dry red chilies	
20 to 25 (5 grams) bay leaves	
1/3 cup (15 grams) mace	
7 big pieces (25 grams) cinnamon	
Little oil to fry	

MILK MASALA (MAKES 1-1/4 CUPS)

A masala which can make delicious cold drinks with milk or can be used to garnish many Indian sweets.

INGREDIENTS

1/2 cup (70 grams) almonds

1/2 cup (65 grams) pistachios

15 cardamoms

1/2 teaspoon nutmeg powder

2 teaspoons saffron

METHOD

(1)   Make a coarse powder of almonds, pistachios and cardamoms.
(2)   Lightly roast saffron and crush.
(3)   Mix all the ingredients together and fill in an airtight bottle. Store in fridge.

GHATI MASALA (MAKES 3 KGS.)

A time saving complete masala for curry or dry vegetable preparations.

INGREDIENTS

1 kg. onions, sliced, dried on cloth for an hour

1/4 kg. cloves garlic, crushed

200 grams ginger, crushed

Oil as required

3 cups (1/4 kg.) dry coconut, grated

2-3/4 cups (1/4 kg.) coriander seeds

1/2 cup (50 grams) cummin seeds

3-1/2 tablespoons (20 grams) caraway seeds

1/4 cup (30 grams) black peppercorns

2 big pieces (10 grams) cinnamon

3 tablespoons (20 grams) poppy seeds

2 tablespoons (10 grams) cloves

5-1/2 cups (3/4 kg.) red chilli powder

15 cardamoms

2 tablespoons asafoetida

3/4 cup (1/4 kg.) salt

METHOD

(1)   Saute onions till golden brown in oil. Keep aside.
(2)   Saute crushed garlic and ginger in little oil till dry. Keep aside.
(3)   Saute grated coconut in little oil till light brown and crisp. Keep aside.
(4)   Saute coriander seeds, cummin seeds, caraway seeds together in little oil. Keep aside.
(5)   Saute peppercorns, cinnamon, poppy seeds, cloves in little oil., Keep aside.
(6)   Take out seeds from cardamoms.
(7)   Make a fine powder of all these sauted spices.
(8)   Mix with all the remaining ingredients and fill in an airtight bottle. Store in fridge.

BLACK MASALA (MAKES 1 KG.)

A typical Maharashtrian masala used for vegetables as well as rice preparations.

INGREDIENTS

1-1/4 cups (100 grams) dry coconut, grated
Oil as required
5 cups (350 grams) coriander seeds
1/4 cup (50 grams) sesame seeds
1/4 cup (30 grams) cummin seeds
1/4 cup (30 grams) caraway seeds
3/4 cup (100 grams) poppy seeds
10-12 bay leaves
2 teaspoons mustard seeds
1 teaspoons fenugreek seeds
4 teaspoons (10 grams cloves)
8-10 pieces (30 grams) cinnamon
15 cardamoms
4 teaspoons asafoetida
2 tablespoons turmeric powder
3/4 cup (100 grams) red chilli powder
1/4 cup salt
2 tablespoons mace

METHOD

(1) Saute dry coconut in little oil till light brown and crisp. Keep aside.

(2) Saute coriander seeds, sesame seeds, cummin seeds, caraway seeds, poppy seeds together in little oil. Keep aside.

(3) Saute bay leaves. Keep aside.

(4) Saute mustard seeds, fenugreek in little oil. Add cloves, cinnamon and saute for half a minute more.

(5) Remove cardamom seeds.

(6) Make powder of all the sauted spices and mace. Mix this powder with coconut, asafoetida, turmeric powder, red chilli powder and salt.

(7) Store black masala in an airtight bottle.

DRY ONION LOTUS BUD

(1) Select a white cone shaped dry onion. Peel off dry skin. Taper the top and keep the base intact.

(2) Starting at the root end, cut small pointed half moon shaped petals around the onion. Keeping only this area of petals, peel off carefully the remaining layer of the onion.

(3) Alternating the position of the petals, cut the second group of petals on the second layer and again peel off the remaining layer of onion. Repeat this till you complete the lotus bud.

(4) Put this lotus bud in ice cold water with a few drops of red colour. Keep for an hour. The lotus bud will become firm and petals will have a pinkish margin.

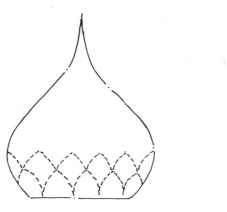 

FANCY CARROT CONES

(1) Cut out required length of a fresh carrot for carving a cone. Shape it into a smooth, tapered cone.

(2) With a sharp narrow knife, cut out pointed petal shapes around the carrot on its broad side. To elevate each petal, cut out narrow wedges from the sides and the centre as shown in the diagram.

(3) Continue alternate layers of petals right upto the top.

 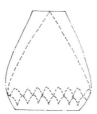 

WATERMELON ROSE

(1) Cut watermelon into half and put on a plate. Peel thick skin and white flesh to make a perfectly round shape. Only the pink flesh should be seen. Trim the lower edge inwards.

(2) Carve the first round of five to six petals. Put the first cut straight, about 1/4 inch deep. Then put the second cut at 45° angle from the top, so that the petals look separated.

(3) Carve the second layer of petals alternating with the first one.

(4) Cut all petals till you reach the top, changing the angle of the knife. The knife angle makes a petal look turned inside or outside.

(5) Remove any seeds that are seen on the surface.

(6) Carefully separate the first two layers of petals with a long sharp knife. But hold them in position. It will be easier for the guest to pick up one petal as one serving.

(7) Cut out assorted sizes of leaves from the watermelon skin (see Pg. 49) and arrange them around the watermelon rose.

  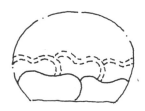 

WATERMELON DAHLIA

(1) Select a perfect round watermelon. Cut a slice from one end to make a base. Make it stand in a plate.

(2) Carve out six big leaves on the lower side of the melon. Peel out green skin from three petals showing white flesh from inside. Trim serrated edges and veins on green as well as white leaves.

(3) Now peel off skin and white flesh from the remaining watermelon and make the surface round and smooth.

(4) Carve 'V' shaped petals by holding knife at 90° angle to the surface of the melon. Make second cut a little lower at 45° angle, so that the petals look separated. Cut a wedge in each petal. Make alternate layers of petals, almost upto the top. Carve a round on the top to make centre of the dahlia flower. Carve a check pattern by cutting wedges in the centre of the round.

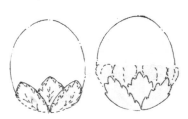  

292

Dust Jacket Front Side

1. Alu puries   p. 108
2. Spinach pullao with paneer   p. 111
3. Green peas dahivade   p. 121
4. Kadhi with pakoda   p. 99
5. Khata curry   p. 101
6. Amrut curry   p. 90
7. Paneer makai Kheer   p. 138
8. Tricolour dhokla   p. 131
9. Beetlenut leaves, cardamoms, cloves etc. as mouth freshners
10. Carved fruits leaves and

Dust Jacket Rear Side

1. Cream of spinach soup   p. 71
2. Macaroni rissoto   p. 156
3. Mexican cutlet with salsa verde   p. 151
4. Golden salad with cucumber flower and fancy tomato wedges   p. 51
5. Bread sticks   p. 78
6. Pungent tomato juice   p. 31

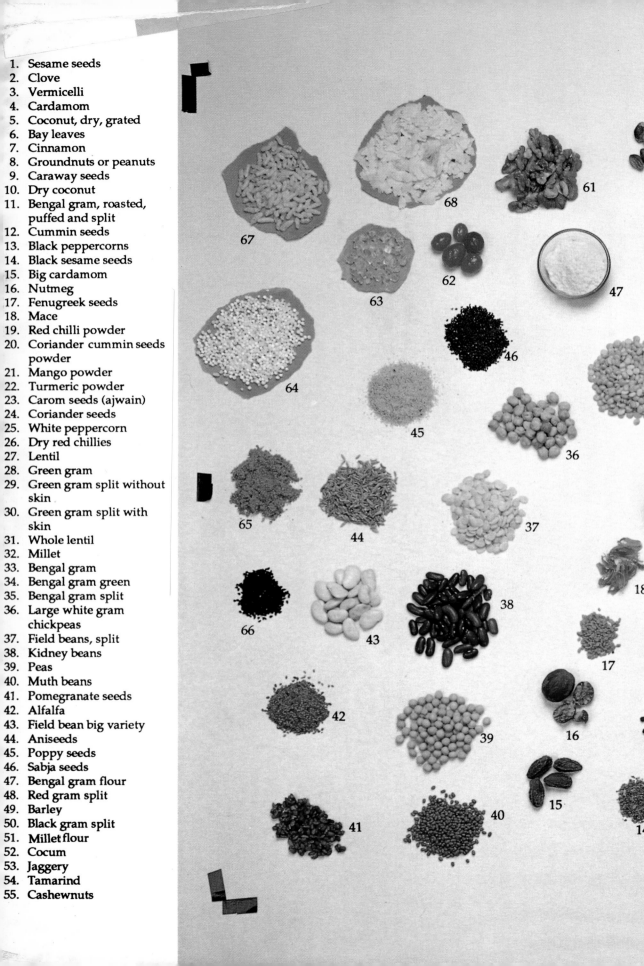

1. Sesame seeds
2. Clove
3. Vermicelli
4. Cardamom
5. Coconut, dry, grated
6. Bay leaves
7. Cinnamon
8. Groundnuts or peanuts
9. Caraway seeds
10. Dry coconut
11. Bengal gram, roasted, puffed and split
12. Cummin seeds
13. Black peppercorns
14. Black sesame seeds
15. Big cardamom
16. Nutmeg
17. Fenugreek seeds
18. Mace
19. Red chilli powder
20. Coriander cummin seeds powder
21. Mango powder
22. Turmeric powder
23. Carom seeds (ajwain)
24. Coriander seeds
25. White peppercorn
26. Dry red chillies
27. Lentil
28. Green gram
29. Green gram split without skin
30. Green gram split with skin
31. Whole lentil
32. Millet
33. Bengal gram
34. Bengal gram green
35. Bengal gram split
36. Large white gram chickpeas
37. Field beans, split
38. Kidney beans
39. Peas
40. Muth beans
41. Pomegranate seeds
42. Alfalfa
43. Field bean big variety
44. Aniseeds
45. Poppy seeds
46. Sabja seeds
47. Bengal gram flour
48. Red gram split
49. Barley
50. Black gram split
51. Millet flour
52. Cocum
53. Jaggery
54. Tamarind
55. Cashewnuts